DEVELOPING COUNTRIES AND REGIONAL ECONOMIC COOPERATION

DEVELOPING COUNTRIES AND REGIONAL ECONOMIC COOPERATION

M. Leann Brown

PRAEGER

Westport, Connecticut
London

Library of Congress Cataloging-in-Publication Data

Brown, M. Leann.
    Developing countries and regional economic cooperation / M. Leann
Brown.
        p. cm.
    Includes bibliographical references and index.
    ISBN 0-275-94960-5 (alk. paper)
    1. Developing countries—Economic integration—Case studies.
    2. Developing countries—Economic policy—Decision making—Case
studies.   I. Title.
    HC59.7.B6893   1994   94-8314
    338.9'09172'4—dc20

British Library Cataloguing in Publication Data is available.

Library of Congress Catalog Card Number: 94-8314
ISBN: 0-275-94960-5

First published in 1994

Praeger Publishers, 88 Post Road West, Westport, CT 06881
An imprint of Greenwood Publishing Group, Inc.

Printed in the United States of America

The paper used in this book complies with the
Permanent Paper Standard issued by the National
Information Standards Organization (Z39.48-1984).

10 9 8 7 6 5 4 3 2 1

Copyright Acknowledgment

The publisher and author are grateful to the following source
for granting permission to reprint:

An earlier version of Chapter 4 appeared in a 1989 *Journal of Modern African Studies* article, "Nigeria and the ECOWAS Protocol on Free Movement and Residence," XXVII,
No. 2: 252–273, and is reprinted by permission of Cambridge University Press.

To my parents
Ruth Moak and Leroy Bradford Brown
With love, respect, and gratitude

Contents

Abbreviations   **xi**

1. Introduction   **1**

The Performance Record of Regional Cooperative Efforts
Among Less Developed Countries   4

Theoretical and Methodological Approach   4

The Chilean Decision   7

The Nigerian Decision   8

The Philippine Decision   8

Summary   9

Notes   10

**2. Explaining Regional Economic Cooperation: The Case for a
Cognitive Framing Model**   **13**

Realist and Liberal Explanations for International Cooperation   15

A Cognitive Framing Model   21

The Framework of Utilities Suggested in Free Trade, Regional
Integration, and Customs Union Theories   31

The Cognitive Framework of Developing Country Elites   36

Notes   39

3. **The Andean Case: The 1976 Chilean Decision to Withdraw from the Pact**   **43**

   The National Economic and Political Context of the Decision   43

   Chile and the Andean Pact   47

   D24 and Chile's Decision to Withdraw from the Pact   51

   Summary   65

   Notes   68

4. **The ECOWAS Case: Nigeria's 1983 Decision to Expel Alien Workers**   **73**

   The 1983 Nigerian Decision to Expel Alien Workers   74

   Protocol on Free Movement of Persons, Right of Residence, and Establishment   76

   Nigeria and ECOWAS   79

   National Short-Term Economic Concerns   83

   National Short-Term Societal Stability Concerns   87

   National and Personal Short-Term Political Concerns   88

   Summary   92

   Notes   95

5. **The ASEAN Case: The 1977 Philippine Decision Concerning Sabah**   **99**

   The Sabah Controversy   100

   The Philippines and Regional Economic Cooperation   105

   National Short-Term Political Stability Needs   111

   Potential Long-Term National Security Benefits from Regional Cooperation   114

   Potential Long-Term National Economic Benefits from Regional Cooperation   117

   Summary   120

   Notes   122

6. **Conclusions and Policy Recommendations**   **125**

   Divergent Decision Framing   126

   A Cognitive Framing Model   127

   Effective Institutions—A Solution to Incongruent Payoff Structures   133

Political Leadership and Entrepreneurship—A Solution to
    Incongruent Payoff Structures   136
Recommendations for Enhanced Institutional Effectiveness and
    Intellectual and Political Leadership   138
Notes   142

Appendix   **145**

Bibliography   **155**

Index   **169**

Abbreviations

ASA	Association of Southeast Asia
ASEAN	Association of Southeast Asian Nations
CEAO	*Communaute Economique de l'Afrique Occidentale*
CEDE	Center for Studies on Company Development (Chile)
D24	Decision 24 (Andean Pact)
ECOWAS	Economic Community of West African States
LAFTA	Latin American Free Trade Association
MNLF	Moro National Liberation Front
OPEC	Organization of Oil Exporting Countries
SEATO	Southeast Asia Treaty Organization
SOFOFA	*Sociedad de Fomento Fabril (Chile)*
TNCs	Transnational corporations
UN	United Nations
US	United States

1 Introduction

Over the past 30 years, less developed countries[1] have established several regional economic organizations to address their poverty, underdevelopment, and external dependency. Economic imperatives and the rationales for cooperation intuitively seem sufficient to ensure that national political leaderships would engage in the give and take necessary to achieve their stated goals. Yet, the historical record reveals a faltering pattern for most regional cooperative efforts. At best, they have experienced uneven results; many are now defunct. Why is this the case?

During the 1940s through the 1970s, functionalist and neofunctionalist theorists identified a plethora of factors that may contribute to the success of economic cooperative schemes during their startup, operational, and output phases. However, even the most successful integration effort among advanced industrial countries, the European Communities, was buffeted by the economic upheavals of the 1970s and early 1980s. Regional economic integration efforts among developing countries were even more severely affected. Despairing of achieving progress via regional strategies, many developing countries turned their energies to lobbying for reform of multilateral institutions in such futile efforts as the call for a New International Economic Order.

The international political economy of the 1990s provides qualitatively different challenges to national economies and their governments. Global interdependence is more pervasive and complex than ever before. Advanced industrial countries suffer from structural rigidities that foster the decline of formerly mainstay industries and chronically high unemployment. Trade competition is fierce, and volatility plagues global currency markets. The command economies have collapsed, and any credibility that central planning and extensive state involvement in national economies may have enjoyed has been dashed. The "compromise of embedded liberalism," that is, the consensus that the state should practice free trade in the international arena while simultaneously assuming responsibility for insulating its domestic economy against the destructive forces of the free market, has proved difficult to sustain (Ruggie, 1982).

Among several trends becoming discernible in this highly fluid era is the evolution of regional trading blocs. The most institutionally sophisticated among these is the European Union. The increased scope and depth of cooperation stipulated in the 1991 Maastricht Treaty provides evidence of this trend. Another example is the recently concluded North American Free Trade Agreement, which presently conjoins the economies of North America, but soon will include the more liberalized economies of the Western Hemisphere. Thus, developed countries are banding together in cooperative efforts to stabilize the economic environment within which they operate and to preserve the standard of living expected by their citizenry. In most cases, developing countries are excluded from the decision-making circles which seek to consolidate these trading blocs. Individually, they bring little or no economic leverage to the negotiating tables. If they do not counter this trend with their own regional integration schemes, they will be effectively shut out of major world markets.

A second post-Cold War trend, which renders essential the revisiting of the issue of economic cooperation among developing countries, is that with increased economic pressures of stagnating growth rates in industrialized countries and existing assistance funds being diverted to the former Soviet bloc, less foreign aid will be available to meet the needs of traditional foreign aid recipients. Monies will no longer be forthcoming from the United States and the Soviet Union to guarantee these countries' "proper" alignment in East-West competition.

This latter trend dovetails with current philosophical orthodoxy among economic development and assistance theorists and practitioners. These experts doubt the long-term utility of foreign assistance in achieving appropriate and sustainable economic development. The current wisdom is that economic development must be a "grass roots" initiated and supported process. That is, economic progress must be undertaken from the ground up, rather than orchestrated by outside agents and resources. To facilitate appropriate (economically rational) and sustainable development, self-reliance strategies that economically and politically empower the people are advocated. In short, these trends suggest that developing countries will be increasingly forced to join together in regional integration schemes as a defensive measure against the global tendency

toward trading blocs and to provide a regional alternative to shortfalls in
aid from the industrialized world. Regional cooperation must move again
to the forefront of the agendas of less developed countries. This study
aspires to contribute to that discussion in theoretical and practical terms.

As noted, earlier research into this issue was generated out of the
functionalist and neofunctionalist literature and tended to focus on the
characteristics and processes of the regional economic organization itself. For example, analysts assigned importance to such attributes and
processes as membership size, symmetry of members' power capabilities, quality of regional leadership, decision-making style, level of organizational autonomy, and distributive outcomes of regional policy.

In contrast, this study approaches the question of economic cooperation among less developed countries as a comparative study of foreign
policy decision making. The decision to cooperate or not to cooperate
within regional economic organizations is made by elites within the
member states on a case-by-case, project-by-project basis. A cognitive
framing model is used to examine how national elites decide to cooperate or not to cooperate with regional economic initiatives. The way that
decision makers conceptualize the issue to be addressed; whether utilities are assessed on the regional/collective, national, or personal basis;
the framing of the issue in terms of gain or loss; and the influence of
probability, risk, survival needs, ideology, and time are primary ingredi-
ents comprising the cognitive frameworks of member-state elites. In the
final analysis, the aggregated consequences of such national elite-level
decisions determine the overall viability of regional cooperative efforts.

The cognitive framing model is used to examine three decisions made
by the governments of Chile, Nigeria, and the Philippines with regard to
participation in the Andean Pact, the Economic Community of West African States (ECOWAS) and the Association of Southeast Asian Nations
(ASEAN), respectively. The decisions were detrimental to regional economic cooperation in the Chilean and Nigerian cases but facilitated regional cooperation in the Philippine case. The literature confirms that
the 1976 Chilean decision to withdraw from the Andean Pact, the 1983
Nigerian decision to deport alien workers, and the 1977 Philippine decision regarding territorial claims over the Sabah region had long-term implications for the well-being of the regional organizations of which they
were a part. It is the thesis of this study that developing country elites
frame decisions regarding regional cooperation in terms of short-term,
national, and personal loss avoidance. In many cases, incongruity between the long-term, regional, economic framework of benefits inherent
in the regional integration schemes and the cognitive framework out of
which member-state elites assess the utility of cooperation results in a
decision not to cooperate. However, the Philippine case will demonstrate that although developing country elites frame their decisions in

terms of short-term, national loss avoidance, the decision outcomes do not always run counter to regional cooperation goals. This finding points the way to specific policy recommendations presented in the final chapter. Through a combination of conscious institutional design and political leadership, the short-term, national, and personal needs of member-state elites to avoid loss may be addressed to improve their ability to frame decisions in terms of long-term, regional economic benefits which will foster regional cooperation.

THE PERFORMANCE RECORD OF REGIONAL COOPERATIVE EFFORTS AMONG LESS DEVELOPED COUNTRIES

Before proceeding with a summation of the cases at hand, it is necessary to address the claim that the performance record of regional integration efforts among developing countries has not been as dismal as has been implied. There are areas of successful policy undertakings that may be pointed out. For example, ASEAN has been instrumental in assuaging political disputes among its members, and the ECOWAS is currently involved in a (highly controversial) conflict melioration effort in Liberia. In the main, however, the economic achievements of these organizations have been limited. Table 1.1 is a partial listing of regional economic organizations among developing countries with the dates of their establishment and their current institutional status. More complete information regarding their goals, membership, major accomplishments, and operating difficulties can be found in the Appendix.

This inventory of regional integration efforts among less developed countries provides evidence that national decision makers believe that enhanced benefits may be derived from regional integration. However, nearly 45 percent of the efforts are superseded, inactive, or defunct. It is difficult to sustain the momentum of cooperation across multiple issue areas over the long haul. In many instances, the discrepancy between the predominantly long-term, economic structural benefits conferred by regional cooperation and the framework of needs out of which member-state elites make their decisions results in institutional stagnation and paralysis.

THEORETICAL AND METHODOLOGICAL APPROACH

The goal of this study is to describe, explain, and compare, in a theoretically meaningful way, the processes and causes[2] associated with foreign policy decisions on selected issues in three developing countries— the 1976 Chilean decision to withdraw from the Andean Pact, the 1983 Nigerian decision to expel alien workers, and the 1977 Philippine deci-

Table 1.1

ORGANIZATION	DATE ESTABLISHED	STATUS
Mali Federation	1959	defunct
Asociacion Latinoamericana de Libre Comercio	1960	replaced
Mercado Commun Centroamericano	1960	defunct
Organisation Commune Africaine et Malgache	1961	defunct
Union Douaniere et Economique de l'Afrique Centrale	1964	operational
Caribbean Free Trade Association	1965	replaced
East African Community	1967	defunct
East Caribbean Common Market	1968	replaced
Communaute Economique de l'Afrique de l'Quest	1970	operational
The Caribbean Community	1973	operational
Mano River Union	1973	operational
Sistema Economico Latinoamericano	1975	operational
Communaute Economique des Pays des Grands Lacs	1976	operational
Southern African Development Coordination Conference	1979	operational
Preferential Trade Area for East and Southern Africa	1981	operational
Communaute Economique des Etats de l'Afrique Centrale	1981	operational

sion to relinquish territorial claims on Sabah—and to derive conclusions about the foreign policy choices of developing country elites regarding their participation in regional economic organizations.

Chapter 2 will make the case for using a cognitive framing model to explain member states' cooperative or noncooperative decisions in contrast with more systemic explanations provided by the realist and liberal traditions. Particular note is taken of earlier functionalist and neofunctionalist explanations for the success or failure of integration efforts. The postulated elements of the decision makers' cognitive framework, not necessarily in order of importance or relevance to a specific decision context, that influence utility assessment are:

1. Issue *conceptualization*[3];
2. The *level* of utility assessment, i.e., regional/collective, national, or personal;

3. Association of the issue with *gain* or *loss;*

4. The influence of perceived *probability* and/or *risk;*

5. Association of the issue with the need for political, economic, or personal *survival;*

6. The influence of *ideology* on utility assessment; and

7. The influence of *time* on utility assessment.

Ten propositions relevant to these components are derived from the theoretical literature to suggest how these components should affect decision making regarding participation in regional economic organizations. It is assumed that congruity between the frameworks of benefits implied in participation in regional economic schemes and the cognitive framing of utilities by developing country elites facilitates regional cooperation and, obversely, that incongruity between these frameworks is a major source of these organizations' difficulties and failures.

The three historical cases of elite decision making with regard to regional cooperation are presented in Chapters 3–5. Case studies differ from quasiexperimental and quantitative approaches in their heavy reliance on within-case analysis to evaluate propositions about causation. Within these cases, the way each decision is framed by developing country elites is the focus of the inquiry. George and McKeown (1985: 34) describe this "process-tracing" approach:

The process-tracing approach attempts to uncover what stimuli the actors attend to; the decision process that makes use of these stimuli to arrive at decisions; the actual behavior that then occurs; the effect of various institutional arrangements on attention, processing and behavior; and the effect of other variables of interest on attention, processing, and behavior. . . . *The framework within which actors' perceptions and actions are described is given by the researcher, not by the actors themselves* (my emphasis).

A stream of behavior through time is the research focus rather than a single behavior. In a sense, the case serves as its own "control," because changes in the stream of behavior can be identified by the researcher immersed in the unfolding of the process and explained in terms of theoretically relevant factors. Thus, each case study possesses its own explanatory power with reference to the proposed model. In-depth, qualitative case studies possess particular utility for inducing an understanding of the cognitive processes of foreign policy elites.

Comparative analysis[4] allows us to structure and examine specific propositions across cases, countries, and institutions. The selected cases constitute a single class of foreign policy behavior, decisions with regard to participation in regional economic organizations. The decision making by Chilean and Nigerian government officials are "most similar" cases in that they both involved instances of extreme noncooperation with an Andean Pact decision and ECOWAS protocol, respectively. The Philippine case is a "most different" comparison in that Philippine decision makers announced a policy change facilitating cooperation within the ASEAN (Przeworski and Teune, 1970: 31–46). The institutions involved (the Andean Pact, ECOWAS, and the ASEAN) exemplify regional cooperation efforts across three continents, with varying records of accomplishment. Thus, the thesis and propositions associated with the model's components will be tested within and across cooperative and noncooperative decisions made by national elites within three regional institutional contexts. A summary of these cases is provided below.

THE CHILEAN DECISION

When the military Junta assumed power in Chile in September 1973, it began to implement liberal, "free market and free trade" policies to redress Chile's desperate economic situation. Although Chile had actively participated in the Andean Pact since its establishment in 1969,[5] the ideology of its economic leaders in 1973 placed the Junta immediately at odds with Decision 24 (D24, ratified in June 1971), the Statute on the Common Treatment of Foreign Capital, Trademarks, Patents, Licensing Agreements, and Royalties. The Junta also disagreed with pact plans for instituting common external tariffs. The most salient provisions of D24 prohibited foreign investment in specific sectors of the member-states' economies, provided for gradual "fadeout" of foreign ownership of business ventures to 49 percent within 15 years, and limited foreign firms' profit remittance to 14 percent of their original capital investment. D24 was perceived by the Junta economic leadership as deterring badly needed foreign investment in Chile. The Junta first sought to identify loopholes in D24 wherein their more liberal foreign investment policies might be pursued. When this failed, they lobbied for revision of D24. But, as relations with the pact deteriorated over 2 years of bitter controversy, the Chilean government gradually concluded that the country's developmental needs could best be met outside of pact participation.

Most analysts agree that Chile's withdrawal in August 1976 affected long-term negative consequences for the Andean Pact. Progress was delayed in most areas, including agreement on sectoral industrialization and a common external tariff, during the 2 years of acrimony over D24. Momentum toward further integration of national economies was lost with Chile's withdrawal. The scope of Andean Pact activities has continued to expand, but the level of integration remains relatively stalemated in the wake of the Chilean pullout.

THE NIGERIAN DECISION

On January 17, 1983, without prior public discussion or warning, the Nigerian Federal Minister of Internal Affairs, Alhaji Ali Baba, announced that all aliens residing and working illegally in Nigeria had 14 days to leave the country. At the time of the expulsion, an estimated 1 million Ghanaians and an additional million citizens from other West African countries were illegally employed in Nigeria. The forced exodus took place in great haste and disorder, resulting in extreme hardship and some loss of life among the evictees. It also set back cooperation within the Economic Community of West African States.[6]

In 1983, Nigeria was suffering severe economic dislocations due to a glut in world oil markets. Domestically, Nigeria suffered from low economic growth and high levels of inflation and unemployment. Government elites feared these factors would exacerbate religious and political tensions in an election year. They singled out alien workers as the source of Nigeria's crime, social unrest, and unemployment.

Although legal according to domestic immigration and ECOWAS law, the Nigerian decision to expel the alien workers directly contravened the spirit of the 1979 ECOWAS Protocol on Free Movement of Persons, Right of Residence, and Establishment. Nigeria had played a central role in the founding of the economic community in 1975, and Lagos hosted its headquarters. Community accomplishments had been few, however, and many Nigerians regarded the above-mentioned ECOWAS protocol as contributing to Nigeria's unemployment and social instability. Although ECOWAS officials and most heads of the member states rushed to refute the charge that Nigeria's policy struck a serious blow to community cohesion, the expulsion of alien workers constituted a clear case of national elite interests taking precedence over regional policies. The act demonstrated that cooperation with community initiatives was expendable when Nigeria's leaders faced immediate threats to their political survival.

THE PHILIPPINE DECISION

The ongoing dispute between the Philippines and Malaysia, both members of the Association of Southeast Asian Nations,[7] over the territory of Sabah (known as North Borneo under British colonial administration) disrupted diplomatic relations between the two countries and affected association activities between 1968 and 1977. In 1977, the Philippines was experiencing increasing unrest in the southern islands from Moro National Liberation Front-sponsored insurgency. Approximately 10,000 persons had died, and it was widely acknowledged that Sabah served as a rebel training site and conduit for weapons. In August 1977, President

Ferdinand Marcos announced at Kuala Lumpur that "the Government of the Republic of the Philippines is . . . taking definite steps to eliminate one of the burdens of ASEAN, the claim of the Philippine Republic to Sabah." (Marcos, 1977: 308–310) With this gesture, the Philippines ostensibly chose to forgo long-held claims over Sabah to enhance cooperation within the regional economic organization. More important to Philippine reckoning on the issue was the fact that removing the territorial dispute from Malaysia-Philippines relations would possibly secure Malaysian cooperation in ending the illicit trafficking of men and weapons across the frontier.

Additional long-term economic and strategic considerations encouraged greater Philippine cooperation within ASEAN. A reduced British and U.S. military presence threatened to alter the strategic balance of power in Southeast Asia. ASEAN was perceived by association members as useful in filling the political vacuum created by their reduced commitment. The five noncommunist members of ASEAN increasingly relied on the political and economic confidence generated by the association to address matters of regional stability and security. The association's potential as a catalyst for economic development and growth was also generally accepted.

SUMMARY

It is the thesis of this study that developing country elites frame decisions regarding regional cooperation in terms of short-term, national, and personal loss avoidance. Incongruity between the framework of benefits implied in regional economic cooperation and the framework out of which developing country elites make these decisions more often than not results in decisions that deter the progress of integration and deprives member states of an enhanced pool of economic and political resources. However, this is not always the case. The three cases of this study present examples of disparate framing, but the Philippine decision facilitated regional cooperation. In essence it may be said that the "right" choice, cooperation, was made for the "wrong" reason. This suggests that positive long-term collective economic consequences may derive from decision making framed in terms of short-term, national, and personal loss avoidance.

Previous investigation into the causes of regional organization failures in the main focused attention on the characteristics and processes of the institution itself. This study assumes that there is a relatively objective environment of benefits and constraints imposed by the international system, the member state's position within that system, and its attributes and capabilities. There is a particular framework of benefits deriving from the characteristics, processes, and policies of the regional organization. And there is a framework of utilities perceived by national elites which is the most immediate determinant of the issue-specific decision. Member-state elites operate within the systemic and regional frameworks, but their cognitive framework is also heavily influenced by personal considerations, risk and loss aversion, survival needs, and ideology. Both traditional and contemporary realist and liberal explanations for international cooperation fail to take cognitive framing into consideration adequately.

This study explores the potential framework of utilities implied in cooperation with specific initiatives of regional cooperation with the Andean Pact, the ECOWAS and the ASEAN. It then analyzes decisions made by Chile, Nigeria, and the Philippines relative to those initiatives, which resulted in contravention of regional initiatives in the Chilean and Nigerian cases, but facilitated regional cooperation in the latter case. The three cases support the proposition that developing country elites take decisions to cooperate or not to cooperate with specific programs and initiatives of their regional economic organization based on calculations of their need to avoid short-term, national, and personal loss. Theorists have suggested that effective institutions may serve an intervening variable to bridge the gap between the framework of benefits offered by regional cooperative efforts and the cognitive frameworks out of which member-state elites operate. Effective political leadership on the regional level is postulated as an essential element in the ultimate success of these organizations. Effective institutions may provide these elites with an alternative framework which redefines personal or national self-interests in terms of conjoint and enhanced payoffs while allowing them to meet their immediate personal and national needs to avoid risk and loss. The concluding chapter presents practical recommendations for making regional economic organizations among developing countries more effective in light of the findings of the study. Effective political leadership on the regional level is postulated as an essential element in the ultimate success of these organizations.

NOTES

1. Categorizing countries on the basis of economic development is a controversial and inexact science. There is always the potential for ethnocentric or normative considerations to color both the devising of the original taxonomy and the classification of countries on the basis of the scheme. Poor countries, relative to advanced industrialized ones, have been variously labeled the "Third World," the "South," "less developed," "developing," etc. (One undergraduate textbook labeled them the "other world.") The ideological and geographical implications of the first two referenced classifications are not appropriate to this study.

The Overseas Development Council classifies "developing" countries as those with a per capita annual income of less than US$2000 or a standard of living less than 90 on the Physical Quality of Life Index. The PQLI is calculated by averaging percentages associated with the average life expectancy at 1 year of age, infant mortality, and literacy rates. See McLaughlin (1979: 132) for further explication of these criteria for categorizing nations by developmental level.

Although the conceptual difficulties associated with the use of labels is acknowledged, the adjectives *less developed* and *developing* will be used interchangeably in this study to designate countries less bountifully endowed with economic assets and/or those that have failed to rationally exploit these resources to the maximum benefit of their citizenry. E. Bradford Burns (1987: 8) provides a straightforward, human-needs–oriented definition for economic development: ". . . the use of national resources for the greatest good of the largest number of inhabitants. . . ."

2. There are several types of explanation and competing notions of "causation." This study assumes that cause (the independent factor) is related to effect (the dependent factor) in terms of tendency or probability. Cause is temporally antecedent to effect.

3. We are dealing here with "issues" rather than "issue areas." Rosenau defines an issue area as consisting:

of (1) a cluster of values, the allocation or potential allocation of which (2) leads the affected or potentially affected actors to differ so greatly over (a) the way in which values should be allocated or (b) the horizontal levels at which the allocations should be authorized that (3) they engage in distinctive behavior designed to mobilize support for the attainment of their particular values.

Rosenau differentiates issues from issue areas by describing the former as temporary and situational while the latter are persistent and general (Rosenau, 1966: 77, 81).

4. The benefits of comparative cross-national research are expounded by George (1974 and 1979), Eckstein (1975), and Lijphart (1971, 1975).

5. Bolivia, Chile, Colombia, Ecuador, Peru, and Venezuela constituted the Andean Community.

6. The members of the Economic Community of West African States are Cape Verde, Dahomey (Benin), the Gambia, Ghana, Guinea, Guinea-Bissau, Côte d'Ivoire, Liberia, Mali, Mauritania, Niger, Nigeria, Senegal, Sierra Leone, Togo, and Upper Volta (Burkina Faso).

7. Indonesia, Malaysia, the Philippines, Thailand, and Singapore were founding members of ASEAN in 1967. Brunei joined the association in 1983.

2 Explaining Regional Economic Cooperation: The Case for a Cognitive Framing Model

A state's accession to membership in a regional integration scheme implies some level of commitment to cooperate within the institutional framework to affect policy coordination and/or collaboration. Its leaders agree to inform, consult, and consider the preferences of fellow members in the formulation of policy, and/or to promulgate common policy with harmoniously combined or interacting functions or parts. When members' interests are congruent, formal institutions are not required to ensure cooperation.[1] However, occasions are rare when several members' interests completely coincide over multiple issue areas. Thus, as each policy decision arises, member-state leaders must decide whether to comply with the regional policy. What influences and determines these decisions?

Realist and liberal interpretations of international phenomena posit that countries make these decisions within the context of an anarchical world order on the basis of some "rational" designation of objectives and utilitarian assessment of the effectiveness of policy alternatives to bring about the preferred outcomes at acceptable cost. However, rational actor models are based on some relatively circumscribed assumptions. They assume that the decision-making unit's ultimate objective is an absolute or relative improvement in final welfare, and that an "objective" value exists which utility maximizers will assign policy alternatives. The most parsimonious rational actor models of international transactions ignore attitudes toward probability, risk, and loss; ideological considerations; and how time affects decision making. In short, rational actor models ignore subjective aspects of decision making and assume an objective payoff structure imposed by the external environment. Although acknowledging that a structure of utilities is imposed on national decision makers as a consequence of the nature of the international system and their country's attributes, capabilities, and domestic political system, this study further posits that the cognitive framework within which foreign policy decision makers interpret and assess these factors ultimately determines what is deemed a rational choice. A cognitive framing model will be used to examine decision making regarding cooperation within regional economic organizations.

Cognitive framing models assume that policy makers take decisions within a more subjective structure of utilities configured by such factors as how they conceptualize the policy issue; the level of analysis; their attitudes toward gain and loss, probability and risk; whether they perceive their political, economic, or personal survival is at stake; their ideology or "world view"; and the time frame in which they believe costs and benefits are likely to accrue. This approach is context dependent. Decision makers' cognitive frameworks are predominantly shaped by their roles and the national domestic contexts and only to a lesser extent are influenced by idiosyncratic factors. Although any decision maker is likely to calculate the utilities in the same way given the context, no single rational choice exists for the policy question (McKeown, 1993: 204). What is rational is a function of the way utilities are framed within the thought processes of policy elites. A rational choice in terms of conjoint utilities provided by regional economic cooperation may lack rationality within the cognitive framework of a political elite seeking to maximize individual political goals.

This is the crux of the dilemma of developing countries' cooperation within regional economic organizations. Regional integration schemes offer a collective framework within which member states assess the utility of cooperation. They are undertaken to provide economic benefits that member states cannot or have difficulty accomplishing alone. This study will demonstrate, however, that the framework of conjoint and national benefits implicit in cooperation within regional economic schemes is in many instances incongruent with the cognitive framework within which national elites decide to comply with regional initiatives.

This chapter first considers realist and liberal explanations of interstate cooperation or the lack thereof. Potential components of an alternative cognitive framing model are presented. Then, the benefits and costs associated with regional economic cooperation as delineated in trade union and economic integration theory are outlined. These payoffs tend to be structural in substance, regionally distributed, long-term, and therefore only potential. The framework within which elites of developing countries are likely to take foreign policy decisions is then considered. Because of desperate economic, political, and societal conditions, this framework is often dominated by immediate and specific elite or national needs. Policy makers' personal or national political and economic survival may be at risk. They must make decisions to deal with these concerns before regional collective ones. Finally, conditions are such that policy makers cannot choose to address long-term needs at the expense of short-term exigencies. If short-term needs are not met, there is often no future for the political elites of developing countries.

REALIST AND LIBERAL EXPLANATIONS FOR INTERNATIONAL COOPERATION

Classical realists posit the state as the primary unitary international actor, a "black box" from which decisions emit without regard for distinctive national attributes, domestic political and social systems, the cultural characteristics of its citizenry, or the personality traits of its leadership. Acting as a single cognition and will, the state automatically prioritizes its "national interests" and then calculates costs and benefits associated with various policy options to achieve the desired ends. Realists acknowledged, however, that these tasks are undertaken under conditions of uncertainty, without sufficient resources, including information and time, to fully survey all possible courses of action. Thus, realists conceptualize state behavior as a consequence of bounded rationality (Keohane, 1989: 62; Simon, 1955, 1957, and 1958).

Realists believe that the structure of the international system is the principal determinant of interstate transactions. Structure encourages certain actions and constrains others. Understanding the structure of the international system allows the analyst to explain patterns of state behavior, including cooperation and noncooperation. States identify their national interests and plan strategies on the basis of calculations about their relative positions within the international system. The realist rationality assumption provides the critical link between the structure of the system and the behavior of the individual state. The assumption of nation-state rationality allows the analyst to predict how statesmen will respond to system-imposed incentives and constraints. Morgenthau (1966: 5) elucidates:

We put ourselves in the position of a statesman who must meet a certain problem of foreign policy under certain circumstances, and we ask ourselves what the rational alternatives are from which a statesman may choose . . . and which of these rational alternatives this particular statesman, acting under these circumstances, is likely to choose. It is the testing of this rational hypothesis against the actual facts and their consequences that gives meaning to the facts of international politics and makes a theory of politics possible.

Assuming rationality is constant permits the realist to attribute variations in state behavior to changes in the international system (Keohane, 1989: 41).[2]

Because the international system is anarchical, that is without central-ized authority to enforce agreements among the parts, relations among states are inherently competitive and conflictual. Self-preservation is of necessity the first among a nation's priorities. Stanley Hoffman (1965: vii) describes international politics as "a competition of units in the kind of state of nature that knows no restraint other than those which the changing necessities of the game and the shallow conve-niences of the players impose." This constant threat to survival con-strains states to seek maximization of relative as well as absolute ad-vantage.[3]

Under these conditions, cooperation between and among states is un-usual. States cooperate only when they cannot independently achieve the benefits they seek. Cooperation within a coalition or alliance is the result of a common threat, short-term congruence of power interests, or an artifact of global polarity. Within these transitory relationships, states must guard against allies' benefiting more than they from the arrange-ment. International organizations are therefore epiphenomenal at best. Classical realism sheds very little light on countries' decisions to cooper-ate within regional economic organizations. Cooperation in areas for-merly referred to as "low politics," such as monetary management, health, humanitarian efforts, and the environment, are not accounted for (Stein, 1990: 5, 25; Keohane, 1984: 7).

Liberals also conceptualize the foreign policy choices of states in terms of rational cost and benefit analysis. Rooted in 19th century *lais-sez faire* economics, liberalism envisions international transactions not in relative or constant sum terms; instead, the reserve of benefits in-creases as states interact. There is a "natural" harmony of states' inter-ests. States' choices and behaviors in the international political arena aggregate in the long term to yield cooperation, just as in the economic realm individuals' and firms' choices to maximize personal welfare and profit constitute market forces that facilitate growth and generalize pros-perity. Cooperation and peace are the normal state of affairs; conflict is a periodic aberration that disturbs economic exchange. It is a conse-quence of shortsightedness, miscalculation, misperception, the absence of quality information, or disfunctional institutions (Stein, 1990: 8). Lib-erals anticipate that converging interests will give rise to a variety of international cooperative schemes.

Theoretical explanations for cooperation between and among states did not culminate with classical realist and liberal thought. Liberals' op-timistic assumption of the possibility of international cooperation under-went four major transformations between the 1940s and 1980s relevant to this study: functionalism in the 1940s and early 1950s, neofunctional-ist regional theory in the 1950s and 1960s, and interdependence theory in the 1970s.[4] In the 1980s, a synthesis of realist and liberal thought emerged in the various configurations of regime theory.

Functionalists observed that political authority was becoming decentralized within the modern state, and comparable processes were underway internationally. Specialized agencies and the technical experts that served them represented important new actors on the international scene. Agencies, such as the International Labor Organization, enhanced cooperation because they performed valuable tasks without directly challenging the authority of the state.

In the 1950s and 1960s, neofunctionalists added labor unions, political parties, and trade associations to the list of important transnational actors. Cooperation among technical experts on a single issue was expected to "spillover" into other issue areas (Haas, 1958). Neofunctionalists were particularly interested in the benefits to be gained from regional economic cooperation. The creation of supranational bodies, such as the European Economic Communities, was viewed as an appropriate response by states increasingly unable to meet their citizens' needs through autonomous means. Neofunctionalists provided in-depth analysis of factors that may influence the success of regional economic cooperation during various stages of the process in the context of advanced industrial and developing country participation. Listed below is a partial accounting of these factors and exemplars of the relevant theoretical literature.

I. Factors Identified as Significant at the Onset of the Cooperative Process
  A. Geographical proximity (Etzioni, 1965; Spaak, 1968; Nye, 1971b)
  B. Symmetry in members' power, size, and economic capabilities (Deutsch, 1957; Etzioni, 1965; Russett, 1967; Haas, 1971; Nye, 1971b; Hazlewood, 1980)
  C. Congruency of governmental types/forms (Bond, 1978)
  D. Quality of individual-level leadership (Haas, 1967; Nye, 1971b; Boyd, 1984)
  E. National regional leadership (Ojo, 1980; Boyd, 1984)
  F. Elite value complementarity (Lindberg, 1971; Nye, 1971a; Krause and Nye, 1975; Haas, 1976; Hazelwood, 1980)
  G. Existence of pluralism, autonomous modern associational groups, and transnational nongovernmental organizations (Nye, 1970; Scheingold, 1970; Schmitter, 1970; Nye, 1971b; Sweeney, 1984)
  H. Capacity of states to adapt/respond (function of interdependency, absolute economic capabilities, power capabilities, available information, and internal political stability) (Deutsch, 1964; Haas, 1971 and 1976; Nye, 1971)
  I. Level of political integration (Nye, 1971b)
  J. Level of security integration (Nye, 1971b)
  K. Level of social and cultural integration (Lindberg, 1971; Nye, 1971a; Mazrui, 1972; Nyong, 1983)
  L. Influence of external actors, regional and superpowers (Schmitter, 1969; Nye, 1971b; Haas, 1976; Hazlewood, 1980; Boyd, 1984)
  M. Systemic economic environment

II. Perceptual Factors
   A. Low/exportable visible costs (Nye, 1971a)
   B. Perceived equity in distribution of benefits (Haas, 1971; Lindberg, 1971; Nye, 1971b; Healey, 1977; Hazlewood, 1980; Yeats, 1981)
   C. Perceived external cogency (Schmitter, 1969; Nye, 1971b; Haas, 1976)
   D. Level of nationalism (Anderson, 1967; Lindberg, 1971; Nye, 1971b; Bond, 1978)
III. Characteristics of the Regional Economic Organization
   A. Number of member states (Riker, 1962; Olson, 1965)
   B. Structure of the decision-making body (Lindberg, 1971; Bond, 1978; Boyd, 1984)
   C. Style of decision-making/bargaining modalities (Haas, 1970 and 1976; Lindberg, 1971)
   D. Depth/scope of decision making (Schmitter, 1970; Lindberg, 1971; Nye, 1971a; Groom and Taylor, 1975)
   E. Level of institutionalization/authority/organizational autonomy (Haas, 1958; Huntington, 1968; Nye, 1968 and 1971a; Taylor, 1968; Schmitter, 1970; Lindberg, 1971; Haas, 1976; Sweeney, 1984; Keohane, 1989; Sandholtz, 1993)
   F. Policy implementation capabilities (Puchala, 1970; Lindberg, 1971)
IV. Process Factors
   A. Functional linkage of tasks/"spontaneous spillover" (Haas, 1958 and 1971; Lindberg, 1965; Nye, 1971a)
   B. Deliberate linkages/"cultivated spillover"/coalition formation (Nye, 1971b)
   C. Increased transactions, particularly trade (Deutsch, 1953 and 1969; Robson, 1971; Haas, 1971; Nye, 1971b; Yeats, 1981)
   D. Elite socialization/support (Mitrany, 1966; Haas, 1964; Sweeney, 1984)
   E. Regional associational/transnational nongovernmental group formation (see I.G)
   F. Ideological or identitive appeal/development of regional identity (Segal, 1967; Schmitter, 1970; Nye, 1971b)
 V. Policy Outcomes/Distributive Consequences
   A. Equity in distribution of benefits (see II.B)
   B. Industrial allocation policy (Lanfranco, 1980)
   C. Shared services (Nye, 1971a)
   D. Labor migration (Nye, 1971b)
   E. Joint ventures
   F. Monetary coordination
   G. Judicial coordination

This research effort, which uses a cognitive framing model, may be regarded as simultaneously contrasted with and contributing to the neofunctionalist tradition. On the one hand, with the exception of the perceptual factors listed above (under II), most neofunctionalist literature focused on attributes and processes of the regional economic organizations themselves to provide explanation for the sources of member-state cooperation. This research assigns primary causation to the cognitive framework within which developing country elites assess the utility of regional cooperation. Neofunctionalist and liberal neoinstitutionalists predilections are reflected, however, in the conclusion that effective institutions can bridge the gap between the framework of utilities implied in regional cooperation and that out of which developing country elites are forced to take decisions.

The interdependence literature of the 1970s sustained the focus on transnational and transgovernmental coalitions and added transnational corporations to the list of actors challenging the state for international dominance. This literature also described the modern state as increasingly characterized by "multiple channels of access," which weakened its control over foreign policy. As increasingly ineffective states confronted issues of increasing quantity and complexity, their need for international institutions grew (Grieco, 1988: 486, 489, 498–490; Keohane and Nye, 1977: 35–36, 232–234, 240–242).

Regime theory evolved as a distinctive analytical perspective in the early 1980s. The literature most often cited as pioneering these ideas is Axelrod's *The Evolution of Cooperation* (1984), Keohane's *After Hegemony: Cooperation and Discord in the World Political Economy* (1984), and Krasner's *International Regimes*, an edited volume published in 1983. As previously noted, regime analysis may be regarded as a synthesis of the realist and liberal traditions. It incorporates a number of realist assumptions such as its anarchical conception of the international system, the designation of states as primary actors, and its reliance on the central tenets of instrumentally rational decision making. Regime analysts argue, however, that realism overemphasizes conflict and underestimates the capacity of international institutions to promote cooperation. States' behavior is not just a reflection of the anarchical world order and/or the result of self-interested utility-maximizing behavior. Instead, patterns of states' interests and capabilities and the level of global interdependence may foster cooperation. International institutions constrain and socialize states and render their actions intelligible to others. Regime theorists concede that difficulties in monitoring compliance with international agreements and policies may impede states' inclination to cooperate. To the extent that international institutions put into place procedures to monitor behavior, they reduce members' information costs, uncertainties, and over time, transaction costs. Ultimately, international institutions succeed to the degree that they are able to establish norms, rules, and principles and facilitate the convergence of expectations and interests (Stein, 1992: 207–208).

Regime theorists come in various stripes. Those whose conception of international interactions more closely resembles the realist than the liberal tradition believe that the anarchical and conflictual nature of the international system hinders cooperation to an extreme degree. They acknowledge, however, that cooperation is present within the international system and requires explanation. Furthermore, they acknowledge the dangers inherent in realism's pessimistic interpretation, which provides little hope for dealing with the ubiquitous threat of war in an age of nuclear technology and the collective goods problems characterized by the prisoners' dilemma. (That is to say, when collective goods are involved and individual nation-states rationally pursue their egocentric interests, a suboptimal outcome may be achieved.) Therefore, analysts with realist inclinations believe that a hegemon is necessary for the creation of international regimes. They accentuate the utility of sanctions in guaranteeing cooperation within international institutions.

The existence of a hegemon may increase the likelihood of regime creation in two ways. The benevolent hegemon may possess sufficient systemic and issue-specific interests to make it willing to bear disproportionate costs associated with regime creation and maintenance. In the international economic sphere, the United States' willingness to adhere to (relatively) free trade policies while its trading partners practiced trade protectionism in the wake of World War II, and its allowing use of the dollar as global currency, are often provided as examples of a benevolent hegemon at work. Analysts also point out, however, that the role of the hegemon is not always benevolent. By definition, the hegemon possesses the means to coerce compliance of weaker states by denying them the benefits of the regime and/or applying sanctions in other issue areas.

Regime analysts with realist suppositions believe that states will defect or cheat on regime rules if the opportunity presents itself. They regard this behavior as the "rational choice" and point out that this rationality is the basis of the free rider problem in providing collective goods. It logically follows from this interpretation that monitoring and sanctions are requisites for successful institutions. The literature that focuses on these functions discusses costs associated with monitoring and sanctioning behavior and how these factors might best be incorporated into regime procedures at acceptable cost levels.

Rather than accentuating the importance of shared and converging interests, regime theorists with realist inclinations regard reciprocity as the most potent guarantor of cooperation. Cooperation is best sustained among egocentric states if exchanges are constituted on a mutually conditional basis. In successive interactions, a state's cooperation is contingent on the cooperative behavior of its partners in a tit-for-tat interaction. Effective reciprocity depends on three conditions: the state must be able to identify and sanction defecting partners, and sufficient long-run incentives must exist for the state to assume responsibility for administering punishment.[5] Effective institutions reinforce and legitimize the conditions that formalize interactions and facilitate reciprocity.

In summary, neorealist regime theorists recognize that there are instances of cooperation in the international arena unexplained by classical realist theory. They also acknowledge the existence of collective needs and problems, which may be unmet and exacerbated if states act autonomously to maximize utilities. Because this body of thought regards defecting, cheating, or free riding as the state's natural inclination, a hegemon likely will be required to create and/or maintain the regime. The institutionalization of monitoring, sanctioning, and reciprocity is essential to creating and maintaining cooperation (Axelrod, 1984; Taylor, 1987: 61, 65).

Liberal regime theorists differ from their realist colleagues in emphasis. They acknowledge the difficulties in cooperation in the anarchical world system and the increasing prevalence of collective goods problems. They believe, however, that states, sharing common interests and goals, desire cooperation, and that creating effective institutions is the means to facilitate this cooperation. Liberal regime theory relies less on the existence of a hegemon, monitoring, and sanctioning. It contends that such factors as increasing interdependence, common or converging interests, the enhancement of available information, and norms are sufficient to foster cooperation (Grieco, 1988: 497). This study embraces the liberal concept of effective institutions as the solution to the discrepancy between the framework of payoffs provided by cooperation in regional economic efforts and the framework out of which developing country elites choose cooperation or noncooperation. The following section outlines an alternative cognitive framing model that will be used to structure the analysis of the three case studies.

A COGNITIVE FRAMING MODEL

Neither classical realist nor liberal concepts of rational decision making take into account how decision makers perceive the decision scenario and how they formulate assumptions about utilities or the payoff structure.[6] They assume that the payoff structure is objectively determined by the character of the global system and possibly influenced by international institutions. However, cognitive psychology and related sciences[7] maintain that the way individuals perceive and frame decisions determines in large part how they assess benefits and costs. Cognitive psychologists' assumptions about the significance of decision framing are outlined in prospect theory.

Kelley and Thibaut (1978: 17) distinguish between the "given matrix," which defines the payoffs structured by the environment and attributes of the actors, and the "effective matrix" out of which actors actually make their choices. The effective matrix is the payoff structure perceived by decision makers. The social psychologists write: "There is no close causal nexus between the *given* matrix and the behavior it elicits." Instead, actors respond to payoffs in the given matrix to generate the effective matrix, "which is . . . closely linked to their behavior." Actors may make decisions that seem irrational given the objective decision context. To understand actual decision making, it is necessary to know the effective matrix out of which actors assess the objective payoff structure (Stein, 1990: 118).

In "framing" a decision, an actor first makes several "metadecisions," which establish points of reference for subsequent utility assessment. These points determine the criteria the decision maker deems appropriate for analyzing and assessing a particular issue. The framing decisions pertain to the essential nature of the policy question such as: What is the issue at hand? On which level should utilities be assessed—a regional, national, or personal basis? Does the issue involve welfare enhancement and maximization or loss avoidance? What probabilities are attached to the potential positive and negative outcomes? Does the policy question entail some risk or threat to political, economic, or personal survival? Are the prescriptions of my world view and ideology relevant to the issue? What time horizon is involved in cost and benefit realization?

Analysts must be alert to the possibility that reference points may shift during the course of decision making. The location of a point of reference is determined by all possible outcomes known to the decision maker, either by direct experience or by observation of others (Kelley and Thibaut, 1978: 9). This choosing of reference points and subsequent cognitive and decision-making processes shape the decision to cooperate or not to cooperate (Stein, 1992: 213, 226; Stein, 1990: 193). There is no formal framing theory that identifies the cognitive framework leaders are likely to choose under different conditions. The cognitive framing model used in this study, however, emphasizes the importance of how actors frame policy questions in terms of issue conceptualization, the level of utility assessment, and whether utilities are calculated in terms of loss or gain. The need for political, economic, and personal survival and ideology are posited as two potentially lexicographic influences on utilities assessment. The influences of probability and risk and the time horizon on utility assessment are also posited as important constituents of the cognitive framing model. Propositions as to how these components may be expected to influence decision making are provided to guide the consideration of these framing components in the case studies to follow. It is assumed that congruency between the framework of utilities offered by regional economic initiatives and the way developing country elites frame their policy decisions and utility assessment facilitates cooperation.

1. Issue Conceptualization

It may seem self-evident that the initial conceptualization of the substantive content of the policy question is crucial to how decision makers
assess utilities. It must be pointed out, however, that particularly within
the context of crisis decision making, whether a policy question even
exists may be the object of debate. A common illustration of this possibility is the 1962 Cuban Missile Crisis when US Secretary of Defense
Robert McNamara was initially unconvinced that the basing of Soviet
ballistic missiles in Cuba constituted a novel threat to US national security.

Particularly because regional and national decision makers may be formulating policy to address problems on different levels of analysis, regional versus national and personal, congruence in the conceptualization
of the policy question cannot be taken for granted. The case studies that
follow clearly demonstrate that issue delineation is a crucial first step in
decision framing. For example, in the Andean case, the primary policy
question for Chilean decision makers was how to avoid losing direct
foreign investment and how to facilitate economic recovery and growth,
whereas for regional policy makers, the most salient objectives in formulating Decision 24 were guaranteeing indigenous control over economic
development and decreasing foreign economic dependence. Thus, the
first cognitive framing proposition to be investigated is:

Proposition I: *Divergence may obtain between the regional economic
organization and member-state elites' conceptualization of the substantive content of the policy question.*

2. The Level of Utility Assessment

A second, possibly self-evident, framing issue, which relates directly
to Proposition I, is the metadecision regarding the level of analysis on
which utilities are to be assessed. From the perspective of the regional
initiative, utilities should be assessed in terms of *regional* and *national*
benefits. However, it will be demonstrated that member-state elites are
more likely to assess utilities in terms of *personal, national,* and then
regional concerns. The second and third propositions to be investigated
in the study are:

Proposition II: *Regional decision makers undertake policy initiatives to
maximize regional and national gains.*

Proposition III: *Member-state elites assess the utilities of regional cooperative schemes on* personal, national, and regional bases, *consecutively.*

3. Association of the Issue with Gain or Loss

Whether decision makers frame the foreign policy question in terms of gain or loss is crucial to the decision output. Laboratory research reveals that people are generally more concerned about loss than gain. Pain is a more powerful motivator than pleasure. In framing choices, people weigh potential losses more heavily than gains. For example, greater pain is experienced on losing $100 than pleasure derived from discovering the same amount.

Decision makers may select the status quo or an aspirational state as the point of reference for gain or loss. In general, human perception is attuned to evaluate changes or differences rather than to evaluate absolute magnitudes. Attributes such as brightness, loudness, or temperature are perceived in relation to the past and present context of experience. Values assigned to these attributes are a function of the reference point and magnitude of positive or negative change relative to that point (Kahneman and Tversky, 1979: 277).[8]

Persons' sensitivity to gain and loss decreases as the decision question moves away from their primary reference point. Certain or potential losses closest to the reference point are most weighted when decision options are evaluated. If loss is threatened close to the primary reference point, even if it is not a particularly large loss, it may be highly weighted in the mind of the decision maker and may induce risky behavior (Stein, 1992: 218, footnote 40, 221). A decision maker's perspective also may be affected by incomplete adaptation to recent losses experienced outside the context of the immediate decision scenario (Kahneman and Tversky, 1979: 288).

Decision makers' decisions to cooperate reflect a general tendency toward loss aversion. Decision makers may decide to cooperate not because the venture promises substantial absolute or relative gains that cannot be realized independently, but because they anticipate that failure to cooperate will bring losses. As will be noted in all three of the following case studies, the decision regarding the regional economic organization can be interpreted as an attempt to avoid loss rather than enhance welfare. In the case of Chile, decision makers' choices were shaped by the desire to avoid loss of direct foreign investment. Nigerian leaders feared for their political survival, and the Marcos regime feared loss of political control over the Muslim insurgency in the south. Propositions IV and V summarize the gain/loss component to be considered in this cognitive framing model:

Proposition IV: *Certain or potential losses are more highly weighted than those associated with gain in member-state elites' decision making. That is to say, developing country elites are loss averse.*

Proposition V: *Certain or potential loss very near the decision maker's primary point of reference may induce risk-acceptant behavior.*

4. The Influence of Perceived Probability and/or Risk on Utility Assessment

Probability refers to the ratio of the chances favoring an event to the total number of chances for and against it. Persons have limited ability to comprehend and evaluate probabilities, particularly extremely high or low ones. Editing, coding, and other cognitive processes are likely to be used to deal with these uncertainties and, thus, will affect how probability is calculated. The decision maker may simplify the array of choices by "rounding off" probabilities. The probabilities of identical outcomes may be combined. Highly likely outcomes may be coded as certain and unlikely outcomes discarded as insignificant.[9] A prevalent phenomenon, the "certainty effect," occurs when persons underweight outcomes that are merely probable in comparison with outcomes that are certain.

The probability framing component will be particularly important in the three cases of this investigation, because the time horizon for realization of benefits implicit in the regional cooperation schemes are long-term and therefore associated with only moderate to low levels of probability. The needs facing developing country elites, however, are immediate and highly probable. Because decision makers' editing and coding processes are difficult to discern without in-depth psychological analysis, Proposition VI of this investigation will focus exclusively on decision makers' heavy weighting of more certain policy options.

Proposition VI: *Developing country elites place a premium on high probability in utility assessment in their foreign policy decision making.*

Prospect theory differs from many versions of utility theory by treating the decision maker's response to potential loss, risk, as a function of the characteristics of the situation rather than the personality of the decision maker. Risk-averse or -acceptant policy choices are conceived as responses to the decision context confronting the elites within their governmental roles rather than idiosyncratic factors (McKeown, 1993: 208).[10]

Choices among risky prospects exhibit several effects that are inconsistent with the tenets of utility theory. People are generally risk averse with respect to gains and risk acceptant with regard to losses. Prospect theorists refer to this "mirror imaging" in preferences as the "reflection effect." As previously noted, potential losses are assessed relative to the initial reference point rather than final welfare enhancement (Kahneman and Tversky, 1979: 263–264; 268–269).[11] Proposition VII encapsulates the reflection effect regarding perceived risk:

Proposition VII: *Developing-country elites exhibit risk acceptance with regard to potential losses and risk aversion with regard to potential gains.*

5. Association of the Issue with the Need for Political, Economic, or Personal Survival

Risk and loss aversion are most pronounced when a decision involves political, economic, or personal survival. The framework of rationality is greatly affected when the decision maker is maximizing payoffs to ensure survival. Survival is given preeminent weight, and other options are considered only after this fundamental objective is ensured. Such preference sequencing is referred to as lexicographic. Actors with lexicographic preferences maximize in sequence rather than make trade-offs. A policy option that fails to maximize survival will not be considered, regardless of how well it addresses secondary priorities.

Rosecrance (1973) provides a lexicographic conception of the prioritization of "national interests" in his "onion theory" of international relations. He argues that security is the state's fundamental objective, and that only subsequently does it pursue material and ideological preferences. It follows from this that it is more difficult to achieve cooperation on security issues than economic ones (Stein, 1990: 90–91).

The cognitive process that assigns first priority to survival is a conservative rationality. It is fully rational to avoid an option with positive expected returns to avoid an option that greatly threatens survival. Stein (1990: 109) writes: "States that fear for their survival may rationally depart from the otherwise rational. Not wishing to risk their very national existence, they may be conservatively rational, eschewing gambles with higher payoffs."

As will be shown, this primary need for survival makes it irrational for states to take risks, even in cases with potentially high payoffs. Options involving high levels of risk to political survival, whether from a potential coup or insurgency, are choices that political elites are not likely to consider. A successful military coup d'etat may result in death or, at best, political and financial ruin for the ousted leaders.

States' leaders whose survival is ensured can afford to think in the long term and accept risks implied by potential options. Less secure elites are more likely to think in terms of immediate payoffs and risk minimization. They approach the decision process lexicographically, with survival, high probability, and immediate payoffs dominating their frameworks.

In the Nigerian case, the Shagari government was fighting for its political survival. The fact that the regime succumbed to a military coup within months of the deportation decision provides irrefutable evidence of the validity of elite concerns. Decision makers in the Chilean and, to a lesser extent, the Philippine cases were also concerned with political survival. As will be discussed, the Pinochet regime came to power in a bloody coup which overthrew the socialist Allende government. The economic disorder that facilitated its illegal assumption of power remained the most formidable challenge to its continued rule. In the Philippine case, although Muslim insurgency was a chronic source of political and societal instability rather than an immediate threat to the Marcos regime, it represented a potential challenge to the elites' long-term political survival when coupled with other problems. However, only in the Nigerian case did survival concerns dominate the framing of the policy decision.

Proposition VIII: *Political, economic, and/or personal survival are given preeminent weight by member-state elites in utility assessment; other policy objectives are considered only after these objectives are attained.*

Ideology is a second crucial component of cognitive framing with potentially lexicographic influence.

6. The Influence of Ideology on Utility Assessment

Another potentially important component of cognitive framing is developing country elites' belief systems, world views, or ideologies. Because the decisions to be taken are political and economic in nature, ideology is likely to exert significant influence. As used in this study, *ideology* subsumes several basic concepts: ideas, beliefs, and values cohering in a theory or system with the implication of some political goal(s) or action(s).[12] Goodwin (1987: 22–23, 27) elaborates:

. . . ideology is a doctrine about the right way, or ideal way, of organizing society and conducting politics, based on wider considerations about the nature of human life and knowledge. The "action-guiding" aspect of such doctrines derives from the fact they claim to establish what is politically true and right, and so give rise to imperatives which are essentially moral. They inevitably include the recommendation that their ideals should be realized, or should continue to be realized.

Ideological tenets may be inherently persuasive to the extent that they lexicographically influence the prioritization of policy options; options at odds with the ideological constructs may be eliminated *a priori* (Stein 1990: 234). Ideology may be used as an editing, coding, or heuristic device. Ideological tenets may decrease the stress of policy making by simplifying and clarifying political-economic phenomena. They may suggest solutions to problems. Political-economic phenomena are very complex; many economic relationships are yet to be understood; and the areas of controversy among economic theories are substantial. Furthermore, there is no objectively correct answer to political questions of resource allocation. And the costs associated with economic crises and policy failure are high. Thus, policy makers seek ways to reduce uncertainty and solve their economic and political problems. Ideological tenets advance this purpose; they purport to render comprehensible complex social, economic, and political phenomena. They provide a "template or blueprint for the organization of social and psychological processes;" they are "maps of problematic social reality and matrices for the creation of collective conscience" (Geertz, 1964: 62, 64). They also may serve as catalysts or binding agents that allow policy ideas to combine in new ways.

Ideologies may facilitate policy compromise by generating consensus and solidarity within the international organization or within the domestic politics of member states. Of course, it is also possible that ideology may be used as a tool of and/or mask the intent of particular interest groups. For purposes of this study of cognitive framing, however, ideology will be regarded as a component in decision framing with the potential for lexicographic significance:

Proposition IX: *Ideology may exert lexicographic influence on developing country elites' framing of the costs and benefits of cooperation.*

The establishment of regional economic organizations is an indicator that the founding leadership embraced the tenets of customs union and integration theory, both derivatives of the ideology of classical liberal economics. However, the Chilean case will provide the strongest illustration of the importance of ideology in decision framing. Upon assuming power in 1973, Chilean governmental officials, heavily influenced by Friedmanite-style, free trade ideology, were immediately at odds with the Andean Pact's Decision 24, which sought to limit foreign content of investment in the region.

7. The Influence of the Time Horizon on Utility Assessment

A critical aspect of the cognitive framework within which elites formulate policy decisions is the time horizon used when calculating their interests. Do decision makers act to maximize immediate payoffs at the expense of future ones, or do they practice self-denial in the present to maximize prospective payoffs (Stein, 1990: 21)? Psychological research suggests that people tend to give more weight to immediate and certain gains at the expense of long-term, less certain ones (Stein, 1992: 212).

The most widely used model of intertemporal choice is the discounted utility or exponential discounting model. Future time is divided into discrete periods; the present value of a payoff to be made some time units from the present is called the discount rate. The higher the discount rate, the lower the present value of future payoffs.

Exponential discounting occurs at a constant rate. This implies that the decision makers discount a unit of future time to the same degree regardless of when it occurs (Taylor, 1987: 21).[13] With exponential discounting, a 1-day delay in gratification has the same significance whether the delay is 24 hours or a year and a day from today. The exponential discount model assumes that choices are consistent over time.

Many cognitive scientists now regard the discounted utility model as descriptively and normatively flawed. It is widely believed that discounting tends to be hyperbolic rather than exponential. Hyperbolic discounters are subject to "time inconsistency;" their preferences change systematically with the passage of time. For example, when faced with a choice between an inferior early option and a superior later option, the hyperbolic discounter will tend to prefer the later, superior option when both are remote, but the earlier, inferior option as both approach in time. The inferior option becomes disproportionately tempting when it is imminent. Time-inconsistent behaviors differ from high time discounting. High time discounting signifies that outcomes experienced earlier are more highly valued than those experienced later. Time inconsistency refers to changes in time discounting as a function of delay. A high rate of time discounting is possible without inconsistency. The behavior of misers who plan to splurge in the future but fail to follow through in the end illustrates time inconsistency associated with negative time discounting.

The first empirical evidence that individuals' choice patterns were incompatible with the discounted utility was provided by Richard Thaler in 1981. Researchers are divided about the pervasiveness of decision makers' tendencies to discount future outcomes and how the phenomena may be overcome to produce optimal decisions. Some view time inconsistency as a pervasive problem to be overcome through intricate and energetic efforts at self-control. Others regard it as aberrant behavior exhibited only when normal cues are absent (Loewenstein and Elster, 1992: xi–xvii). Loewenstein and Elster (1992: xxiii) imply that in the political realm, potentially negative effects of time inconsistency in decision making may be overcome by effective institutions:

While individual discount rates, to the extent that they exist, may be high, humans possess remarkable capabilities to overcome these rates. Social and political organization, elaborate strategies and tactics of self control, social norms, and emotions arising from memory and anticipation all mitigate the otherwise pernicious effects of hyperbolic discounting.

Stein (1992: 107) writes: "If actors have different time horizons when they interact, their varying perspectives can become the bases for conflicting assessments of self-interest and so generate dilemmas of cooperation and conflict." The discrepancy in time horizon calculations of developing countries' elites and the long-term commitment required for most regional integration schemes to achieve fruition are major deterrents to the success of regional economic organizations.

The discount rate applied to the future often is influenced by interaction patterns. Most interstate transactions are ongoing; they have a history and a future. Interactions occur within a historical and issue-specific context that includes information about the trustworthiness and agreeability of actors. Nations will be required to deal with each other in the future, particularly those in regional proximity. The certainty of future interactions affects the payoff structure perceived by policy makers and makes cooperation rational. Iteration allows the incorporation of future returns into the current calculations of utility. Under repeated iterations, policy makers must weigh the immediate benefits of self-interested, uncooperative behavior against the benefits of iterated cooperation (Stein, 1990: 98–100). If government leaders anticipate repeated transactions within the organization, they may elect to cooperate to preserve access to future transactions. It also follows that leaders with few prospects for political survival are likely to discount the future more than those more certain of retaining their positions (Oye, 1985: 13). Multiple factors interacting within effective institutions may "lengthen the shadow of the future": iteration, reliable information about others' intentions and actions, quick feedback regarding changes in others' intentions and actions, clear rules and procedures, effective monitoring and sanctioning, etc. (Axelrod and Keohane, 1985: 232).

Stein (1992: 164) is dubious of the suggestion that political decision makers' apparently self-abnegating behavior is a reflection of the incorporation of future payoffs into the current decision equation. To assume that self-sacrifice is attributable to future payoffs is to assume that actors believe they have a reliable sense of future payoffs. Foreign policy actors rarely can know or even estimate future payoffs. They know the opportunity and actual costs of self-sacrifice and the payoffs others derive from their sacrifice. Instead of self-sacrifice being an indicator of postponed gratification, it may signal that the decision maker has chosen collective rather than autonomous strategies to meet her needs. Stein

(1992) contends that what a state is willing to do for its allies is a measure of the quality of the collective relationship, specifically the usefulness and effectiveness of the organization. Thus, seemingly non–self-interested behavior may be attributed to immediate self-interest by attaching some value to the regional cooperative effort.

Proposition X: *Developing-country elites act to maximize immediate payoffs at the expense of future ones.*

Thus, 10 propositions have been provided that are associated with potential constituents of the cognitive framing of the decision to cooperate on a regional basis. The segment to follow suggests in general the payoff structure implied in participation in regional integration organizations. These payoffs are delineated in trade union and regional integration theory.

THE FRAMEWORK OF UTILITIES SUGGESTED IN FREE TRADE, REGIONAL INTEGRATION, AND CUSTOMS UNION THEORIES

Developing countries' success in the early stages of industrialization, which has been the most commonly embraced model of economic development, is contingent on the generation of investment capital in principle sectors of the economy and the availability of markets for the sale of the commodities produced by these sectors. Thereafter, it is important that incentives and protection be provided to ensure the profitability of the primary enterprises, and that intersectoral interaction is unencumbered. The expansion of export activities is usually considered crucial to generate surplus for investment in manufacturing and industrialization activities. Transportation and communication infrastructure must exist for the export sector to function properly. Regional cooperation addresses these needs in several ways: by pooling resources to undertake infrastructural and complementary industrialization schemes; by establishing free trade areas or common markets and customs unions; and by harmonizing monetary, fiscal, and social policies.

The pooling of resources to deal with infrastructural inadequacies provides a means to attack one of the root causes of underdevelopment. Economic activities and sectoral integration within countries often remain stalemated because of inadequate, inappropriate, or irrational infrastructure. Intraregional trade is often minuscule not only because the region's countries export competitive goods, but also because roads, railway, and shipping routes and facilities link the countries with their former colonial owners rather than each other. Storage facilities, distribution networks, and communication are often lacking. The benefits of such regional infrastructural projects as the building of roads, dams for water management or hydroelectricity production, or telecommunication systems transcend national boundaries and make resources available to the entire region. Rational allocation of infrastructural improvements is an investment in short- and long-term national and regional development.

Liberal economic theory holds that productive efficiency is maximized and costs and prices are rationalized if each country engages in economic production in those areas in which it possesses comparative advantage. Regionally devised, complementary industrial schemes permit the member states to pool scarce resources, technology, and marketing expertise to undertake projects with the capacity to benefit from the economies of scale generated by the expanded market and tariff protection. To the benefits of economies of scale also may be added the benefits of vertical and horizontal specialization. Needless duplication of investment and competition within the region is avoided.

The regional economic organization often undertakes infrastructural and industrialization projects first because their costs and benefits provide regional leadership with relatively clear-cut choices, and the completion of such projects provides immediate and tangible evidence of the organization's efficacy and usefulness. A sector-by-sector, project-by-project approach is usually compatible with the members' inclination to make limited commitments. Furthermore, the geographical distribution of the projects offers concrete evidence of the equity of distribution of organizational benefits, assuaging nationalistic concerns (Balassa, 1961: 15).

Classical liberal economic theory contends that the existence of such constraints as tariffs and quotas between states hinders the expression of naturally harmonious economic transactions and reduces trade. However, the "infant industries" of developing countries are not as efficient and competitive as transnational enterprises and therefore require protection from imports from the global arena. Regional economic organizations generally aspire to gradually reduce intraregional tariffs to create a free trade zone or common market among the member states, to erect common external tariffs against foreign imports, and to apportion customs revenue among the members according to an agreed formula (Viner, 1950: 5). The free trade area may be distinguished from the customs union in that tariffs and quantitative restrictions among the member states are abolished, yet member states can fix separate tariff rates on imports from the rest of the world. The area is equipped with rules of origin designed to confine free trade to products originating in the region (Robson, 1980: 20). Custom unions involve the same provisions and, in addition, tariffs on nonmember goods are equalized usually by way of a rather elaborate system of common external tariffs. Common market schemes also include abolishment of restrictions on factor movements and harmonization of national economic policies. Complete economic integration, well beyond the immediate aspirations of the regional economic organizations of this study, also involves the unification of monetary, fiscal, and social policies under the control of a supranational authority (Balassa: 1961: 2).

The primary purpose and value of these approaches is that they redress the problem of inadequate market size. The combined populations of the member states allow manufacturing and industrial enterprises to take advantage of economies of scale and create proportionate demand for goods. This lowers prices and makes domestic goods competitive with those of exogenous large national economies. Larger markets promote the shift of developing economies from exporting primary products to finished or higher–value-added ones. The larger the range of goods produced, the greater the possibilities for trade creation and diversification (Yeats, 1981: 32, 34).

Regional partners may engage in bulk purchasing as well as enhanced economies of scale in marketing, distribution, and service. It is frequently infeasible for individual, small-scale exporters and importers to conduct the research required to determine the best price offered by alternate suppliers, etc. Resources may be pooled for research, information shared, and joint purchase orders placed.

Collaboration often yields impressive savings on freight costs. Freight liner firms normally grant reductions for larger consignments because they require fewer calls. Bulk shipments may make more attractive charter or contract arrangements feasible. If cargoes are aggregated on a regional basis, they may derive the benefits of a containerized, unit-load transport system.

Combining resources and expertise permits the developing countries to confront their technological and managerial deficiencies. As mentioned in conjunction with market data, extant technological and managerial expertise can be pooled to address the needs of all participants. Collective action by the developing countries can provide countervailing power in negotiating with transnational corporations for all of their needs, whether for direct investment, technology, manufactured products, or equitable tax benefits (Yeats, 1981: 27–28).

In implementation, the full value of free trade and custom union schemes is difficult to realize because of the multitude of factors that interact to yield optimum results. If commodities are newly imported from regional partners because the price of the formerly protected domestic product was lower than any foreign source plus the extant duty, then the consumer benefits, efficiency is rewarded, and trade is created (Viner, 1950: 44). If, however, the customs union operates simply to divert trade from its former lower-cost external source to more expensive partner sources, no competition is created, and consumers remain at the mercy of inefficient producers. Among the factors that determine whether trade is truly facilitated are the complementarity or competitiveness of the economies, their size, propinquity and transportation costs within the union, the degree of economic intercourse before integration, and the level of tariffs before and after the union (Balassa, 1965: 22).

Greater overall benefits are derived from customs unions with competitive economies and where large cost differentials among commodities exist. The height and structure of the common external tariff must be designed to promote efficient industries. The adoption of a common tariff on imports from nonmember countries and the harmonization of other measures affecting trade will eliminate distortions in competition among the partner countries only if exchange rates are allowed to adjust freely. Distortions in competitiveness occur, however, if the speed of inflation differs among countries, and devaluation takes place only intermittently. Thus, the benefits of tariff reform can be realized only if monetary and fiscal policies are brought in line with the overall objectives of the organization (Balassa and Stoutjesdijk, 1975: 42–43).

Theory dictates that the average tariff level on imports from outside the custom union area should be lower than it would be in the absence of a customs union. From a theoretical and practical standpoint, a customs union is positive only to the extent that it facilitates a more extensive and efficient division of labor.

Despite the convincing theoretical rationale for economic integration and the wealth of advice as to how it best might be achieved, many proponents conclude their discussion with the caveat that their generalizations and recommendations are best applied where market mechanisms are allowed relatively free expression. As previously outlined, several self-evident factors make the direct implementation of integration theory among developing countries problematic. Many sources of the problems can be traced directly to the structural residue of the countries' colonial pasts. Theory would have it that the removal of artificial barriers to free trade, the permitting of unfettered mobility of the factors of production, the enlarging of the marketplace, and pooling of natural and technological resources automatically will yield economic efficiency and increased output. No such quick fix is sufficient to rationalize the economies under consideration, however. As previously noted, these economies are designed to produce and export a single or few primary commodities; the infrastructure is geared for that export economy; and the country's agricultural and manpower potential is underutilized. Removing tariffs, quotas, and other trade barriers to create a free trade zone, and/or the implementation of a common external tariff, usually the first steps advocated by classical economic and integration theorists, do little to remove the aberrations of the colonial structure or change the realities of poverty and underdevelopment. National tariffs and customs are often a primary source of foreign exchange and revenue for the developing countries. Removing intraregional tariffs and/or the imposition of a common tariff often results in unacceptable income shortfalls for some members.

There is usually relatively insignificant intraregional trade, because the countries of the region export similar primary agricultural or mineral commodities. And in most cases, either the goods they import, manufactured and industrial goods, are unavailable from their regional partners, or goods of equal or superior quality can be imported from industrialized countries for lower prices. In many instances, it is simply less costly to import goods from the geographically more distant industrialized countries, because inadequate transportation exists among the regional countries.

The conclusion that must be drawn is that commitment to an integration scheme founded solely on the calculation of gains and losses accruing to individual member states from the implementation of some variation of a regional free market zone with a common external tariff will destine the organization to moribundity. The commitment of the political leadership and the political will to sustain and expand regional cooperation must derive instead from integration's central role in the process of restructuring and rationalizing the economies to set the stage for future generalized and long-term development. Broadening the area of unfettered activity of competitive enterprises creates opportunities for innovation and encourages new products, processes, and methods of distribution (Mikesell, 1982: 204–5). Because plans for customs unions or free trade areas require long time horizons for implementation and benefits realization, the impact of expectations of future market opportunities is often more important than their effect on existing trade patterns. By creating customs unions and free trade areas, political leaders demonstrate that they wish to bring about fundamental change in the structure of their production and trade and work together to construct a mechanism to orient their economies in the direction of regional specialization. Robson (1980: 146, 160) makes this point:

The argument for regional integration among developing countries is . . . largely based on the prospective gains from rationalizing the *emergent* structure of production. The lower is the level of development attained by the integrating countries at the time of integration, the greater will be the importance of the gains from *prospective* realization . . . (Robson's emphasis).

He continues: "it is necessary to consider integration as a part of development policy, subjected to a planning process and utilizing appropriate planning techniques."

Table 2.1
Framework of Utilities Suggested in Trade Union and Regional Integration Theory

ISSUE CONCEPTUALIZATION	Economic development and growth • industrialization • infrastructure improvement • market enlargement • trade liberalization • protection of regional industry • harmonization of monetary policy • fiscal policy coordination • labor mobility Foreign economic intervention
LEVELS OF ASSESSMENT	Regional National
GAIN/LOSS	Gains from economic development and growth Avoid losses associated with foreign exploitation and dependence
PROBABILITY/RISK	Moderate probability gain Low risk
SURVIVAL	Not applicable
IDEOLOGY	Free trade, customs union, and dependency theories
TIME HORIZON	Long-->short-term

To summarize, the framework of payoffs suggested in this literature contains some or all of the components listed in Table 2.1.

Again, these components constitute the potential matrix associated with cooperation within regional integration schemes. More important and immediate to the actual choices made is the effective framework, that group of factors that shape the cognitive frameworks of foreign policy elites in developing countries. These frameworks may be dominated by perceived threats to political and economic survival, risk aversion, and short-term payoff needs.

THE COGNITIVE FRAMEWORK OF DEVELOPING COUNTRY ELITES

The cognitive framework out of which many developing country elites approach issues of regional economic cooperation, and indeed all other policy questions, is highly personalized and nationalistic. Analysis of the foreign policy processes of developing countries suggests that the perceptions and beliefs of top governmental decision makers are more significant in the shaping of policy decisions than within the policy processes of advanced industrial states. Rosenau (1966: 27–92) writes that, "the potency of an idiosyncratic factor is assumed to be greater in less developed countries," than in developed ones because there are, "few of the restraints which bureaucracy and large scale organization impose in more developed economies." It is not the intent of this study to imply that decisions concerning cooperation within regional economic organizations derive exclusively from the personality traits of individual political leaders. Instead, it is posited that the point of reference and payoff structures perceived by policy elites are shaped "closer to home" than the inducements and constraints presented by the regional organization or the anarchy of the international arena. The cognitive frameworks of policy elites are shaped first by the fact that they are often at political, economic, and possibly even physical risk. Therefore, the need to survive dominates their list of personal and national priorities. Huntington (1968: 179) asserts that, "The prime requisite of any government is to remain a government, and political leaders give first priority to staying in power. They are likely to rate the goals of internal order and external security above that of economic development."

In two of the three cases to be examined, the political leadership perceived itself at risk. In the Nigerian case, political, economic, and societal disorder threatened the Shagari regime. The fact that the regime succumbed to a military coup within months of the decision to expel alien workers is solid evidence of the validity of its concern. In the Philippine case, the Marcos regime's decision to cooperate, shaped by its need to deal with the chronic but escalating civil war in the southern islands, coincided with regional interests to resolve the territorial issue over Sabah. A strong case may be made that the Shagari government's approach to the policy decisions was lexicographic; survival dominated its cognitive framing.

Second, developing country elites often frame the issues associated with regional cooperation in terms of loss rather than gain. Because their countries are so resource-poor, the leadership is hypersensitive to possible loss; potential loss is heavily weighted in utility calculations.

Third, because they operate within high levels of political and economic risk, decision makers are likely to eschew potential and long-term benefits in favor of immediate payoffs. They simply cannot afford the luxury of waiting for a long-term payoff. They may not be available to reap the benefits of such delayed gratification.[14]

Developing countries are often sadly lacking in resources required for economic development. Many legitimate developmental demands compete for limited national resources: education, health, the building of infrastructure, some level of reimbursement for land redistribution, and agricultural and industrial investment. Advanced industrial states are better able to forgo absolute, short-term payoffs in favor of potential long-term or conjoint benefits. It is often beyond the capacity of the political leadership of less developed countries to agree to share meager

Table 2.2
Contrasting Framework of Utilities Suggested in Theoretical Literature

FRAMING COMPONENT	TRADE UNION AND REGIONAL INTEGRATION THEORY	DEVELOPING COUNTRY ELITES
ISSUE CONCEPTUALIZATION	Economic development and growth • industrialization • infrastructure improvement • market enlargement • trade liberalization • protection of regional industry • harmonization of monetary policy • fiscal policy coordination • labor mobility Foreign economic intervention	Survival • political • economic • personal Political stability Economic development and growth Societal stability
LEVELS OF ASSESSMENT	Regional National	Personal National Regional
GAIN/LOSS	Gain in economic development and growth Avoid losses associated with foreign dependence	Loss avoidance Seek political and economic gains
PROBABILITY/RISK	Moderate probability gain Low risk	Preference for highly certain options Risk averse
SURVIVAL	Not applicable	Not applicable
IDEOLOGY	Free trade, customs union, and dependency theories	Nationalism; dependency, mercantilist, customs union, free trade and integration theories
TIME HORIZON	Long--> short-term	Immediate/short-term

resources with its regional partners and to delay gratification of often desperate economic needs with only the promise of long-range greater benefit. Developing states need immediate and dramatic gains from integration. Because the benefits of integration are slow in coming, other avenues to economic development may be perceived as more attractive than regional economic cooperation. The three countries of our study are among the most resource-rich and industrially developed among the regional partners. The temptation for them is to forsake group developmental strategies and to proceed on their own, and/or to form economically beneficial liaisons with trading partners outside of the region. This, as will be discussed, was true in the Chilean case.

The integration process also involves a political and psychological

commitment that the leadership of developing countries may find difficult to sustain. In some cases, the effort to secure independence necessi-
tated the generation of extremely nationalistic, often revolutionary sentiment among the elite and general population. The leadership may have
sought to sustain this nationalistic fervor to assuage the political impact
of ideological, ethnic, and class cleavages and economic hardship so that
state building could proceed. The psychological and political momentum
implicit in tossing off the colonial yoke and accruing legitimacy for gov-
erning the new state is not congruent with relinquishing sovereignty for
economic decision making to a regional entity.

In most cases, after the immediate burst of enthusiasm and political
will that accompanies the establishing of the organization, it may lan-
guish in an extended embryonic state. The mission of the organization
may be unclear and the recruiting of effective leadership and personnel
often difficult. In this early state of institutionalization, expectations
have yet to converge; collective norms are not yet in place; institutional
legitimacy is in question; and there is little elite commitment to the regional enterprise or collective goals. The literature suggests that the cognitive framing of developing country elites may be contrasted with the
framework of benefits implied in regional economic integration as shown
in Table 2.2.

The case studies to follow demonstrate that the long-term perspective
required to realize the economic benefits from the regional economic
organization is in many cases incongruent with immediate and specific
needs that dominate national decision makers' cognitive frameworks.
The issue-specific framing of these decision scenarios will be considered
in Chapters 3 through 5.

NOTES

1. Cooperation is not necessary if interstate relations are harmonious. The
concept of cooperation implies a conscious effort to adjust policies to meet another's preferences, needs, or demands. It proceeds not only from shared interests but also from discord or potential discord. Without discord or its potential,
harmony obtains rather than cooperation (Keohane, 1984: 12).

2. This is an illustration of instrumental rather than procedural rationality.
This approach claims to explain the consistency of choices with one another and
the underlying preferences of decision makers rather than decision processes.

3. Stein (1992: 203, 209, footnote 17) writes that states behave as "defensive
positionalists." This interpretation of states' motivations derives at least in part
from the fact that realist analysis traditionally has focused on disputes over territory in the Westphalian system. Territory is a fixed quantity good, and therefore,
disputes are, of necessity, constant-sum games.

Snidal (1991: 387–398, 401) denigrates the usefulness of distinguishing between
states' struggle for relative and absolute advantage. In cases with large numbers

of participants, relative gains have little effect on cooperation. As the number of transactions increases, relative gains become increasingly irrelevant to the prospects for cooperation. Realists claim that relative gains inherent in the nature of the international system create zero-sum conditions, which preclude cooperative behavior. Snidal's examination of the evolution of international conditions from relative anarchy to cooperation reveals that initiating cooperation is no more difficult under conditions of relative gains than absolute gains. The importance of relative gains decreases significantly in cases involving more than two states. Thus, aside from issues such as bipolar security transactions, there is little to be gained by distinguishing between relative and absolute gain seeking. Sophisticated interpretations of state behavior avoid the implication that states seek solely relative or absolute gains. Many choices ostensibly driven by motives of relative gain are in reality shaped by aspirations of long-term absolute gain.

4. Exemplars of functionalist literature include David Mitrany's *A Working Peace System* (London: Royal Institute of International Affairs, 1943) and Ernst B. Haas' *Beyond the Nation-State: Functionalism and International Organization* (Stanford, CA: Stanford University Press, 1964). Haas' contributions to neofunctionalist theory included such works as *The Uniting of Europe: Political, Economic, and Social Forces, 1950–57* (Stanford, CA: Stanford University Press, 1965) and "Technology, Pluralism, and the New Europe," pp. 149–176 in Joseph S. Nye, Jr., ed. *International Regionalism* (Boston: Little, Brown, 1968) and Joseph S. Nye, Jr.'s "Comparing Common Markets: A Revised Neo-Functionalist Model," pp. 192–231 in Leon N. Lindberg and Stuart A. Scheingold, eds. *Regional Integration: Theory and Research* (Cambridge, MA: Harvard University Press, 1971).

The interdependence literature includes such works as Richard C. Cooper's "Economic Interdependence and Foreign Policies in the 1970's," *World Politics* 24 (January 1972): 158–181, Edward S. Morse's, "The Transformation of Foreign Policies: Modernization, Interdependence, and Externalization," *World Politics* 22 (April 1970): 371–392, and Keohane and Nye's *Power and Interdependence*, 1977.

5. Axelrod and Keohane (1985: 235–236, 250) acknowledge the difficulties associated with identifying and sanctioning defectors. When multiple actors are involved in the cooperative effort, it may be impossible to identify defectors. Even if states possess the capabilities to punish cheaters, they may have little incentive to expend the resources to execute the role of policeman. Privatizing punishment is one way to deal with the difficulties of imposing sanctions. Formalized arrangements may provide for those directly transgressed against to assume responsibility for punishing transgressors. A danger associated with both the privatization of punishment and tit-for-tat interactions is that acrimonious retaliation may escalate to a level that any prospect for a convergence of interests or internalization of norms associated with cooperation will be destroyed. To preclude this, Axelrod (1984: 138) suggests the state return "only nine-tenths of a tit for a tat." The internalization of norms makes cooperation among the options considered first by the state rather than contingent on its partners' cooperation in the immediately preceding transaction.

6. "Payoffs" are usually measured on a cardinal scale, that is, one featuring an arbitrary zero, equal units, and replaceable by any positive linear transformation of itself. Payoffs are identified with utilities in that the player prefers one

outcome to another if the first yields a greater payoff (utility) than the second. The player is indifferent between them if they yield equal payoffs (Taylor, 1987: 63).

7. Psychiatry and behavioral and social psychology investigate how people make their decisions and how these processes influence the choices they make.

8. The Weber-Fechner law, which holds that change in physical stimulus is perceived as a ratio of change to the prior condition rather than proportionately to its absolute amount, has been known since the 19th century (Loewenstein and Elster, 1992: 71).

9. Cognitive psychologists have identified an array of editing, coding, and heuristic processes that may be used, consciously or unconsciously, by a decision maker to deal with complex questions. In one such process, the *isolation effect,* components common to all policy options may be eliminated, which may result in distortions in assessment. This tendency may produce inconsistent preferences, because options may be separated into common and distinctive components on the basis of multiple criteria, and different decompositions may lead to different preferences.

10. This is not to discount the possibility that decision makers' personalities may well affect their responses to risky policy options. Risk-assuming and -avoiding behavior may be sensitive to a bevy of idiosyncratic factors such as the decision maker's level of knowledge, experience, or general sophistication (McKeown, 1993: 216–217).

11. Decision makers use editing, coding, and/or heuristic devices to simplify and transform incoming data and the payoff structure. The available information may be incomplete, ambiguous, and/or contradictory. It may be forthcoming in such quantity, speed, and complexity that the decision maker may lack the capacity to use it. Its substance may be incompatible with previously held policy beliefs and generate cognitive dissonance, anxiety, and frustration in the decision maker. Many of these characteristics are discussed in the literature dealing with crisis decision making. However, within the context of noncrisis decision making, when information is of very high quality, and the decision making unit possesses optimal capacity to process the data, human beings tend to use various devices to expedite the assessment of policy options. Because editing, coding, and heuristic devices facilitate decision making, it may be assumed that they are used, consciously or unconsciously, whenever possible.

In considering policy options, decision makers may separate risk-free components from riskier ones and then evaluate the former. This editing may result in inconsistent preferences when the same choice is presented in a different form. The decision maker's preferences among policy options will not be consistent across contexts, because the editing operations used may vary according to context. This study does not extend these phenomena as suppositions to be investigated because of the difficulty in documenting instances of this cognitive coding (Kahneman and Tversky, 1979: 284–285; Tversky and Kahneman, 1986: S257).

12. An idea is a thought, concept, or image in the mind; it may be more or less well formulated. A belief or an opinion is more organized; it is the expression of something deemed actual or true. In addition to embodying what is regarded as truth, values likely contain normative and emotive content; they designate what is desirable or good.

13. Loewenstein and Elster (1992:x–xi, 4–5) provide a good summary of the evolution of this thought. P. Samuelson first proposed the discounted utility model in 1937; however, the debate over how individuals discount time well preceded this date. In the 19th century, economists contemplated man's baseline or "natural" time discounting. One school of thought, exemplified by W. S. Jevons (1871), insisted that ignoring the future is a natural human tendency. Another approach, first propounded by N. W. Senior (1936), asserted that equal treatment of the present and future is natural. The myopia school focused on emotions experienced in the present but associated with future pleasures and pain. These emotions were thought to give the future immediate impact, overcoming what would otherwise be a total preoccupation with the present. In this view, discounting occurred because of the relative weakness of such emotions and from an inability to imagine the future in vivid and accurate detail.

Nineteenth-century economists who assumed that human beings weight the present and future equally argued that the temptation of immediate consumption distorted the individual's natural inclination toward a balanced weighting of the present and the future.

A second phase, dominated by the writings of Bohm-Bawerk (1889 and 1914) and Fisher (1930), viewed intertemporal choice in cognitive terms, as a trade-off between present and future benefits. Bohm-Bawerk (1889: 261) writes: "*These imagined future emotions are comparable*. Indeed, they are comparable not only with present emotions experienced at the moment, but also with each other; and that comparability, furthermore, obtains irrespective of whether they belong to the same or different future periods of time" (his emphasis). Discounting was predominantly attributed to the decision maker's inadequate ability to imagine the future. Again, Bohm-Bawerk (1889) wrote:

We feel less concerned about future sensations of joy and sorrow simply because they do lie in the future, and lessening of concern is in proportion to the remoteness of that future. Consequently we accord to goods which are intended to serve future ends a value which falls short of the true intensity of their future marginal utility. *We systematically undervalue our future wants and also the means which serve to satisfy them.* . . . It may be that we possess inadequate power to imagine and to abstract, or that we are not willing to put forth the necessary efforts, but in any event we limit a more or less incomplete picture of our future wants and especially of the remotely distant ones (his emphasis).

A further stage emerged at the beginning of the 20th century. Reacting to new trends in psychology such as Freud's theory of unconscious motivations, economists sought to supplant psychological explanations with mathematical and graphical analysis of such nonevocative concepts as time preference. These concepts consciously strove to avoid reference to underlying psychological causation. The present work on hyperbolic discounting represents a reintroduction of psychological literature into the intertemporal choice debate.

14. Specifically with reference to new democratic governments, the distinguished political analyst Alexis de Tocqueville commented on the influence of social instability on the time horizons of citizens' thinking: "Social instability favors the natural instability of desires. Amid all these perpetual fluctuations of fate the present looms large and hides the future, so that men do not want to think beyond tomorrow." (from *Democracy in America,* quoted in Loewenstein and Elster, 1992: 48)

3 The Andean Case:
The 1976 Chilean Decision to
Withdraw from the Pact

The first case in our study of national decision making regarding participation within regional economic organizations examines the most absolute form of "noncooperation," formal withdrawal from organizational
membership. The immediate and specific concern of Chile's military
government in the mid-1970s was economic recovery and growth. Every
indicator (i.e., the country's balance of payments, external debt burden,
inflation, productivity statistics, and unemployment levels) confirmed
that Chile's economy was in deep distress.

Junta economic officials, steeped in Friedmanite ideology, were convinced that free market remedies, including elimination of restrictions
on trade and foreign investment, were the proper antidote for Chile's
economic difficulties. However, these strategies ran counter to regional
development plans to which Chile was already committed within the
context of its participation in the Andean Pact. Among other things, the
Andean Pact's Decision 24 (D24) placed ownership and profit repatriation restrictions on foreign investors in the region. The pact was also
considering adopting a comprehensive system of common external tariffs. After 2 years of negotiations aimed at reconciling national and pact
policies, Chile withdrew from the pact on October 30, 1976. This chapter
examines the incongruity of cognitive frameworks that precluded cooperation between Chile and its pact partners.

THE NATIONAL ECONOMIC AND POLITICAL CONTEXT
OF THE DECISION

Within the global community of states, Chile is a relatively small
country (292,257 square miles) with a medium-sized economy, but it

ranked with Colombia as the most developed within the Andean group. The population (more than 10 million at the time of the 1976 decision to withdraw from the Andean Pact) is a racially homogeneous Indian-European mix and is fairly well educated. A cataloging of Chile's natural assets, including its citizens, would suggest that it possesses a resource base sufficient to place it among the developed countries of the world.[1] However, export dependence, structural irrationalities, and economic mismanagement have combined to produce a less successful economic history than an objective accounting of productive factors would explain. The long, narrow country (2600 miles long and 110 miles wide at the maximum point), seemingly supported by the Andean spine, is dominated economically by mineral extraction in the north, industry in the center around the capital, Santiago, and agriculture in the south.

At the beginning of the 1970s, 70% of the population could be classified as middle class; 22% lived in extreme poverty; and 8% made up the upper class. Chile is an urban society. At the time of the 1976 decision, 61% of the working population were manual or industrial workers; 21% engaged in agriculture; and the remaining 18% were petty bourgeoisie—shopkeepers, artisans, truck owner/drivers, and small peasantry (Mendez, 1979: 331).

Chile gained political independence from Spain in 1818, but efforts to achieve economic independence began in earnest in the post-World War II era. Many of the ups and downs in Chilean economic history may be traced to its dependence on the export of mineral commodities—primarily copper and nitrates. When world demand and prices for copper are high (particularly during periods of war), resources exist for economic development, and Chilean governments can postpone making structural adjustments to balance Chile's developmental course. When, however, demand and prices for Chilean copper decline, funds are unavailable to further developmental goals, the population suffers deprivation, and political instability often results.

Chilean economic policy between 1940 and 1955 was aimed at decreasing the country's vulnerability to vacillations in the world copper markets. Import substitution industrialization (in iron, steel, electricity, and consumer goods) was the preferred instrument for attaining conomic growth. Between 1949 and 1953, the gross national product experienced sharp growth partially attributable to a dramatic increase in copper prices caused by Korean War–induced demand. Inflation accelerated during this period, however, and agrarian reform came to a virtual standstill. With an end to the war came an end to the era of prosperity; the price of copper fell 30%, and inflation reached 83.8%.

To deal with these problems, the political leadership sought the advice of the Chicago-based Klein-Saks consulting team. The Klein-Saks mission suggested classical economic remedies for inflation—lowering demand and prices. These policies resulted in lower inflation but also a decline in wages, employment, economic growth, and increased foreign borrowing. Chile experienced its worst short-term recession since the 1930s. However, the economy eventually stabilized, and the economic policies of President Carlo Ibanez del Campo (1952–1958) were more balanced in their sectoral orientation, including providing incentives for agricultural production.

Chile experienced economic progress during the 1960s. Ibanez's successors (Jorge Alessandi, 1958–1964, and Eduardo Frei Montalva, 1964–1970) were proponents of the government playing a relatively active role in facilitating economic growth across the various sectors. Their economic policies called for gradually restructuring and rationalizing the economy. Extensive public works, housing projects, and improved education and nutrition were high priorities. The Christian Democrats pushed through a measured program of copper nationalization.

Yet, inflation persisted; the public debt mounted; and the country's balance of payments deteriorated. The promulgation of land reform laws did little to shore up the stagnant agricultural sector or to rectify the grave economic inequities within the society. As the 1960s ended, Chile was a net importer of agricultural goods, and total foreign indebtedness had reached levels exceeded worldwide only by Israel. Unemployment was at 8%. The Santiago shanty town population exceeded 500,000. In 1969, these slum dwellers and the *campesinos* (small landowners and landless farm workers) began mobilizing. Union membership rose, and there were strikes and land seizures. In October, students rioted, and there was an isolated military revolt. In 1970, the Popular Unity Government[2] of Salvador Allende was elected.

The Summer 1974 issue of *Latin American Perspectives* (p. 70) informed that, "The central objectives of the united popular forces are to replace the current economic structure, ending the power of national and foreign monopoly capitalists and large landowners, in order to initiate the construction of socialism." Most of the Allende government's economic plans centered around improving the lot of the country's 61% manual workers. Import substitution industrialization of intermediate goods was to continue. Complete nationalization of the country's extractive and financial sectors was to be carried out. Agrarian reform began with the expropriation of all agricultural estates larger than 80 hectares (197.68 acres).

Allende's government raised wages, made credit more readily available, and increased government spending. Chile's chronic inflation increased. The nationalized copper industries experienced tremendous losses. Initially, confusion reigned over which companies were to be nationalized. After nationalization, the enterprises were poorly managed. Workers' discipline declined; there were absenteeism and wage disputes. The process of land expropriation and the expropriated estates were also badly managed. Workers began seizing properties smaller than 80 hectares, and the government was forced to legalize their acts after the fact. Expropriated estates were held and run as collectives rather than distributed among individual farming families. The Allende government continued to provide inadequate investment for the agricultural sector, so the massive food imports increased.

In November 1971, Allende's government was forced to declare a moratorium on debt repayments until they could be rescheduled. Chile's first default on a US$20 million loan from the EXIM Bank led to the immediate suspension of American credit. Seventy percent (US$243 million) of Chile's debt payments with the Club of Paris was rescheduled in April 1972. Although the US government and financial institutions expressed displeasure with the Allende regime by cutting off credit, Chile found other credit sources in the International Monetary Fund and European, socialist, and other Latin American countries (Taylor, 1981: 63–64). Throughout 1973, Chile experienced economic anarchy and recession; in September, inflation levels reached 320%. On September 11, a military coup led by General Pinochet Ugarte overthrew the Allende government.

The Pinochet government practiced a combination of Ricardian economics and Friedmanite monetarism. Market mechanisms were permitted as much free rein as possible. Minimal control was exercised over prices, banking operations and interest rates, and exchange rates. Tariffs were lowered and direct foreign investment encouraged. Comparative advantage was sought in mining, agriculture, agribusiness (particularly fruits), forestry, fisheries, and labor-intensive industrial manufacturing. Exceptions to liberal economic theory were made in some sectors. During the first few years in power, the government continued to control more than 95% of the banking and financial institutions, 90% of the mining sector, 40% of the manufacturing sector, and 60% of the distribution sector; bringing the state's share of the gross domestic product to 45% (Taylor, 1981: 97–106). The market was not allowed to set salaries. Workers' wages remained under rigid government control, and collective bargaining and strikes were prohibited.

In 1974, high world copper prices afforded the Pinochet regime some economic maneuverability. In 1975, however, copper prices declined, reducing export earnings by US$1 billion.[3] The Junta itself was partly responsible for the fall in copper prices. In November 1974 and 1975, the Intergovernmental Council of Copper Exporters called for decreasing copper production by 10% and 15% respectively. The Junta did not comply with these recommendations, allowing that prices were best determined by market forces. Meanwhile, oil prices continued their upward spiral, exacerbating chronic balance of payments deficits. Imports account for 75% of Chile's oil consumption.

In March 1974, agreement was reached with the Club of Paris to re-schedule the $700 million in debt service payments due that year and in 1975 (*Latin America,* March 29, 1974: 99). However, in May 1975, in an unprecedented move, West European nations, among Chile's largest creditors, refused to consider renegotiating payments on the foreign debt until there was clear evidence that progress was being made in human rights (*New York Times,* May 12, 1975: 1:5). In November, a secret World Bank study was publicized, which concluded that the Chilean economy was worse off than under the Allende regime. The report's primary recommendation was that less money be spent on armaments. Between 1971 and 1975, per capita income in Chile declined an average of 2.7% per year, and by the fall of 1976, when the Junta withdrew Chile from the Andean Pact, the economy had bottomed out some months before. Unofficial unemployment stood at 25% (Taylor, 1981: 122–124).[4] There is little question that recovery measures were drastically needed. The liberal economic philosophy and strategies of the Junta, however, were at variance with development strategies already in place within the Andean Pact.

CHILE AND THE ANDEAN PACT

The Andean Pact was born out of frustration with the cumbersome machinery[5] and extreme inequity in benefits distribution of the larger Latin American Free Trade Association (LAFTA). Between 1962 and 1967, the economic giants of LAFTA (Argentina, Brazil, and Mexico) accounted for more than 72.5% of production and trade in manufactured and semifinished goods, and the medium-sized and less developed LAFTA economies found themselves increasingly dwarfed (Bond, 1978: 405).

Ironically, in 1965, then-Chilean President Eduardo Frei Montalva (the Latin American statesman probably most influenced by West European integration efforts) wished to improve Chile's economic perfor-mance but recognized that the country had reached the limits of its growth potential within the parameters of an import substitution strat-egy. He assumed the initiative and sought the recommendations of four prominent Latin American economists as to how LAFTA's inertia might be overcome. When the economists' recommendations failed to generate any enthusiasm outside of Chile, in 1966 Frei arranged further discus-sions with Peru's Fernando Belaunde-Terry. Their meeting resulted later that year in Colombian President Carlos Lleras Restreop's bringing to-gether in Bogota representatives from five of the future six members of the Andean Pact (Fontaine, 1977: 12–13). The resulting Declaration of Bogota called for a general agreement on trade concessions and comple-mentary industrial agreements to promote balanced economic develop-ment within the LAFTA framework (Taylor, 1984: 68). On May 26,

1968, after 3 years of detailed negotiations, the Agreement of Cartegena (*Acuerdo de Cartegena*), formally bringing into existence the Andean Pact, was signed by Bolivia, Chile, Colombia, Ecuador, and Peru. Gabriel Valdes, the Chilean Foreign Minister, was quoted in the Bogota daily *El Tiempo* as strongly supporting the Andean scheme and the economic, social, and political results that would accrue. Salvador Lluck led a Chilean delegation to Lima to convince the Peruvian military government to join the pact (*Latin America,* January 10, 1969: 13), and a delegation of Chilean industrialists representing the *Sociedad de Fomento Fabril* (SOFOFA) traveled to Caracas to persuade their Venezuelan colleagues of the advantages of pact membership. While there, Raul Saez (who would later figure prominently as an opponent of D24) made "brilliant" presentations before governmental and labor groups in support of the new Agreement.

In February 1969, *Latin America* reported rumors circulating in Ecuador's private sector that Chilean private industry was reconsidering its initial support for pact participation. It was said that Chilean industry was coming to accept the views of some Venezuelan, Ecuadorian, and Peruvian businessmen that integration should be achieved gradually via the allocation of new industrial capacity, rather than by rapid and automatic lowering of tariff barriers (*Latin America,* February 21, 1969: 58). Despite some private sector trepidations, Frei's government was a major force behind ratification of the Andean scheme. The agreement entered into force October 16, 1969.[6]

The geographical area of the Andean Pact is approximately two-thirds the size of the United States. At the time of ratification, the member states' combined gross national products equaled $30 billion, a sum larger than that of Argentina and Mexico, and one-half that of Brazil. Andean Pact member nations represented 90% of Latin American copper and tin production, 50% of its coal exports, 65% of its iron exports, and, after Venezuela's incorporation, 86% of Latin America's crude oil production. The group was, however, vulnerable in the agricultural sector. It accounted for only 15% of Latin American beef and wheat, 12% of the wool and raw cotton, and 8% of the corn produced. Pact countries were net importers of meat, cereals and dairy products (*New York Times,* January 26, 1970: 77:1).

The Agreement of Cartegena provided for a program of trade liberalization more ambitious than that undertaken by LAFTA. It included automatic elimination of intraregional tariffs and establishment of a joint external tariff, common treatment of foreign investment, harmonization of economic and social policies including industrial sector agreements, and preferential treatment for Bolivia and Ecuador as the least-developed members.

As the most economically advanced members of the pact, Chile and

Colombia were consistently enthusiastic supporters of rapid and irreversible trade liberalization. The two countries' domestic markets were saturated, and they sought external markets to competitively export their goods. The Chilean and Colombian economies were generally complementary rather than competitive. The countries initially requested only 240 exemptions each from the pact's list of items to be freed from tariff restrictions. Even though Chile's industrialization was more advanced than other pact members', it was enthusiastic about the planned sectoral development schemes and bargained aggressively for plant allocations (Fontaine, 1977: 31).

By most observers' estimations, the Andean Pact enjoyed 4 years of successful decision-making and policy implementation. Trade liberalization successes included approval of the initial tariff reduction plan (D22) and nomenclature (D58), and implementation of a common minimum external tariff (D12) (Mytelka, 1979: 37). The original agreement's signers seemed intent on establishing a workable regional economic scheme to avoid the pitfalls experienced by the larger LAFTA organization. Momentum from the initial exercise of political will that generated the organization permitted national governments to make significant concessions in early Commission negotiations on the assumption that short-term sacrifices would ultimately result in long-term benefits.

Political stability within the participating countries ensured national delegates to the commission relatively long terms and considerable negotiating autonomy. "Clubbism" characterized commission meetings between 1969 and 1973. The collegial atmosphere allowed for discussion and compromise among the delegates; integration issues were debated as differences of opinion among friends with compatible frames of reference. As a function of their long tenures and personal ties, commission delegates developed a supranational identity, which depoliticized sensitive integration issues and gave regional interests high priority in the decision-making process.

When Allende's Socialist government came to power in Chile in 1970, private sector organizations in Venezuela and Colombia alleged that Chilean economic and social policies were no longer compatible with the pact, a claim Chile vigorously denied. Allende's government was committed to reducing Chilean economic dependence on the United States, its vulnerability to transnational corporations, and avoiding political isolation. During Allende's tenure, Chile remained fully participatory in Andean Pact affairs. Other pact members expressed solidarity with Chile in the face of the "economic aggression" of the Kennecott embargo (*Latin America,* February 21, 1969: 58).[7]

The year 1973 is regarded as a turning point in Andean Pact progress. The organization's momentum slowed as the complexity and full implications of integration decisions became apparent. Small and medium-sized manufacturers protested the loss of economic position after feeling the impact of the tariff reduction schedule. Other national interest groups pressured member governments to secure tangible benefits as compensation for the immediate costs of economic integration.

Increased political instability in member countries redefined the environment within which the commission operated. The September 1973 overthrow of the Allende government wrought an immediate change in Chilean participation. Chile's commission delegation experienced a complete turnover. The new delegation used commission meetings as a forum for political attacks on D24. And tariff liberalization was another area of disagreement between Chile and the Andean Pact.

At a round table sponsored by the Center for Studies on Company Development in Santiago in August 1976, Chile's Finance Minister, Sergio de Castro, provided a detailed summary of the regime's stance on the external tariffs issue. Castro associated the pact's common tariffs with regional policies on foreign exchange. He opined that common tariffs should fall outside the purview of the Andean Pact, because the member states had divergent economies and approaches to economic policy. Pact officials, of course, saw regional harmonization of tariffs and exchange policies very much within the domain of the pact precisely because of the close link between tariffs and exchange rates.

Castro provided data to support the position that high tariffs can result in imbalances between protected (principally manufacturing industries) and unprotected (usually agriculture and export industries such as mining) sectors. He maintained that 10% to 35% was a sufficiently high tariff to protect local industries (*Andean Report*, Vol. 11, No. 9, September 1976: 171).

Disputes with Chile were not the only difficulties experienced by the pact during this period. Bolivia began to use the commission to publicize its long-sought demand for an exit to the sea (*salida al mar*). Integration became increasingly politicized as delegates sought to advance national priorities over regional interests.

After 1973, the commission reached fewer decisions, and nonimplementation of decisions became frequent in 1974 and 1975. D40 on double taxation, D47 on the minimum state investment permitted a firm classified as a mixed corporation rather than a foreign firm, and D46 on the formation of subregional industries were never ratified (Mytelka, 1979: 38). The commission attempted to reassert decision-making authority via organizational flexibility and expansion of international contacts. In June 1974, the commission created three "ad hoc intergovernmental committees" to study Junta proposals for sectoral development programs in the automotive, petrochemical, and metalworking industries. The goal was to eliminate the controversy and conflict obstructing high-level negotiations by appointing national specialists in each industrial area to serve as intermediate negotiators. The committees helped the commission reach final agreement on the metalworking and petrochemical programs, but approval was delayed on other regional development proposals.

Contact with foreign countries and international organizations was actively cultivated to expand Andean Group commercial relations and to bolster the commission's image as a legitimate supranational agent for the conduct of regional transactions. In 1973, the commission appointed delegates to represent the region's interests at United Nations' Economic Commission for Latin America, the General Agreement on Tariffs and Trade, and LAFTA meetings (*Business Latin America,* November 30, 1972). "Mixed commissions" were established to link the Andean Pact with Argentina, Comecon, the European Communities, Japan, Mexico, and Spain (Middlebrook, 1978: 68–71). None of these initatives yielded particularly significant benefits.

Although it cannot be claimed that transnational interest groups with economic and political clout to significantly affect Chilean policy existed, by early 1975, various industry-specific associations were springing up to complement the integration efforts of the Andean Pact. One interesting example of these was the *Asociacion Espanola de Empresas de Ingenieria y Centros de Investigacion (Tecniberia)* created to study the possibilities of integrating the region's engineering and shipbuilding industries, and to forecast the demand for shipping over the next 7 years. A second example, the *Asociacion Andina del Cuero y del Calzado,* held its first general assembly in January 1975 in Lima. This group's goal was to promote cooperation among the footwear-related industries in the subregion (*Bank of London and Latin America,* IX, No. 1/75, January 1975: 19).

In 1976, analysts were divided as to the likely consequences to Andean integration of Chile's withdrawal. Some predicted dire consequences for the pact, because the departure deprived the organization of the Chilean market and industrial leadership. However, others claimed that the removal of this derisive member would allow the organization to focus its energies on the tasks it had set for itself. At minimum, it was clear that the metalworking and petrochemical agreements required renegotiation, and the automotive agreement under consideration was adversely affected (*Business Latin America,* February 2, 1977: 30).

D24 AND CHILE'S DECISION TO WITHDRAW FROM THE PACT

The Andean Pact's D24 (ratified in June 1971), the Statute on the Common Treatment of Foreign Capital, Trademarks, Patents, Licensing Agreements and Royalties, was clearly among the most controversial of Andean Pact promulgations. Proponents of the decree claimed that D24 represented an ambitious and successful example of policy coordination by developing countries within the context of a regional economic organization.

The reasoning and sentiment that prompted the D24 legislation were pervasive among developing countries faced with a juxtaposed need for investment capital and a desire to cast off external economic dependence. The developing countries sought to retain control over their developmental course and profits from the labor of their citizens. Without some form of foreign investment code, it was feared that pact members would engage in unhealthy competition, that they would be tempted to use "beggar-thy-neighbor" tactics to attract foreign capital. This approach/avoidance behavior, and the general opinion that the motives of foreign sources of investment capital were suspect, were prevalent in the 1960s and 1970s. Transnational corporations were viewed by many in the developing world as irresistible entities on the international economic scene, their economic resources dwarfing those of many governments.

D24 authorized the establishment of national agencies to register and review all direct foreign investment contracts (articles 5 and 6). Taking cues from nationalization and indigenization schemes underway in the individual member states, it prohibited new foreign investment in commercial banking, insurance, communications, public services (particularly utilities), advertising, and internal transportation sectors (articles 41–44). Restrictions were placed on medium- and long-term local credit available to foreign investors (article 17).

National enterprises were defined in D24 as those with more than 80% of their capital held by domestic public or private investors. Domestic capital controlled less than 51% of the total interest or was reflected in less than 51% of the management of foreign firms. National capital was to hold the primary interest in mixed enterprises.

All foreign enterprises were required to gradually "fade out" foreign ownership to 49% within 15 years (22 years in less-developed Bolivia and Ecuador) to be eligible to participate in the Andean Pact's tariff reduction scheme (articles 27–30). D24 restricted foreign firms' remittance of profits to 14% of registered capital investment (article 37) and established restrictions on technology transfers (articles 18–25). Certain extractive industries, notably oil, were exempted from D24 fade-out requirements and profit remittance limits. Member governments could not offer oil depletion allowances. Oil and gas exploration and exploitation ventures were to be carried out in conjunction with state oil corporations. Until 1981, foreign investors were permitted concessional contracts which could remain effective for up to 20 years (Fontaine, 1977: 20).

As noted earlier, Chile's Christian Democratic government under

Eduardo Frei Montalva (1964–1970) wholeheartedly endorsed the D24-embodied notion of control and limitation of the influence of foreign capital in the Andean Pact and Chilean economies. Frei's nationalization efforts focused on copper, the most important source of government revenue and the most prominent symbol of foreign exploitation. "Chilianization" of the copper mines provided for 51% government ownership of the giant industries, with generous compensation provided to the original owners.

The Socialist government of Salvador Allende that succeeded Frei in 1970 also strongly supported D24. However, Allende was forced to ratify the decision by presidential decree in the face of fierce opposition from the Congress and the *Contraloria* (*Latin America*, August 23, 1974: 257).[8] The Socialist Popular Unity Government aspired to more radical change than incumbent in D24. Allende's nationalization policies did not include "adequate compensation" for the original owners, completed government acquisition of the copper industry, and extended to other industries and the agricultural sector. Industry was nationalized in one of five ways: expropriation, public acquisition of shares (most banks were acquired in this manner), direct agreement with owners, and intervention or requisition that involved a change in control but not ownership.

Great confusion and disorder surrounded Allende's nationalization program. For example, Anaconda originally received US$174.5 million in promissory notes from the Frei regime for 51% of its shares. However, Allende and others felt the terms negotiated were too generous, and on July 11, 1971, constitutional reform gave the Chilean government complete ownership of the copper mines. Provisions for compensation to the copper companies included deductions for "excess profits," i.e., greater than 12%, garnered by the companies for the previous 15 years, and further deductions were allowed if the facilities were found to be in a state of poor repair. When all deductions were calculated after expropriation, the copper companies owed the Chilean government.

Once under government control, the enterprises were badly run. The state enterprises were administered by large bureaucracies with political objectives taking precedence over economic ones. For example, the El Teniente, which under private management employed 8,000 people in 1971, took on 4,000 new employees after expropriation to meet employment objectives. Worker discipline fell off, absenteeism rose, and wage disputes proliferated.

The Pinochet regime, which came to power as a result of the September 1973 coup, adhered to Friedmanite economic philosophy, and was immediately at odds with D24. Friedmanite free trade theory maintains that economies function best when the market forces of supply and demand are permitted free expression. Economic conditions inherited from the Allende regime were bleak, and Pinochet and his economic advisers were convinced that only by eliminating barriers to interaction with the industrialized world, including transnational corporations, could Chile achieve some kind of "take off" toward economic recovery.

If the case is to be made that Friedmanite economics assumed lexicographic importance in the way Chilean political leaders framed the decision to cooperate or not to cooperate with the Andean Pact's D24, the prevalence of these beliefs among the relevant decision makers must be established. Within the four-man Junta, the official responsible for economic affairs was Admiral Jose Toribio Merino Castro. Rear Admiral Lorenzo Gotuzzo was the first Minister of Finance. However, the Junta almost immediately acknowledged its lack of expertise in the area, and although the "economic team" underwent several personnel changes, economic policy remained firmly under civilian control. *El Mercurio* (March 16, 1980: A3) described the relationship between the military and its economic technocrats in this way: "The military established public tranquility and ensured the full execution of the norms dictated by the government while the civilians accompanied by the military elaborated and applied an economic scheme of immense projections for the stability and development of the country." Many of those involved in economic planning had previous affiliation with management of the right-wing daily *El Mercurio* or were economists at the University of Chile and the Catholic University of Santiago.

The Ministries of Economics and Economic Coordination enjoyed the most long-term influence over Chile's economic decision making, including the decision to withdraw from the pact. Fernanda Leniz was the Junta's first Minister of Economics. Leniz's conservative economic credentials were well recognized at the time. He had served as head of the *Sociedad de Fomento Fabril* (SOFOFA),[9] was chairman of the board of *El Mercurio,* and had been a long-time employee of the powerful Edwards family [10] (*Latin America,* October 12, 1973). It is generally assumed that failure to deal with Chile's runaway inflation precipitated his dismissal. Sergio de Castro succeeded Leniz when the new cabinet was put into place in April 1975.

Raul Saez, the Minister of Economic Coordination appointed after the July 1974 resignations, came to eclipse Leniz' role as chief governmental spokesman on pact affairs. Saez had enjoyed a varied past. A graduate of the University of Chicago and former Christian Democrat, he had served as Finance Minister under the Frei administration and had been one of the Alliance for Progress's "nine wise men." Exiled in Venezuela during the short-lived Allende regime, he acted as adviser to the antipact businessmen's organization *Fedecamaras* (*Latin America,* October 12, 1973: 328; November 1, 1974: 343). As pointed out earlier, Saez was an early supporter of the Andean Pact but came to passionately oppose D24 and worked diligently to circumvent its influence on the Chilean economy. Saez's resignation preceded the decision to withdraw from the pact by nearly a year (*Andean Report,* December 1975: No. 6: 15).[11]

The Foreign Ministry played a lesser role in deliberations concerning pact participation. The naval officers occupying the top post in this ministry during the period under consideration were Vice Admirals Ismael Huerta Diaz and Patricio Carvajal. Ricardo Claro served as economic adviser to the ministry and toured the United States in 1974 to explain D600 foreign investment rules (*Wall Street Journal,* September 10, 1974: 7:2). Throughout the course of the debates, the Foreign Ministry maintained the position that compromise would be reached and that Chile would retain membership in the pact. It was reported that elements within the Foreign Ministry objected to withdrawal from pact membership because such action could only exacerbate the international isolation Chile already suffered because of its human rights violations.

Although they were not primary players in decisions concerning pact participation, the Chilean delegation to the Andean Pact and support personnel had a vested interest in their country's continued participation in the organization. In 1975, the Chilean government provided a budget of US$1,107,000 for pact-related activities. Fifteen professional-level staff and 15 support personnel constituted the delegation, one-half of the 1973 level. Chilean staffers regarded the declining level of activity in their agency as a temporary reflection of Chile's economic difficulties. In fact, a content analysis of *Grupo Andino* accounts (The sample involved a 30-month period between 1971 and 1975) of the Junta's verbal behavior toward the pact yielded the following distribution: 79% positive, 10% neutral, and 10% negative (n = 57). In 1974 and 1975, Chilean nonverbal activity within the pact actually increased because of the increased number of trade missions (Ferris, 1976: 78–83, 105).

An increasing number of other governmental agencies had formally affiliated with their Andean Pact counterparts. Chile's Communications Minister, Leopoldo Porras, participated in the first meeting of the Ministers of Communication in May 1974. Earlier meetings of the *Ministros de Trabajo del Grupo Andino* had been attended by Chilean representatives. It is unlikely that voices from these agencies held much sway in the decision to withdraw.

The only governmental institution operating in Chile outside of those created by the Junta was the court system. The Supreme Court, headed by an extremely conservative president, Enrique Urrutia Manzano, had legitimized the coup on the grounds that the Allende regime, although legally elected, had "lost its legality by acting on the margin of the law" (*New York Times,* April 18, 1974: 3:1). No indication of the court's position on withdrawal from the pact was found. Chile, however, had allied itself with Peru as the strongest opponent of the proposed Andean tribunal. Officials from the other member nations also regarded this stance as a product of the current regime. It was believed that Chile's historical tradition of legalism under different circumstances would have manifested itself in support for such a supranational entity (Ferris, 1976: 123).

The authoritarian nature of the Chilean government and the extremely doctrinaire perspective of its top office holders were strong influences in Chile's decision to leave the pact. Within the government, only the Foreign Ministry provided weak support for continued participation in the regional economic organization, and it seems that its advocacy was ineffectual. The Junta had disbanded the legislature and placed in recess the political activities of the more centrist parties. No institutionalized means existed for authoritative supporters of the pact (i.e., Frei and the Christian Democratic Party) to gain access to the decision-making process. Frei and his associates expressed their views on the issue via the press and other publications, but this proved inadequate to affect the decision.

The military Junta had no philosophical problems with simply ignoring the troublesome decision but could not promulgate contradictory legislation without offending their pact partners. Technicians were assigned the task of identifying a loophole in D24 provisions. Admiral Toribio Merino announced that Chile would seek to revise the Cartegena Agreement (*Latin America,* June 28, 1974: 193).

Business International, a group of foreign businessmen, met in Santiago in late June 1974 and received widespread attention from both Chilean governmental officials and the sanctioned press. Spokespersons from this group made it clear that they regarded D24 as a serious impediment to foreign investment in Chile. Eldridge Haynes of Business International focused his comments specifically on the 14% profit repatriation limit: "The New York banks, where most of the investment capital comes from, have an interest rate of 11.8%. Consequently, to secure a return of only 14% is hardly attractive to investors." The businessmen acknowledged that the modification of D24 would prove a lengthy and difficult process (*Latin America,* July 19, 1974: 218). Similar views were espoused by the Council of the Americas; it predicted negative consequences from D24.

It is an empirical question, of course, whether the Junta's ideologically driven expectations of negative consequences from D24 implementation were valid. In 1971, Harvard business school students interviewed 20 North American corporations within the Fortune 500 group, almost all with investments in Andean Pact countries as well as other Latin American countries, to ascertain their opinions on Andean Pact restrictions. The Harvard study concluded that although the corporations did not view favorably some aspects of the D24 provisions, no major shift

in investment policy was likely to occur. The potential for political instability in the subregion was of greater concern to them than D24 provisions. The corporations were assuming a wait-and-see attitude. Most
doubted that the decision would be strictly implemented. With a single
exception, the corporations confirmed that they would comply with joint
venture and fade-out aspects of the decision if required to do so (*Inter-
American Economic Affairs*, 1971: 55–65). A survey by Guy B. Meeker
(1971: 25–42) of businessmen working in the Andean region concurred
with the Harvard group's findings that D24 would have little impact on
foreign investment activity in the region.

Mytelka (1979: 99–105) reports that Andean industrial programming
activities mitigated any dampening effect D24 may have had on direct
foreign investment and produced a net increase in affiliates in sectors
involved in the industrial programming. Before pact formation, there
were 762 foreign affiliates operating in the Andean Pact area, 13% of
which were located in Chile. By 1975, 9.8% of those firms had been
liquidated, nationalized, sold, or absorbed by other affiliates; 813 new
foreign affiliates had been created within pact member states, bringing
the total to 1,372, an increase of 80.1%. The data further suggest that the
least developed members of the pact, Bolivia and Ecuador, gained more
direct foreign investment than might have been expected given their undeveloped economies and global economic conditions. For those countries, the negative consequences of global economic recession were partially offset by integration.

A 1981 Hojmann study concluded that foreign investment in the pact
countries increased between 1970 and 1978 by US$250 million. The in-
crease in loans to the subregion exceeded the increase in the value of
direct investment, but the percentage increase in loans to Andean Pact
nations was no greater than to all Latin American countries. The rise in
direct foreign investment in Andean Pact countries during that period
was comparable to that of Mexico and Brazil, which had no D24-type
legislation (Hojmann, 1981: 153–154). Despite the persuasive evidence
that D24 implementation had little negative effect on direct foreign investment in the region, the Junta's ideological framing of the issue made
it unalterably opposed to the legislation.

On July 13, 1974, a new Chilean foreign investment statute, Decree
Law 600 (D600) was issued. The law established the *Comite de Inversi-
ones Extranjeras* (CIE) to deal with all matters pertaining to the inflow
of foreign capital and to register approved foreign investments. The law
permitted the granting of contracts for 10 years from the beginning of
production with the possibility of a second 10-year extension. In special
cases, the initial period could be 20 years. D600 guaranteed governmental nondiscrimination against foreign capital; foreign companies were
permitted to remit profits and repatriate their capital. Investors in Chile

before the promulgation of the new law were to continue to function under previous regulations but were required to apply to the CIE for new status before July 1975. If the application was judged acceptable, the capital was classified as new foreign investment annulling the previous contract (*Bank of London and South America Review,* Vol. 8, August 1974: 490).

D600 drafters hoped that the terminology of the new decree was sufficiently ambigious to avoid open conflict with D24. Raul Saez, the "economic warlord" in the Chilean cabinet, immediately set off to tour the Andean capitals to explain the implications of the new law. Some elements within the Chilean private sector were alarmed by the vagueness of the new statute. They feared it would deny Chilean exports access to the rest of the Andean market (*Latin America,* August 23, 1974: 257).

Chile's partners in the Andean Pact were firmly committed to the major precepts of D24 but at first seemed willing to hear and understand Chilean objections to the law. Bolivia, Colombia, Ecuador, and Peru had incorporated D24 into national legislation in early July 1971 by decree laws, as had Chile. The Venezuelan Congress approved the decision with its vote to join the pact in September 1973 (Fontaine, 1977: 67). However, at the time of Chile's promulgation of D600, only Peru and Venezuela had fully implemented the provisions of D24. Venezuela had oil income and no difficulty attracting foreign capital, and Peru's national legislation relating to foreign investment was actually significantly more exacting than that of the pact. Peru opposed liberalization of D24, fearing that any relaxation of pact rules would accentuate the differences between Peruvian and other members' legislation. Ecuador more or less ignored the provisions of D24 in search of badly needed investments from abroad, whereas by mid-1976 Bolivia also would press for liberalization of the decision (*Wall Street Journal,* May 24, 1976: 6:2). Bolivia and Ecuador, however, did wish to retain the preferential treatment afforded them under D24 (*Bank of London and Latin America Review,* xiii, November 1974, No. 11/74: 650–61).

At the September 9, 1974, meeting of the Andean Commission, approval of the fertilizer and petrochemical industrial projects was to dominate the agenda, but the debate centered almost exclusively on the new Chilean law. It became clear that other pact members regarded D600 in violation of D24. Four of the five members openly attacked Chile's new law. Peru's Premier General Edgardo Mercado Jarrin and its industrial and commerce ministers strongly criticized the Chilean law as an infraction of pact agreements. The Peruvian press mirrored that judgement. Peru and Bolivia issued a joint statement supporting D24. Much of the five's unease concerning Chile's D600 arose out of concern for the general malaise of the organization. Bolivia's Minister of Coordination, General Juan Lechin Suarez, declared that Chile's position "creates disloyal competition which endangers the unity of the subregion." Colombia's Congress accused Chile of "trying to disregard the main objective of Andean integration." (*New York Times,* September 9, 1974: 52:1)

Chile proposed a compromise formula under which Andean rules would apply only to investments in manufactured goods for export to pact members, whereas D600 rules would apply to investments whose products were to be marketed domestically or exported outside the Andean Group. The others said no; Chile either was or was not to be a part of the pact. In the face of such united opposition, the Chilean delegation walked out of the meeting. They eventually returned, but the meeting was suspended to allow the delegates to consult with their governments (*Latin America,* September 20, 1974: 296).

At the end of September, an Andean group mission labored for 3 days in Santiago to resolve the differences to no avail. Peru and Venezuela threatened to expel Chile from the pact, and even Colombia joined in the criticism. There were basically five areas of disagreement between the D24 and D600 legislation. D24 placed far stricter limits on the sectors open to foreign investment and provided for disinvestment of shares to domestic investors over a period of 15 years. D600 required no fade-out by foreign investors. D24 set a 14% ceiling on profit returns on capital investment by foreign firms; D600 set no limits. D24 forbade member governments to guarantee foreign credits unless the government had some stake in the operation; D600 put no restraints on governmental loan guarantees. Foreign firms were granted access to only short-term domestic credit under D24 rules; the Chilean law did not restrict local credit for foreign corporations. And D24 imposed significant controls on the import of foreign technology, a provision lacking in D600 (*Latin America,* November 1, 1974: 343). The remaining five pact members stressed that D24 guidelines actually worked to the advantage of foreign investors in that they clearly spelled out the conditions under which investment could be undertaken.

By late 1974, all parties seemed willing to effect a compromise. In November, Bolivia, Colombia, Ecuador, Peru, and Venezuela resolved that Chile's new law did not directly violate D24 and that the CIE was indeed competent to administer D24 provisions. The pact expressed its willingness to consider a marginally higher profit remission than 14%. In April 1975, the pact allowed Chile to sell CORFU (the state development corporation) industries to foreign investors, a venture previously impossible under D24.[12] Furthermore, the pact postponed for 2 years deliberations on tariff agreements, another source of Chilean animosity.[13]

Despite these compromises, Chile was forced to modify D600 to meet D24 provisions in August 1975. This created a legacy of bitterness in Chile toward the pact. It was speculated that Chile, at that time, wished to avoid further diplomatic isolation; much negative world opinion was being generated by the Junta's human rights violations (*Latin America,* February 22, 1975: 364). The compromises of 1974–1975 did little to address the primary differences in the way the two parties framed the problem. Pact leaders supported D24 on the grounds that it would avoid unhealthy competition for foreign investment among its members and would decrease foreign dependence. The ideology of Chile's leadership led them to conceptualize the question in terms of avoiding the loss of direct foreign investment.

Eduardo Montalva Frei, former Chilean president and founding father of the Andean Pact, remained committed to Chile's continued participation in the pact and adherence to D24.[14] In May 1975, Frei granted an interview to *Ercilla* in which he criticized the Junta's economic programs. He disagreed with the Junta's decision to sell to private-interest business enterprises established by CORFU between 1939 and 1970 (*Latin America,* June 6, 1975: 174).

In January 1976, Frei began in earnest a publication campaign to oust the Junta. In a 112-page booklet published in Santiago and distributed by Christian Democrats in Argentina, Frei denounced Junta violations of human rights, the torture and assassination of political dissidents, and the repression of labor organizations. He also strongly criticized the economic policies of the regime. Frei concluded that the Junta was being guided by "extremist groups who openly display their fascist character," and in effect called on the armed forces to end a regime "with many totalitarian characteristics" (*New York Times,* January 19, 1976: 2:4; January 22, 1976: 34:1).

In an August 28, 1976, *El Mercurio* article, Frei presented at length the reasons why withdrawal from the Pact would be "an irreversible and irreparable error" for Chile. This decision, based on some incomprehensible rationale, would expose the Chilean market to unrestrained international competition. Chilean industry, already plagued by low demand, high interest rates, decapitalization, and antiquated technology, would be defenseless. It would be unable to compete with foreign competition, as could no other country at a comparable level of development.

Chilean officials promised that once freed from D24 provisions, foreign investors would be waiting at the door. Frei asked, "Who are they?" Investors are influenced by conditions and developmental objectives of the receiving country. Large markets such as those provided by the Andean Pact are always more attractive to investors; they provide a more stable investment environment. Experience reveals that when investment criteria are too favorable for the investor, less reliable investors, those willing to engage in risky ventures in pursuit of quick profits, are attracted.

Frei questioned why the other five members of the Andean Pact were attracting more foreign investment than Chile, as well as experiencing higher levels of development. They clearly did not perceive D24 as detrimental to their development. He said, "It is a curious fact that Bolivia is presently undergoing an investment boom, and to a great extent so are Colombia, Ecuador, and even Peru, which had gone through a series of hardships, and they are still in the Pact."

There is speculation, he wrote, of Chile's entry into the *Cuenca de Plata* Agreement. Regardless of the benefits or disadvantages of this move, Andean Pact participation does not preclude negotiation of an enhanced economic relationship with Argentina. Neither does pact participation restrict trade with Brazil, nor the United States.

D24 was a positive element in the economic development of all members of the pact. Particularly important to the development of domestic entrepreneurship was its provision for gradual conversion of mixed industry to national control. A primary benefit from this process was the exchange of administrative and technological know-how. Twenty years ago, Frei wrote, foreign investors did not favor this approach but were now more receptive to participation by indigenous elements.

Frei specifically addressed the issue of the pact-proposed common external tariff. Some tariff protection was necessary for developing countries, but to neglect to adjust protection rates as infant industry acquired competitive status was an error. Andean Pact–proposed tariff levels, with a ceiling of 60%–70%, were reasonable. The 35% levels proposed by Chilean economists would leave industry dangerously exposed, and all negative effects of such reductions were not immediately predictable.

Frei also considered alarming the possibility that Chile might be excluded from the pact's industrial projects already underway. Leaving the pact, he concluded, would leave Chile more isolated than ever, regionally and internationally (Frei, 1976: 10–20).

At a previously referenced round table organized in Santiago in August 1976 by the Center for Studies on Company Development, Economics Minister Sergio de Castro painted a comprehensive picture of his government's views on continued participation in the Andean Pact and its views specifically on D24. Castro asserted that Andean Pact policy had done nothing to improve Chile's low economic growth rate, but that he fully expected Junta policies to redress the problem if Chile pursued an independent course.

Castro's main attack on D24 centered on its fade-out provisions. He said that it was absurd for Chile's scarce capital resources to be used to buy out existing foreign-owned enterprises when they could be used to create new industries and employment opportunities. A foreign-owned factory using Chilean labor, materials, and energy should not be regarded as a foreign enterprise. He claimed that for Chile to achieve its targeted 7% annual economic growth rate without an infusion of foreign capital would require an additional 15% cut in domestic consumption—

an unreasonable sacrifice to ask of an already impoverished society. He praised the overall contribution of foreign capital to the Chilean economy, which, in addition to capital goods and financing, imported technology, human talent, and management and marketing skills.

Addressing the issue of how the advantages of foreign investment might be retained and control still maintained to prevent structural distortions and excessive outflow of profits, Castro did not consider the potential role of loan financing a long-term alternative to equity participation, which was becoming increasingly more acceptable to both financiers and recipients.

With reference to the problem of technology transfer, Castro said that the fade-out system would mean that after 15 years, pact countries would be left with obsolete technology, not access to progressive technical developments.[15] He summarized the Chilean position, stating that each country should be free to set its own foreign investment rules, and that harmful competition could be avoided by providing local investors the same advantages offered to foreign investors (*Andean Report*, Vol. 11, No. 9, September 1976: 170–171).

In early August 1976, the six countries' foreign ministers met in Lima to ratify the protocol amending the Cartegena Agreement and to extend the deadlines for the industrial sectoral development and tariff programs. The policy differences between Chile and the pact had narrowed to an almost inconsequential level during 2 years of negotiations. Pact members had agreed in theory to increase the profit remittance ceiling on foreign investments to 20% and to compromise on other issues. However, Chilean officials were past the point of cooperation. The Minister of Economics, Sergio de Castro, refused to sign the protocol revision, indicating that this act could take place only after the group modified D24. The other members had come to believe that the Pinochet regime was trying to sabotage the entire organization. Seven hours of private and heated discussion produced no resolution. Chile had 60 days to ratify the protocol to remain within the pact.

Representatives of the five pact members met in Colombia in mid-August to discuss Chile's position on D24. They agreed to propose that the profit remittance limit be revised upward from 14% to 20% and the automatic reinvestment allowance from 5% to 7% (*Bank of London and South America Review*, Vol. 10, September 1976, No. 9/76: 496). At the mid-September meeting, the Andean Commission was unable to formalize an agreement on the proposed changes to D24. Persistent statements by Peruvian officials, particularly the Integration Minister Admiral Jorge Dubois, implied that a reconciliation with Chile was imminent. The Venezuelans expressed a less forgiving view. They stated that because Chile obviously had lost interest in many features of the pact, it must not desire continued membership. They asserted that Chile's departure was for all practical purposes a *fait accompli* (*Andean Report,* September 1976: 170).

As the withdrawal debate intensified, a few Andean Pact supporters appeared in unexpected quarters. The Chilean metallurgical industries' association, in an *El Mercurio* article, stated that it had always "actively participated" in efforts to achieve economic integration "so necessary" to the economies of Latin America, and that the Andean Pact was very important to the metallurgical industry (*Andean Report,* September 1976: 169). The general manager of a firm that exported mechanical products such as motor compressors for refrigeration pointed out that recently cited government economic statistics relating to his industry, used to "justify erroneous decisions," had been inaccurate. He said that the decision to withdraw had been taken with only partially justified data and inadequately researched projections. Writing on the day of Chile's withdrawal from the pact, he lamented: "Today (my company) has lost its subregional market and the US$3.5 million that was invested for this purpose . . ." (*El Mercurio,* November 18, 1976: 2).[16]

Individual opinion as to whether Chile should continue to participate in pact activities can be found in several lengthy articles in the Santiago daily *El Mercurio.* In a September 4, 1976, letter to the editor, Emilio V. Sanfuentes[17] (*El Mercurio,* p. 2) took issue with an earlier Frei editorial supporting continued participation in the pact. Sanfuentes wrote that most analysts concur that larger markets provide enhanced opportunities for manufacturers and investors; therefore, active participation in the global market was more advantageous than the market provided by the united member states of the pact. In reference to claims that D24 provided predictability and stability for prospective investors, Sanfuentes asserted that Chilean D600 provided equal predictability for foreign investors. D24, he wrote, did not make Andean Pact countries an attractive investment area for foreign capital. This negative opinion was shared by the majority of domestic private entrepreneurs and government officials.

Sanfuentes asserted that the D24 requirement that controlling shares of foreign enterprises be gradually assumed by indigenous owners was irrational. He asked: could not these resources be better invested in new enterprises to create additional employment opportunities?

He disputed the notion that the formation of mixed companies was the only way to assure access to foreign technology. In his opinion, the nationalization of foreign enterprises would instead assure that Chilean industry would be left with obsolete technology.

The immediately preceding discussion, printed in the well-censored daily *El Mercurio,* confirmed that the Junta permitted open debate on Chile's continued participation in the pact in the few months immediately preceding the formal October withdrawal. Government officials assumed that pact issues were sufficiently esoteric and technical and of interest to such circumscribed groups that this form of public dissent of Junta policy constituted no threat. Although the opinions being offered on an individual basis came from persons of acknowledged authority and expertise, Chile's withdrawal from the pact demonstrated that this input was inconsequential to the final policy decision.

Beginning in October, a protocol outlining the terms on which Chile would withdraw from the pact was drafted. Although efforts continued until the mandated deadline to find a way to resolve the differences or to devise arrangements for partial membership in the pact, Chile withdrew from membership in the Andean Pact October 30, 1976 (*Bank of London and South America Review,* Vol. 10, October 1976, No. 10/76).

D102, the Chilean decision to withdraw, stated that Chile gave up the rights and obligations of the market, which meant that Chile no longer could benefit from trade liberalization or keep its assignments in the metalworking and petrochemical industries. Chile continued participation with Decisions 40, 46, 56, and 94, which dealt with double taxation, Andean multinational enterprises, heavy road transport, and the Andean highway network, respectively (*Andean Report,* 1976: A:211). In contrast to the earlier atmosphere of conflict, Chile's departure from the pact was carried out with expressions of great regret, with no recriminations expressed by either side.

The immediate economic effects of the withdrawal were not dramatic. Trade with the pact partners represented only 5% of total Chilean trade. One-half of that trade (valued at US$150 million) represented petroleum imports from Venezuela and Ecuador, which were not affected by the withdrawal. Exports to the subregion (US$106 million in 1975) were predominantly raw materials and food: copper, wood pulp, fruit, wine, and edible seeds. It was not anticipated that this trade would be greatly affected by the withdrawal. It was projected that the export of manufactured goods alone (valued at approximately US$10 million per year) would suffer, but they represented only 10% of the exports to the Andean Pact and only a fraction of Chile's total world exports (Fontaine, 1977: 41–42). Analysts predicted that the greatest cost to Chile likely would come in the loss of future investment rather than in existing trade; Chile's departure from the pact meant that it could no longer offer potential investors duty-free access to the Andean market. And, of course, when future pact programs for automobile, electronic, and paper manufactures were implemented, Chile would have no share of the markets (*Andean Report,* XI, No. 10, October 1976: 188).

Despite the rather sanguine early predictions regarding the effect of the Chilean decision, in the wake of the withdrawal the Andean Pact underwent major changes in its most innovative planning and regulatory policies. D103 weakened the provisions of D24. D104 altered the deadlines for the establishment of a common external tariff, and D105 modified the procedures whereby industrial programs were approved. The April 21, 1978 Protocol of Arequipa extended the deadlines even further.

Although the Andean Pact leadership argued that the essence of D24 remained intact after the revisions, the major thrust of its restrictions was altered. Foreign shareholding was now allowed in existing local or mixed companies, provided the companies remained mixed firms with 51% minimum local ownership. Previously, foreign shareholding was permitted in existing companies only to the extent that a firm remained a national firm, with 80% indigenous ownership.

Divestment requirements were also relaxed. Divestment deadlines were advanced by changing the definition of "existing companies" to read "firms in existence as of 1974" rather than December 31, 1970. The transformation of foreign firms into mixed or national corporations could be accomplished via capital augmentation rather than sale of shares. With the high rate of inflation in the economies of the Andean Pact member states, the level of control to be exerted by indigenous shareholders in the existing transnational corporations was severely restricted. The new provisions exempted foreign and mixed firms in Bolivian and Ecuadorian tourism and agribusiness from divestment requirements on the same basis as previously applied to companies that exported 80% or more of their output outside the pact. Profit remittance levels for foreign firms were raised from 14% to 20%, and the national governments were permitted to raise this limit unilaterally. Reinvestment of up to 7% profits without review was permitted; this limit had been 5% under D24 regulations.

TNCs were granted access to short- and medium-term domestic credit. Medium-term credit was available for up to 3 years, which upon refinancing easily could be transformed into long-term credit. National firms were thus undercut by TNCs in the competition for scarce local capital.

D103 returned pact policy to the point where direct foreign investment could be expected to contribute only minimally to net capital accumulation within pact states. For all practical purposes, control of direct foreign investment in Andean countries reverted to early 1960s levels; TNCs operated with few restrictions (Mytelka, 1979: 37, 73–75).

SUMMARY

Chile's October 30, 1976, decision to withdraw from participation in the Andean Pact was the direct result of the new military regime's determination to apply the prescriptions of neoclassical liberal economic theory to Chile's grave economic problems. Chile's dependent economy, although experiencing overall growth in the 1960s, had long exhibited signs of maladjustment, which mired the country in deep economic distress in the 1970s. The Christian Democratic and Socialist governments that preceded the military Junta regarded integration and Andean Pact participation as integral to their overall plans for economic development.

The economic policies of the new military Junta were heavily influenced and managed by graduates of the University of Chicago's School of Economics, an institution renowned for its strong advocacy of liberal Economic doctrine. Many of these policy makers had suffered intellectual and/or political persecution during previous administrations and regarded the Junta's ascendance to power as an opportunity to vindicate themselves and their economic ideology.

Chile's economic policy makers regarded increased foreign investment and trade as the only means to save the economy from sure destruction. Appreciative of the benefits to be derived from the expanded market and planned industrial schemes, they initially wished to remain in the Andean Pact. The Andean Pact's D24 and the proposed common external tariff, however, directly contradicted the Chilean leadership's assumptions regarding the indispensability of increased foreign investment and trade. After years of seeking compromise and revision of D24, the Junta's attitude gradually hardened; withdrawal from the pact was the logical consequence of the two diametrically opposed economic perspectives.

The framework of utilities associated with Decision 24 and Chile's decision to withdraw from the Andean Pact is summarized in Table 3.1. Among the potentially important components of decision framing associated with D24 and the Chilean decision to withdraw from pact membership is the evidence suggesting that congruence obtained only in the two parties' desire to avoid loss. As far as pact leadership was concerned, the primary utility was to decrease foreign involvement and control over their primary developmental assets and to avoid counterproductive competition for foreign investment among the regional partners. The Chilean leadership's framing of the issue, however, was lexicographically influenced by ideology.

The Chilean case provides a classic example of regime change within a member state of a regional economic organization bringing to power a group that not only lacks commitment to the pact, but also identifies and implements strategies for economic recovery and development that contravene premises on which the pact is based. Furthermore, the authoritarian nature of the regime precluded the effective articulation of the views of those supporting continued pact participation.

It may be speculated that had the 1970s not been a decade of global recession, which exacerbated the problems of an already malfunctioning economy, the Chilean population may have been less inclined to seize on socialist solutions for their problems. Although it cannot be assumed

Table 3.1

FRAMING COMPONENT	DECISION 24	CHILE'S DECISION
ISSUE CONCEPTUALIZATION	Decrease dependence Avoid beggar-thy-neighbor competition Enhance economic development and growth	Avoid loss of direct foreign investment Economic recovery and growth
LEVEL OF ASSESSMENT	Regional National	National
GAIN/LOSS	Loss avoidance	Loss avoidance
PROBABILITY/RISK	Moderate to high probability gain driving from increased control over economic development Low risk loss of direct foreign investment	High perceived risk of losing direct foreign investment
SURVIVAL	Not applicable	Economic survival
IDEOLOGY	Dependency theory	Friedmanite economics
TIME HORIZON	Moderate-->long-term	Short-term

that another partisan faction would have undertaken policies sufficient to bolster the Chilean economy to forestall the military coup, the Socialists' economic strategies were inept and resulted in disaster in almost every sector. Economic distress contributed to the polarization of the political environment; the policy alternatives to Allende's were radically right-wing. As will be noted in the Nigerian decision-making scenario, economic hardship is endemic to these developing countries. As vulnerable members of the global economy, they possess few resources and policy instruments with which to shield themselves from forces in the international environment. This, combined with the contemporary undeveloped and dual nature of their domestic economies and decided instances of economic mismanagement, resulted in political instability.

Aside from proceeding expeditiously toward the achievement of long-range economic objectives, the Chilean case suggests that regional leadership may do well to consider measures that facilitate political stability within member states. Socialization of elites (and indeed the member states' general populations) regarding the benefits of participation in the regional economic organization may prove helpful to preserving member-state participation in regional economic efforts in the face of regime change.

This case well supports the thesis of this study that member-state political elites frame their participation decisions to avoid short-term national loss—economic loss in this instance. Chile's Junta identified increased foreign investment and trade as its first priority for achieving economic recovery and development. Compliance with D24 and continued participation in the Andean Pact were regarded as major deterrents to achieving those goals. Although continued participation in the pact assured at minimum the benefits of a larger market, the immediate and future gains from the industrial schemes, and the psychological and status proceeds from pact membership, these advantages, in the Junta's estimation, were outweighed by the need for increased direct investment and trade. Furthermore, a Junta that glibly disregards international outrage about its overt and widespread human rights violations is not likely to count loss of prestige or reputation among regional neighbors as a serious consideration. The Andean Pact's designated objectives of controlled foreign investment and the erection of a common external tariff were congruent with the developmental strategies of Chile's Christian Democratic and Socialist leadership. The liberal economic dogma of the military regime, however, wrought a reversal of Chile's approach toward economic recovery and development. Chile's new developmental strategy did not include participation in Andean Pact integration.

NOTES

1. Chile's mineral resources include copper (accounting for two-thirds of export earnings), water, iodine, nitrates, salt, silver, sulfur, iron ore, manganese, natural gas, and petroleum. The agricultural sector produced fruits, wool, and rice for export.

2. The Popular Unity Government was a coalition of the Communist Party, Socialist Party, Movement of United Popular Action, the Radicals, the Independence Popular Action, and the Christian Left.

3. On the London Metals Exchange the price of copper in US$ per pound varied during the decade of the 1970s as shown in Table 3.2.

4. Mendez provides a helpful summary of Chilean economic indicators during the decade of the 1970s in his 1979 volume (See pp. 299, 325–327, 331), as shown in Table 3.3.

Table 3.2

	1970	1971	1972	1973	1974	1975	1976
NOMINAL PRICE	64.10	49.27	48.57	80.78	93.27	55.94	63.55
REAL PRICE	106.19	79.12	74.59	109.68	106.55	58.51	63.55

(Mendez, 1979: 339)

Table 3.3

INDICATOR	1970	1971	1972	1973	1974	1975	1976
TRADE ACCOUNT BALANCE (M US$)	156	-18	-255	-137	135	-118	460
BALANCE OF PAYMENTS (M US$)	114	-300	-229	-112	-45	-275	455
FOREIGN DEBT (M US$)	3,123	3,196	3,602	4,048	4,774	5,263	5,195
OFFICIAL UNEMPLOYMENT (%)	6.1	3.8	3.1	4.8	9.2	14.5	13.7

5. See the Appendix for a list of LAFTA's members and a summary of its accomplishments and difficulties. Multilateral negotiations on a product-by-product basis in the annual conference were the only mechanism for tariff reduction. Important decisions were subject to a single-member veto. A permanent executive committee of ambassadorial representatives was responsible for implementation of the decisions of the conference with the assistance of a secretariat having virtually no independent functions (Bond, 1978: 404).

6. In September 1967, LAFTA foreign ministers approved the guidelines contained in the Bogota Declaration (Taylor, 1984: 68).

7. Despite the apparent commitment of the Allende regime to pact initiatives, among the member states, Chile was most frequently accused of violating or failing to implement decisions. Chile took 4 months to implement the first stage of the tariff reduction program, and 4 and 15 months, respectively, to implement stages two and three. Twelve months elapsed before implementation of the minimum common external tariff (Puyana de Palacios, 1982: 159, 313).

8. The *Contraloria* supervised the legality of presidential decrees. Its opinions, however, were nonbinding.

9. The SOFOFA, the Chilean Industrial Association, represented the primary business organizations of Chile. Although an early supporter of the Andean Pact, SOFOFA came to oppose the integration effort and D24. Mytelka (1979: 36) explains that the association had rarely articulated the kind of economic nationalism found elsewhere in Latin America even during the 1960s. Militantly opposed to the socialist government of Allende, SOFOFA announced its opposition to D24, and later as hostility to the Allende government escalated, confirmed that the Chilean business community could not support "a process of integration in which the economic policies of the State were incompatible with Chilean private enterprise" (Atria, 1974: 139). It was alleged that SOFOFA served as a conduit for funding from conservative sources in Mexico and Venezuela, used to bring the downfall of the Allende government (*New York Times*, November 24, 1974: 5:1).

10. The Edwards family, who controlled interests in the Banco Edwards, pub-

lished *El Mercurio* and other newspapers, and held interests in the real estate, transportation, and fishing industries, was singled out by Allende as representative of the evils of capitalism. The state took over the Banco Edwards and moved against *El Mercurio* (*New York Times,* September 8, 1970: 7:1; January 18, 1971: 3:1). It may be generalized that most of Chile's 50 aristocratic families regarded the 1973 coup as in their interest. They supported elimination of D24 restrictions because they perceived their interests as coinciding with those of the transnational corporations (Mytelka, 1979: 35).

11. In December 1975, it was reported that Saez was spending most of his time organizing joint ventures between foreign firms and the Chilean government, particularly in the copper and petrochemicals sectors.

12. It was decided that the shares acquired during the Allende regime would be treated as "existing" foreign companies. They were not allowed access to the Andean market tariff reduction program unless they were willing to sell to local shareholders at least 50% of their ownership within the original D24 deadline (*Andean Report,* XI, No. 5, May 1976: 91).

13. Within the pact, Peru and Venezuela traditionally favored higher tariffs. The proposals on the table for the Pact's external tariff levels were not significantly higher than those proposed by Chile. The proposed maximum 70% tariff would apply only in a few select cases (*Andean Report,* XI, No. 9, September 1976: 171).

14. Shortly after the coup, Frei declared the Junta "the only saving solution for Chile" (*New York Times,* October 12, 1973: 3:4). Frei and some Christian Democratic Party (PDC) leaders viewed the coup as a necessary consequence of the "economic disaster, institutional chaos, armed violence, and moral crisis" produced by the Allende regime. They expressed confidence that once the military had accomplished, "the tasks which they have assumed of avoiding the grave dangers of destruction and totalitarianism which threatened the Chilean nation, they will return power to the sovereign people so that they can decide freely and democratically on the future of the nation." However, as the nature of the Pinochet regime became more clearly defined, the PDC split in its attitude toward the government, and Frei fell silent.

A January 1974 letter signed by the PDC's president and vice president, Patricio Aylwin and Osvaldo Olguin, mailed to Pinochet and published shortly thereafter in Buenos Aires, criticized the regime's repressive economic policies. The correspondence read: "In view of the level of prices and fact that the earnings of workers are insufficient to cover the cost of food and other vital items for their families, we feel it is no exaggeration to say that many of these people are simply going hungry." Later that year, Christian Democratic leader Renan Fuentealba criticized the Junta in an *Agence France-Press* interview and was expelled from the country.

In November 1974, eight former PDC members of Congress and five party leaders issued a statement that "categorically condemned the overthrow of the constitutional president of Chile." The party leaders blamed political extremists, who had created a "false impression" that there was "no other recourse, but armed confrontation or a coup d'etat." They singled out "the responsibility of the irresponsibility of the ultra-left" for "special condemnation" (Sigmund, 1977: 249). The Christian Democratic leadership under Frei conducted a poll of 1,000 local party representatives in late 1975; at the time, 98% remained opposed to forming an alliance with leftist groups against the Junta.

With the exception of Frei, Chile's political parties had no perceptible influence on Chile's continued participation in the pact. The seven leftist parties that had supported Allende were banned; all others were declared in recess. The Junta did not deal kindly with its political foes. Most prominent party leaders found it safer to leave the country than remain under Junta rule, and the Junta engaged in a deadly armed struggle with leftist partisans. By the end of the first year of Junta rule, the ranks of the *Movimiento de Izquierda Revolutionaria* were reduced to a few hundred people in scattered terrorist units. Its leader, Miguel Enriquez, topped a most-wanted list until he was killed by police. Another member of the movement, Lumi Videla, was strangled and thrown on the grounds of the Italian embassy (*New York Times,* October 6, 1974: 18:1; December 13, 1974: 431).

Right-wing supporters of the Junta and its conservative economic policies were zealots of the moribund National Party and its political offspring, *Patria y Libertad* (Fatherland and Freedom). Sergio Jonofre Jarpa, a former Chilean Senator who headed the National Party, and the party's daily, the *Tribuna,* expressed fervent support for the military coup as Chile's only salvation from communism. Although Fatherland and Freedom received monetary support from the Confederation of Industrialists and Landowners association, the group was primarily paramilitary in emphasis (it played a role in the unsuccessful military coup of June 29) and had little influence on the Junta's economic policies (*Washington Post,* October 5, 1983: 137).

15. Many Andean Pact officials regarded the technology transfer issue as the most important long-term aspect of the foreign investment question. Various attempts were made to produce an effective technology policy, but these had been limited to attempts to foster local ability to analyze and break down technology packages, to ensure that the Andean countries negotiated the best terms possible for technology acquisition, and to unrealistic plans for developing local technologies (*Andean Report,* XI, No. 9, September 1976: 171).

16. No direct evidence was found of labor's attitude toward the Pinochet government's stance on D24 and Chile's withdrawal from the pact. Organized labor had been the principle political base for Allende's "popular unity" coalition and government. The largest labor group, the Central Workers Confederation (*Central Unica de Trabajadores,* comprising more than 4,000 unions with an estimated 800,000 individual members) was outlawed with the advent of Junta rule. Its Secretary General, Luis Figueroa, a congressman and head of the Communist Party, went immediately into hiding (*New York Times,* October 6, 1970: 17:1; September 26, 1973: 10:4).

There was one effort in December 1973 to organize a replacement organization for the *Central Unica de Trabajadores,* the *Central Nacional Sindical.* Although the military took no action against the *Central Nacional Sindical,* it perished for lack of financial support. Junta law permitted no legal means for unions to contribute to the maintenance of such organizations and no parties or other sources of support existed.

Deterioration of any remaining confidence among early labor Junta supporters was evident by 1975. Shortly after the coup, Edwardo Rios, President of the

Maritime Workers Union, was sent abroad to defend Junta policies at international labor conferences. But by 1975 he refused to do so; he was quoted as saying: "There is no dialogue with the government" (*New York Times,* September 21, 1975: 30:1).

17. Sanfuentes, a sociologist by training, served as professor of sociology and planning at the University of Chile, and during 1966–1968 received US Agency for International Development Fellowship for study at the University of Chicago's School of Economics. Upon his return, he became a researcher at the *Centro de Estudios Sociologia.*

4 The ECOWAS Case: Nigeria's 1983 Decision to Expel Alien Workers

The decision-making scenario to be examined in the Economic Community of West African States (ECOWAS) case involves Nigeria's 1983 expulsion of an estimated 1 million Ghanaians and an additional 1 million citizens from other West African countries illegally employed within its borders.[1] Nigeria played a primary role in the founding of the ECOWAS in 1975, contributes 32% toward the community's budget, and hosts the community's headquarters (Falola and Ihonvbere, 1985: 141). In May 1979, the ECOWAS leadership signed a protocol providing for the "Free Movement of Persons, Right of Residence, and Establishment." Nigeria led the campaign for swift ratification and implementation of the protocol, which entered into force May 20, 1980. However, in 1983, pressing economic, social, and political problems resulted in the government decision to deport alien workers, most of whom were citizens of Ghana and other West African countries, Nigeria's ECOWAS partners.

Although legal according to domestic immigration and ECOWAS law, the deportation is a blatant example of a member state's policy decision contravening the spirit of a regional economic community initiative, in this case the Protocol on the Free Movement of Persons, Right of Residence, and Establishment. The decision was made in a capricious fashion, without prior consultation with ECOWAS members, and resulted in extreme hardship for the deportees. This case reveals that immediate and specific economic, societal, and political difficulties deriving from the global oil glut of the early 1980s and resulting and concurrent societal and political instability superseded in the minds of Nigeria's leaders any concern that the expulsion order might negatively affect the regional economic organization.

THE 1983 NIGERIAN DECISION TO EXPEL
ALIEN WORKERS

The announcement of the Nigerian decision[2] to expel alien workers came as a "lightning bolt from the blue"—without previous public discussion or warning. It constituted the largest forced migration of people since the 19th century. On January 17, 1983, the Federal Minister of Internal Affairs, Alhaji Ali Baba, in a televised broadcast, gave all aliens residing and working illegally in Nigeria 14 days' notice to leave the country. The minister told news personnel in Lagos that citizens from ECOWAS countries without proper papers were employed in private and public sectors in violation of Nigeria's 1963 Immigration Act, and that this flagrant abuse of the law no longer could be tolerated. The Immigration Act prohibits private sector employment of non-Nigerians without the written consent of the Director of Immigration. After 2 weeks, government agents would begin inspecting commercial and industrial establishments as well as households to identify defaulting aliens and repatriate them. Repatriated aliens would be placed on a "stop list" to ensure that they would not return to Nigeria. It was further announced that registration of legal aliens would begin February 14 at immigration headquarters in all 19 states and Abuja (*West Africa,* January 24, 1983: 233).

On January 25, the government, responding to African and international pressure, announced that the deadline to comply with the order had been extended until February 28 for skilled foreigners such as secretaries, nurses, teachers, masons, and carpenters. The Lagos state government alone was forced to fire 2,600 Ghanaian teachers, but employees of the federal, state, and parastatal institutions, as well as citizens of ECOWAS countries, Cameroon, and Chad who had come to Nigeria before 1963, were excluded from the expulsion order "irrespective of what they do" (*New Nigerian,* January 27, 1983: 9).

The immediate cause cited by Baba for the decision was that the excessive number of illegal immigrants had been "one of the remote causes" of Nigeria's social problems. He said that, "The recent Kano, Maiduguri and Kaduna disturbances were traceable to this influx and the whole nation witnessed with dismay the wanton destruction of property and lives." The government would not allow "such unwholesome developments to continually plague the nation" (*West Africa,* January 31, 1983: 245).

At the time of the expulsion order, an estimated 1 million Ghanaian and an additional 1 million nationals from other West African countries were illegally at work in Nigeria in industries associated with oil, construction, the port facilities, textiles, hotels, security, and domestic services. When the eviction order came down, they began pulling up roots and seeking transportation out of the country. Many of the personal injuries resulted from the haste of the forced departure. There were the inevitable diseases (specifically cholera, malaria, pneumonia, and severe diarrhea) and fatigue. There were reports of babies being delivered in sheds on the docks and at the airport. In early February it was reported in Lagos that at least 16 persons had died—10 from starvation and 6 by drowning while trying to board ships. Although estimates vary, probably fewer than 60 deaths overall were directly attributable to the exodus. Had three-quarters of the aliens not been sturdy young men, the loss of life associated with the exodus would have been higher (*West Africa,* February 14, 1983).[3]

The Chadians claimed that some Nigerian employers refused to disburse their final salaries, and in many instances, the departees were forced to leave behind or sell at a loss property accumulated during their stay in the country. The *Daily Times* reported that some female aliens were offering themselves for marriage in Bendel state to avoid deportation. And men in the same area were seeking employment as farm laborers in interior villages (*Daily Times,* February 1, 1983: 17). Those complying with the order left on foot and by ship, car, truck, and plane. Truck owners quadrupled the usual fare for such transportation, charging US$60 per person, and twice that for their luggage. The airfare to Ghana was US$150.

The January 23 *Sunday Punch* reported that, "almost one week after the 'go home' order on illegal aliens in Nigeria, the police are yet to receive a directive from the Federal Government on enforcement." The order was issued so suddenly that the police only learned of it through the newspapers. *West Africa* (January 31, 1983: 245) reported that, "in full glare of the law, some Nigerians have been molesting aliens who are yet to leave the country."

The suddenness of the order caught the receiving nations unprepared. The travelers' difficulties were compounded by Ghana's closed borders, sealed since September 1982 in an effort to control cocoa smuggling and destabilization of President Jerry Rawlings' regime. They were reopened January 29, 1983. Benin (population 3,377,000) and Togo (population 2,472,000) sealed their borders to prevent a logjam of travelers, which would have exacerbated their ongoing economic crises. The line of double-parked trucks at the border between Nigeria and Benin was 2 miles long at times (*New York Times,* February 3, 1983: A12). Some refugees were detained for 12 days in the open bush before being allowed to reenter their own countries. (Gravil, 1985: 523–537)

Ghana, Togo, and Benin set up emergency reception centers for their repatriated citizens. Already mired in severe economic difficulties, Ghana and Chad appealed for emergency foreign aid to help cope with the sudden influx of persons. Pope John Paul II labeled the expulsion "a grave, incredible drama," producing the largest single, and "worst human exodus in this century" (*Sunday Concord,* February 13, 1983).

United Nations (UN) Secretary General Perez de Cuellar urged the countries to open their borders to allow safe passage for those on their way home (*New York Times,* January 29, 1983: A24). The European Community issued a press statement deploring the order. The US State Department described the decision as "shocking" and claimed that it was a violation of "every imaginable human right." The opposition leader in the British House of Commons, Michael Foot, wrote a letter to the Nigerian High Commissioner in London, Alhaji Shehu Awak, labeling the expulsion order and its mode of implementation "an act of heartlessness, and a failure of common humanity" (*National Concord,* February 8, 1983).

The US embassy in Lagos provided UN officials with US$70,000 and 800 tons of food to assist the relief efforts (*New York Times,* February 2, 1983: A1). The International Committee of the Red Cross flew in a shipment of tents, blankets, and 16 tons of food to Accra, and Catholic Relief Services and the Baptist Mission provided additional assistance.

By mid-February the Nigerian Minister of the Interior claimed that approximately 1.2 million aliens had left. That total represented, among others, 700,000 Ghanaians, 18,000 Beninoise, 150,000 Chadians, and 5,000 Togolese (*New Nigerian,* February 16, 1983: 1). This extreme and capricious decision directly contravened the spirit of the ECOWAS Protocol on the Free Movement of Persons, Right of Residence, and Establishment.

PROTOCOL ON FREE MOVEMENT OF PERSONS, RIGHT OF RESIDENCE, AND ESTABLISHMENT

Traditionally, control over the entry and exit of aliens is the exclusive domain of the sovereign state. International law may require the state to admit its own citizens, but not aliens. Aliens, once admitted, may be deported at the discretion of the national authorities, subject, if at all, to judicial review. Liberal economic theory maintains, however, that economic development is facilitated by removing barriers to the free movement of capital, goods, services, and labor. Article 27, Chapter IV, of the Treaty of the Economic Community of West African States provides for the removal of obstacles to free movement and residence of peoples within the community. It states that henceforth citizens of the various member states shall be regarded as "Community citizens" and that "Member States shall by agreements with each other exempt Community citizens from holding visitors' visas and residence permits and allow them to work and undertake commercial and industrial activities within their territories."[4]

At the 1978 Lagos meeting, the ECOWAS Authority of Heads of State and Government decided in principle to adopt an agreement on the free movement of persons within the community and directed the Council of Ministers to propose a text to be considered at the next summit.[5] At the May 1979 Dakar summit, the authority considered and signed the protocol on Free Movement of Persons, Right of Residence, and Establishment, which entered into force May 20, 1980, after ratification by the necessary seven member states.

The new protocol promised very little in terms of immediate implementation. Phase 1, effective in July 1980, mandated the removal of all visa requirements for those "community citizens intending to stay for a maximum of 90 days in another member state."[6] This provision simply allowed ECOWAS citizens to travel to other member states without visas and remain within that country for 90 days if they had appropriate documents from their own countries and could pay for their visits and return tickets.

Article 3 of the protocol stated that ECOWAS member states "shall reserve the right to refuse admission into their territory . . . any citizen who comes within the category of inadmissible immigrants under their laws." The protocol was not designed to negatively affect citizens of the community already residing and working in other member states provided they were in compliance with the member states' immigration laws (Asante, 1986: 151–152). The implementation of phases 2 and 3, pertaining to permanent residence and establishment, respectively, was contingent on the success of phase 1, with a maximum transitional period of 15 years.

The West African past provided significant precedence for the concepts embodied in the protocol. Throughout their colonial past, the peoples of the region regarded themselves as citizens of a single subregion segmented by European-imposed colonial borders.[7] Ethnic affiliations traversed colonial boundaries, and the nomadic lifestyle of many groups provided for constant interaction between colonial holdings. C. M. B. Brann writes that:

Under the colonial regimes there was free professional movement of elites to the territories administered by each power. Many Sierra Leonean and Ghanaian lawyers, teachers, and civil servants served in Nigeria—always a large employer of external manpower by virtue of its expansiveness and population. Similarly many Dahomeyans helped to form the cadres of the erstwhile capital of OAF, Dakar. Further afield, Ghanaian fishermen settled freely on the Bight of Biafra and Benin whilst in the North, pastoralists crossed unimpeded across the colonial frontiers of all three powers as did of course petty traders (*West Africa*, September 8, 1980: 1711).

In 1964, Nigeria entered into bilateral agreements with Cameroon, Chad, Dahomey, Guinea, *Côte d'Ivoire*, Morocco, Niger, and Togo, exempting their visiting citizens from visa requirements. These privileges were suspended during the civil war but on June 4, 1971, the Yakubu Gowon administration signed an order reactivating the agreements in the spirit of "African brotherhood" (*Africa Research Bulletin,* July 15, 1971: 2130).

It is often said that the protocol is the only ECOWAS provision that actually touches the man on the street. The issue generated much debate and acrimony before and after promulgation. In 1978, a Nigerian commentator observed: "if the influx into Nigeria continues and it becomes clear that Nigeria is merely paying the ECOWAS piper without knowing what tune to call, this is likely to further weaken the already weak domestic support for the Community." (*Daily Times,* May 6, 1978: 19). A survey of letters to the editor and editorial opinions in Nigerian newspapers between November 1980 and January 1981 revealed that spillover from the protocol controversy had generated doubts about Nigeria's continued participation in the organization (Onwuka, 1982: 196–197).

A *Daily Times* correspondent wrote that ECOWAS exists "at the expense of Nigeria and yet one hardly finds a Nigerian in any responsible position in that organization" (*Daily Times,* February 20, 1981). Obi Wali, the Senate leader of the Nigerian People's Party, called for a re-evaluation of Nigeria's commitment to ECOWAS because, "the question of security has not been properly assessed in terms of the individual states." (*Nigerian Tribune,* February 26, 1981).

Although opinion was convinced otherwise, there was no formal evidence to support the notion that the free movement protocol produced a sudden upsurge of travel between and among ECOWAS countries. *West Africa* offered the opinion that it was unlikely that the protocol affected in any way the regular and substantial movement of persons and goods, usually illegally, across the remoter sections of the ECOWAS borders (*West Africa,* June 22, 1981: 1393). In 1980, ECOWAS's Executive Director, Aboubakar Diaby-Ouattara of the *Côte d'Ivoire,* pointed out: "Today you will find more Nigerians in the ECOWAS countries than you can find combined ECOWAS countries' citizens residing in Nigeria." (Okolo, 1984: 35).

Support for the community in Nigeria and region-wide was limited to the governmental, business, and academic elites. Nigeria's governmental leadership voiced consistent support for the community. The Federation of West African Chambers of Commerce and Industry had campaigned vigorously for its establishment. An ECOWAS delegation attended the 1981 annual meeting of the federation, and an official of the federation was a member of the ECOWAS study tour to the Association of Southeast Asian Nations in July 1981. In 1982, the chamber was afforded observer status in the economic community (*West Africa,* May 24, 1982: 1369, 1371).

The West African Economic Association, a group of economists and academics founded in April 1978, also maintained close ties with the ECOWAS secretariat. ECOWAS participated at the association's biannual conferences in Lagos (April 1978), Abidjan (April 1980), and Freetown (1982). The dicussion topic for the Abidjan gathering was "Development Planning Priorities and Strategies for the 1980s in ECOWAS" (Asante, 1986: 204).

However, ECOWAS enjoyed no support among the Nigerian general public. The public and the press believed Nigeria benefitted little from ECOWAS and were especially skeptical of the benefits to be derived from the protocol on free movement. With the absence of support for the community among the general population, it might legitimately be asked why Nigeria had so persistently and vigorously supported plans for an all-encompassing economic community for the West African region. What benefits had been anticipated and realized from participation within the community?

NIGERIA AND ECOWAS

Nigeria's leadership in the process that in May 1975 united the 15[8] Arab-, English-, French-, and Portuguese-speaking countries in the ECOWAS is generally acknowledged. Fifteen years before ECOWAS became a reality, officials of the newly independent Nigerian government voiced support for a Nigeria-led integration of West Africa. Nigeria's First National Development Plan (1962–1968), promulgated a decade before the oil boom, outlined the planners' aspirations to make Nigeria "the industrial heart of an African Common Market" (Ojo, 1980: 573).

After the 1967–1970 civil war, General Yakubu Gowon's administration made regional integration a priority foreign policy goal. France had recognized Biafra during the bloody conflict, and the *Côte d'Ivoire* and Dahomey (Benin) along with two other African countries had supported that stance. This act by its neighbors demonstated to Gowon and the military leadership the ineffectiveness of previous Nigerian diplomatic efforts and its influence in West Africa. It inclined them to view economic integration as a means of increased control over regional political affairs. As the *Daily Times* (May 6, 1979: 10) explained, a West African integration scheme would provide the institutional framework for Nigerian leadership and the erosion of French political and economic influence and offer "a rational outlet" for disbursing oil revenues in the form of external aid to African nations. The far-sighted among the military leaders realized that the oil money was finite, and that its earnings must be used to diversify and technologically advance the economy. Economic integration would benefit the Nigerian economy by providing free and guaranteed future markets, particularly for the country's nascent industrial efforts in iron and steel (Ojo, 1980: 584).

In April 1972, Nigeria and Togo announced the formation of an embryonic all-West African Economic Community (WAEC). Two months later, a Nigeria-Togo joint commission met to work out the details and machinery of implementing the WAEC. The almost simultaneous announcement that a preliminary agreement on a customs union, the *Communaute Economique de l'Afrique de l'Ouest* (CEAO), had been initialed by seven Francophone states in the region quickened Nigeria's resolve.

Oil revenues were used to "sweeten the participatory deal" for Nigeria's West African neighbors. Nigeria provided low-priced petroleum and other trade concessions, invested in development projects, and made available grants and loans. Ojo reports: "When Gowon visited Benin in January 1975 in the last rounds of canvassing for WAEC, he introduced a Nigerian phenomenon called 'spraying' into diplomacy; he literally wrote checks on the spot for every cause."

The Francophone countries were made aware that if they suffered financial loss of CEAO monies as a consequence of participation in the larger West African community, compensatory subventions would be forthcoming from Nigeria and even larger amounts of foreign aid (Ojo, 1980: 593). On May 28, 1975, the draft treaty on WAEC was adopted at a summit in Lagos with the slight name modification to Economic Community of West African States.

Ojo concludes that Nigeria's central role in the founding of ECOWAS casts doubt on Haas's hypothesis that states "confident that their size and resource base make them relatively independent of regional partners, take slight interest in regional integration." (Haas, 1971: 11). Nigeria's leadership wished to make Nigeria the industrial center of West Africa, to enhance its economic development and growth, and to decrease future dependence on oil revenues. It believed that a West African community was needed as a bargaining tool with the industrialized world. In addition, Nigeria wished to undermine French and other colonial influence in the area and to garner for itself political power and influence in African and world affairs (Ojo, 1980: 600–601).

Progress toward achievement of ECOWAS goals from its founding in 1975 until the 1983 Nigerian expulsion of alien workers must be described as halting and miniscule. Many of the organization's problems stemmed from political disorder in Nigeria. The two primary architects of the organization were General Yakubu Gowon and Adebayo Adedeji, his Commissioner for Economic Development. Gowon was removed from office in a bloodless coup in August 1975, and Adedeji left Nigeria for Addis Ababa to become Executive Secretary of the United Nations Economic Commission for Africa. Nigeria's new government under

General Murtala Muhammed had to consolidate itself and deal with a host of new and chronic problems. It had little time to devote to the nurturing of ECOWAS. When Nigeria began again to assume a more active role in African affairs, its attention was focused on the Angolan conflict. Then, a failed coup attempt in February 1976 claimed the life of General Muhammed. The economic distress throughout the region caused Muhammed's successor, General Olusegun Obasanjo, to reemphasize Nigeria's commitment to ECOWAS and its goals (Gambari, 1991: 35–36).

Some progress toward achievement of the community's goals was evident. A 1975 border dispute between Benin and Togo was settled amicably because of ECOWAS efforts (*Punch,* January 26, 1982: 4). At the 1978 Lagos meeting, the authority adopted a Protocol on Non-Aggression to create a "friendly atmosphere, free of any fear of attack or aggression of one state by another" (Okolo, 1984: 39). The members agreed to refrain from attacking each other and to recognize their various borders as inviolable.[9] A protocol for Mutual Assistance in Matters of Defense was inaugurated by the community at the May 1981 summit in Sierra Leone; it was signed by all member states save Cape Verde, Guinea-Bissau, and Mali (*Africa Research Bulletin,* July 15, 1981: 6072).

ECOWAS aimed at full market integration within 15 years. First, external tariffs were to be frozen; tariffs were then to be reduced on goods produced within the community; and finally, a common external tariff and the free movement of goods, persons, and capital within the community were to be implemented. Two years lapsed before stage 1 of the plan was implemented. At the May 1979 meeting of the authority in Dakar, Senegal, customs duties within the community were frozen with immediate effect for the next years.

In 1977, the Trade, Customs, Immigration, Monetary, and Payments Commission recommended to the council "that the Executive Secretary be authorized to arrange for research to be conducted into Customs nomenclature, the structure of Customs Tariffs and Trade flows as a preliminary step towards the eventual elimination of tariffs on intra-Community trade and the harmonization of the customs tariffs of Member States of the Community."[10] The commission suggested that the study be completed by the end of 1977. At their April 1978 meeting in Lagos the authority set May 28, 1979, as the effective date for customs tariff consolidation in accordance with Article 13(2) of the ECOWAS treaty. At the May 1981 meeting in Freetown, the ECOWAS heads of state and government decided to eliminate trade restrictions on unprocessed goods and traditional handicrafts. A plan was devised whereby all intra-regional trade barriers were to be eliminated over 8 years. Little progress toward dismantling trade barriers had been achieved by 1983. The CEAO and to a lesser extent the Mano River Union were often cited as obstacles to trade liberalization (see Appendix) (Lancaster, 1985: 71).

Planning was underway for 5-year programs for various sectors: industry, agriculture, telecommunications, transportation, and postal services. The community's industrial program at the time of the Nigerian expulsion order had been confined to two phases. Efforts had been made to gather existing and necessary data on industry in the region and to formulate a legal framework within which regional industrialization might take place. The fund had participated in the construction of a cement factory in Togo; community members participated in the exploitation of uranium in Niger; and schemes for joint investments in agricultural production in Ghana and Benin were progressing.

Concrete action on improving transportation and telecommunication links between the member states was delayed by insufficient information as well as a lack of funds. By 1977 the Commission for Transport and Telecommunications had completed studies coordinated by the executive secretary in three areas: internal networks that are inseparable from interstate and international networks; the practical arrangements necessary for setting up African transit centers; and short-term solutions for links between the states. Having completed this research, the authority decided at the 1978 Dakar meeting that "an improvement and extension program for the telecommunication networks" would be undertaken, and charged the executive secretary to propose the means to carry out the program (Onwuka, 1980: 56). By November 1979, an ad hoc committee of the Pan-African Telecommunications Project comprising Nigeria, Togo, and Benin had undertaken studies on existing telecommunications equipment and tariffs in ECOWAS states (*New Nigeria,* November 15, 1979). The Project, which aimed at providing automatic links among all ECOWAS capitals and within the countries, was the most advanced among the community's schemes. By 1983, commitments to finance the enterprise totaling US$34 million had been received from European banks, the World Bank, the European Development Fund, and the African Development Bank.

The problems that plagued the early years of ECOWAS's existence were a consequence of institutional immaturity and the cultural and political diversity and poverty of its many members. Lagos (later Abuja) is designated ECOWAS headquarters, but the Fund for Cooperation, Compensation, and Development is located in Togo, creating a competitive locus of power.[11] The financial situation of the community also remained precarious because of the members' late payment of contributions. The approved capital of $500 million was considered adequate for the fund's responsibilities. However, in October 1979, members had contributed only NN22 million, and an additional NN2.5 million had been realized from interest on these deposits (*New Nigerian,* October 30, 1979: 1).

In October 1980, the executive secretariat circulated a questionnaire among the member states to assess the level of policy implementation; it elicited no replies (Asante, 1986: 100). As the community approached the end of its first decade, a committee was appointed to assess its progress and shortcomings. The committee's report, made public in January 1983, found that of eight protocols agreed to in formal sessions of the community, few had been ratified by the necessary seven states, and no state had ratified them all. (It should be noted that all 16 states had signed the protocol relating to the free movement of peoples.) The committee concluded that delays in ratification were attributable to "post-verification of the legality of the acts" by the member states. Many protocol provisions were never incorporated into appropriate bills to be submitted to the national legislatures for approval and implementation. The committee lamented the lack of information on ECOWAS development activities in member states even among those persons who might be expected to remain current on its progress. Even more pointed and damaging was the committee's observation that relevant member state officials receiving ECOWAS documents often did not know what steps should be taken to carry out the provisions (*New Nigerian,* January 20, 1983: 5).

A long-term problem of the community was the lack of convertibility of most member states' currencies. The Nigerian naira is the only strong independent currency in the region. The Francophone states' currencies are stabilized by their formal alignment with the French franc through the *Union Monetaire Ouest Africaine.* Inconvertibility, of course, limits foreign investment in the area, and the continued existence of the franc zone facilitates France's traditional penetration and influence on the Francophone economies.

It therefore must be concluded that, aside from prestige benefits from hosting the community's headquarters and occupying a position of "first among equals" in the organization, Nigeria realized no tangible benefits from participation in ECOWAS. The community clearly remained in an embryonic state. However, benefits beyond those associated with prestige were needed by Nigeria's national leaders to deal with pressing economic, social, and political problems.

NATIONAL SHORT-TERM ECONOMIC CONCERNS

In 1982, the year preceding the January 1983 decision to deport alien workers, the world oil market was glutted. Much of the reduced demand for oil was being met by non-Organization of Oil Exporting Countries

(OPEC) sources—Alaska, Mexico, and the North Sea. In 1979, Nigeria's average daily production was 2.3 million barrels of high-quality crude, but by the end of 1982, that total had dropped to 400,000 barrels per day. Nigeria broke with OPEC-established prices, hoping to get a larger share of the market, but this was of little benefit. OPEC solidarity weakened as its members sought to ride out the shortfall in oil revenues. In 1982, Nigeria's gross domestic product dropped 2%, from NN30.5 billion to NN29.8 billion as a result of a 16% decrease in the petroleum sector's contribution to national revenue (*Nigerian Yearbook*, 1983: 100). Oil sales accounted for 80% of governmental income. The fourth five-year developmental plan had projected receipts of US$30 billion in oil income for 1983. Oil export revenues of US$8 million were anticipated when the decision was made to evict alien laborers (*Wall Street Journal*, February 18, 1983: 2).

In March 1982, Nigerian foreign cash reserves fell to US$1.5 billion, a sum the nation was spending each month on imports. In April, President Shehu Shagari proposed the enactment of an Economic Stabilization Bill to reduce the level of imports, conserve scarce foreign currency, and encourage and protect local industries. By the end of the year, imports were down some 20% (80k of every NN1 of federal revenue was still spent on imports), but the overall annual deficit was an uncomfortable NN1.5 billion. At year's end, the government made plans to borrow US$4.5 billion to meet international payments obligations (*Wall Street Journal*, March 24, 1982: 31:8).

The global oil glut only exacerbated the ongoing economic crisis in Nigeria, a crisis fostered by structural irrationalities, underdevelopment, import and export dependence, mismanagement, and corruption. The 1983 situation mocked optimistic post–civil war forecasts of the country's economic future. Nigeria, endowed with bountiful oil revenues, had begun an era of capitalist development. Import substitution objectives in light consumer goods were accomplished relatively early on. By 1973, the ratio of domestic production to total supply was greater than 90% in commodities such as cotton and textiles, beer and soft drinks, soaps and detergents, and roofing sheets. Unfortunately, these activities accounted for only 5% of total employment.

With the boom in oil prices in the early 1970s, Nigerian officials were soon "planning for economic growth with too much money" (Balabkins, 1982: 125–126). Nigerian development plans became a collection of assorted projects lacking coherent rationale and integration; they were "full of contradictions" (Olayiwola, 1987). Billions of naira were poured into "prestige" projects in the infrastructural, military, education, and cultural sectors (Zartman, 1983). Inexperienced and often corrupt officials, planners, managers, and workers sought to grab a piece of the cake in the investment and distribution of oil boom revenues. Money flowing freely into development corporation coffers provided opportunities for misappropriation; these funds became a major source of money for political parties. Overt symptoms of the mismanaged petroleum-led growth were an inadequate and unreliable electrical supply, unsafe roads, port congestion, and inadequate and unwieldy bureaucracies.

Profound cleavages widened between the country's haves and have-nots. Three groups benefitted quickly and conspicuously from the boom: the administrative elites who controlled the government bureaucracies and state-owned productive activities such as petroleum, steel, and irrigation projects; private sector entrepreneurs who accumulated wealth through construction, finance, industrial production, state contracts, and trade; and professional and technocratic personnel who provided liaison between the state and international firms.

Before the 1970s, agriculture contributed 60% on average to the nation's gross domestic product. Agricultural commodities accounted for 80% of the total value of exports. However, with the "petrolization" of the economy, the agricultural sector was left to deteriorate. No producer incentives were provided. The price of bread was fixed; import duties on staples were relaxed; and rising food demand shifted to foreign sources because of shortages, overvalued currency, and modernity-induced changes in taste. Between 1970 and 1976, although the gross national product grew an average of 7.4% per year, total farm output fell by 0.2% per year. Agriculture's share of the national economy decreased by one-half; it accounted for 28% of the national output, whereas the proportion of workers therein employed remained at 64% (Watts and Lubeck, 1983).

It was generally believed that high levels of unemployment in Nigeria figured prominently among the causes for the exit order. Almost one-quarter of the workforce was unemployed or underemployed. Urban workers bore the brunt of Nigeria's economic crisis. They could not find employment, jobs were lost, workers laid off, and companies used the economic crisis as justification for retrenchment (Falola and Ihonvbere, 1985: 150–152). In some cases, salaries were withheld or irregularly tendered to those workers with jobs. A salient example of the latter practice was the public service sector in Bendel State. The Nigerian Labour Congress reported in a press release: "In a public organisation like Bendel State Transport Services, workers have not been paid their wages for over a year. Some of them in the Lagos area got their June 1981 salaries in April 1982 and others their July 1981 salaries in August 1982." (*Liberation News*, I, 3, February 1983: 1, 8, as cited in Falola and Ihonvbere, 1985: 152).

In November 1981 the transport workers took to the streets carrying 12 mock coffins. The demonstrators claimed that 12 workers of the company had:

died of starvation as a result of nonpayment of salaries. "Some of us have almost been deserted by our wives because there is no money to maintain them, while our children have been forced to go begging. . . ." Many of the workers were now squatting with relatives while some sleep in broken down buses in the company's premises after being driven away by their landlords for failure to pay their rent (*New Nigerian,* November 19, 1981: 13).

The unemployed believed that jobs were being denied citizens and given to aliens. This suspicion was particularly strong in the slum areas of Lagos, Ijora and Ajegunle, where the immigrant population was concentrated. Natives seeking employment were at a disadvantage, because immigrants were willing to accept lower wages. The minimum wage for Nigerians was NN120 per month; aliens were willing to work for NN50 per month. Many jobs occupied by the immigrants—those of shoe shiners, farm laborers, domestic servants, chauffeurs, bodyguards, and "night soil carriers"—were considered undesirable by most Nigerians. Cheap immigrant labor had also filled the breach in agricultur created by the urban flight of Nigerian youth. Although the preponderance of jobs occupied by the immigrants was unskilled, as was previously pointed out, some deportees were professionals such as teachers, nurses, and doctors (*West Africa,* February 7, 1983: 307, 309).

The industries in which aliens created the most resentment were hardest hit by the recession—construction and dock labor services. The recession-fostered decline in dock work was further exacerbated by government-imposed import restrictions. In 1981, the Gongola State Branch of the National Union of Construction and Civil Engineering Workers (NUCCEW) vehemently condemned ECOWAS for having made it possible for Nigerian contractors to hire "cheap labor" from ECOWAS member states "while Nigerians roam about without jobs" (*National Concord,* February 27, 1981). After the quit order was implemented, NUCCEW President R. O. Sanyaolu congratulated the government on its decision. He claimed that aliens had completely taken over the 50,000 construction jobs in Nigeria (*Daily Times,* February 7, 1983: 21). Joshua Ogunleye, National President of the Dock Workers Union of Nigeria, announced that the order was much welcomed by union members. Five thousand additional Nigerians were hired as dock workers in the wake of the aliens' departure (*New Nigerian,* February 25, 1983: 2). Sylvester Bassey, Executive Secretary of the Nigerian Dock Labour Board, also applauded the decision (*Punch,* January 27, 1983: 2).

A few industries objected to the expulsion order on the grounds that the order came too suddenly, providing insufficient time for compliance while sustaining their manufacturing and service-related operations. Many of the industries registering this complaint were manufacturing concerns, private hospitals, and hotels. The *New Nigerian* (January 28, 1983: 9) provided a partial list of firms negatively affected by the order: Philip Morris, Prospect Textile Mills, United Match Company, Kwara Furniture Manufacturing Company, Kwara Breweries, and Kwara Metal and Chemical Company. In general, however, the business community supported the government's action. It was also accepted wisdom that the aliens exacerbated Nigeria's crime, ethnic, and religious problems.

NATIONAL SHORT-TERM SOCIETAL STABILITY CONCERNS

Aside from unemployment levels, the most widely circulated and generally accepted justification for the exit order was that the aliens were responsible for recent riots in the northeast, an increase in crime and decline in moral standard within the society. In July 1981, a riot was sparked in Kano when the governor of the state, Alhaji Abubakar Rimi, directly challenged the revered traditional leader, the Emir of Kano, Alhaji Ado Bayero (Wright, 1982: 105–113). In October 1982, serious religious rioting began in Bulumkuttu near Maiduguri (Borno State) and spread to Kaduna and Kano during the last week of that month. Hundreds of people were killed, including nine police officers, and millions of naira worth of property was destroyed. The 1982 violence, caused by the followers of Alhaji Muhammadu Marwa (a Cameroonian also known as Maitasine), began after the police executed a search warrant and arrested 16 members of the sect. Maitasine's unorthodox preachings had sparked two major riots in Kano in December 1980. The subsequent military seige of the city added to the extensive damage; 4,177 civilians, more than 100 policemen, and 35 army personnel were killed (*West Africa*, November 23, 1981: 2756).

A White Paper on the report of the Kano Disturbances Tribunal of Inquiry recommended, among other things, that the "Immigration Department should undertake the responsibility of registering aliens in the country." (*Daily Sketch*, January 18, 1983: 1) Fifty-four aliens had been deported as participants in the Bulumkuttu disturbances (*New Nigerian*, January 28, 1983: 1). *West Africa* reported that the Nigerian Security Organization, police, and other sources had expressed increasing concern about foreigners participation in the civil disturbances.

Preceding and in the wake of the exit order, non-Nigerians were blamed for the general rise in crime and decline in morality in Nigeria. A January 20, 1993, *Daily Times* editorial (p. 3) summarized the attitude of most government officials and certainly the popular press:

Over 80% of their women have no decent and respectable means of livelihood thereby contaminating the moral fabric of the Nigerian society. Recent names of arrested armed robbers showed that over 50% of them are aliens. And in the recent religious disturbances in Kano, Kaduna, and Maiduguri, very many of the fanatics were identified as illegal aliens. So, no doubt, illegal aliens are constituting a stumbling block to the realisation of the lofty ideas of our moral standards.

Almost universally, aliens were singled out as the source of crime in Nigeria, particularly armed robbery and prostitution, although these allegations were never substantiated with reliable statistical data. One western diplomat posited an interesting theory about the timing of the eviction. Three weeks before the order a man carrying Ghanaian documents was killed while attempting to break into the home of Vice President Alex Ekueme. The official said, "That may have been the incident that triggered it, the thing that made Nigerians say 'Look, this crime wave has gone too far.'" (New York Times, February 3, 1983: A12) Aluko (1985: 541) reports that after this attempted armed robbery, senior civil servants of the Ministry of Internal Affairs forwarded a memorandum to Alhaji Ali Baba stating that "enough is enough"; for security reasons, all illegal aliens must be expelled.

This generalized tendency within the government, the press, and the population to attribute societal instability, the increase in crime, the decline in morality, and the nation's economic woes, particularly unemployment, almost exclusively to illegal aliens is a classic example of scapegoatism fraught with high levels of xenophobia. In a tongue-in-cheek West Africa article (March 7, 1983: 591) entitled "Now that the aliens are gone," Nije Osundare points out the absurdity of assigning responsibility for all of Nigeria's economic and social problems to illegal aliens:

At last those illegal aliens are gone! Unemployment has become a thing of the past. Millionaires can now go to bed with their golden doors thrown wide open, without the fear of a Ghanaian gun or a Chadian arrow; prostitutes are now gone, and our country can bounce back to moral health. What's more, since the invaders left, NEPA hasn't suffered a single bout of epilepsy; uninterrupted water supply has greeted every home; no more inflated contracts, no more gubernatorial acrimonies, no more inferno in public buildings; above all, Africa still remains "the centre-piece of our foreign policy."

NATIONAL AND PERSONAL SHORT-TERM
POLITICAL CONCERNS

Before January 17, 1983, the Shagari government's commitment to ECOWAS was not in question. Addressing the ECOWAS Authority in Lome in May 1980, the recently elected president expressed satisfaction with what had been achieved to date toward ECOWAS objectives. He said: "I . . . wish to assure you, Mr. Chairman, that my Administration is fully committed to the Economic Community of West African States. We shall continue to give sure support to the Community in the realisation of its goals and objectives." Ironically, he immediately thereafter urged his fellow members to ratify the protocol on free movement:

. . . there seems to have been too slow progress in the ratification of some of our vital decisions. I would like particularly to refer to the Protocol on Free Movement of Persons. Since this Protocol was signed a year ago, only six countries of our sixteen have so far ratified the instrument. Nigeria has of course signed the Instrument of Ratification and has long started to implement the letter and spirit of the Protocol. Today large numbers of nationals of member states are taking advantage of this Protocol in Nigeria. I urge all member states who have not ratified the Protocol to do so as soon as possible (Tijjani and Williams, 1981: 202–203).[12]

Before the quit order was announced, it had been thought that President Shagari had been resisting the idea of wholesale expulsion of illegal aliens, especially those from ECOWAS member states. However, the western press charged that he wished to capitalize on the widespread resentment against Ghanaians within Nigerian society to gain political points in an election year. It was speculated that the move was designed to demonstrate Shagari and his National Party of Nigeria's (NPN) ability to act decisively given their ineffectiveness in coping with the nation's overall economic problems (*West Africa,* February 21, 1983: 499).

The Economist (January 29, 1983: 44) was straightforward in its assessment of the political motivation of the eviction order; it reported: "At a time when the government's other attempts at economic rescue are having little effect, it (the eviction) gives the impression of firm and purposeful action. There are votes in chauvinism." It continued a few days later: "Their (the aliens) expulsion is the Nigerian president's xenophobic way of courting votes in next summer's election at a time when his country's economy is in well-deserved tatters" (*The Economist,* February 5, 1983: 13).

The Shagari regime never enjoyed firm political control over the sprawling, politically underdeveloped country. Although hopes had run high with the achievement of a peaceful transition from military government to a presidential system, inherited economic difficulties and control over less than one-third of the seats in the National Assembly by the NPN condemned the Second Republic to an inauspicious start. As early as July 1979, the Nigerian People's Party (chaired by Nnamdi Azikiwe), the United Party of Nigeria (led by Obafemi Awolowo), and the Great Nigerian People's Party (chaired by Alhaji Waziri Ibrahim) attempted to forge a "progressive" alliance to challenge Shagari's party. The coalition lacked the cohesion necessary, however, to operate as a single party or field a common slate of candidates. The NPN allied with the Nigerian People's Party to pass the legislation required to make the new government operational, but by July 1981 this accord had broken down (Williams, 1982: 197). Only 7 of the 19 state governors were NPN members, and although Shagari made a conscious effort to present himself as "President for all Nigerians," he was occasionally treated with contempt by non-NPN governors.

The allegedly oppressive tactics used by the NPN and the government to deal with opposition and the regime's reluctance to respond militarily to Cameroonian incursions into Nigerian territory are usually cited as evidence of the regime's vulnerability. Many opponents of the regime occupied government and university posts in the northern states.

In January 1980, the government arrested and attempted to deport to Chad Alhaji Shugaba Abdurrahman, the Great Nigerian People's Party majority leader in the Borno State Assembly. The government alleged that Shaguba was not a Nigerian citizen. A second mishandled attempt to deport a dissident involved Patrick F. Wilmot, a West Indian Lecturer in the department of sociology at Ahmadu Bello University, Zaria. Dr. Wilmot was to be deported on the grounds that he was a foreigner interfering in Nigerian politics. The government canceled the latter deportation plan in the face of protests by the university's students and professors.

In 1981, Bela Mohammad, a distinguished Marxist scholar and political adviser to the People's Redemption Party governor of Kano State, was killed in political riots. Critics charged that the NPN instigated the riots and planned the murder, and that the police ignored the escalation in violence that resulted in Mohammad's death. There were reports of other politically motivated acts of violence. In Bakolori, Sokota State, it was charged that several peasants were killed in an attempt to deprive them of their land (Falola and Ihonvbere, 1985: 75–79).

The Shagari government's reticence to confront Cameroon over violence on their mutual border demonstrated its reluctance to further destabilize the country by allocating resources and manpower to military action. Cameroon never accepted the incorporation into Nigeria, as a result of a plebiscite, of the former UN trust territory of Northern Cameroon. Cameroonian *gendarmes* harassed Nigerian fishermen, had taken over several villages, and in March 1981, killed five Nigerian soldiers who, according to Nigeria sources, were within Nigeria's borders. Nigerian demands for an apology and compensation were ignored. The country was further incensed when a junior-level Cameroonian diplomat was dispatched to Lagos to discuss the issue. There was public outcry for the military to respond to the Cameroonian outrages and recapture the villages. Cognizant of the country's faltering economy and the lack of political consensus, Shagari was not prepared to take his country to war. An initially supportive public could not be relied on to sustain long-term military operations against Cameroon. Shagari appealed to the Organization of African Unity for its assistance; finally a joint commission was set up with Cameroon to study the issues (Falola and Ihonvbere, 1985: 184; Williams, 1982: 210).

Whatever Shagari's original position on the decision to evict alien workers, in public comments after the order he advocated vigorous implementation. Ghanaians living illegally in Nigeria would be "arrested, tried, and sent back to their homes" if they did not leave by the government deadlines. In this context, Shagari mentioned again the rise of joblessness and crime in Nigeria. Later, in response to the shock and outrage registered by the international community, through ECOWAS Chairman Matthier Kerekou, Shagari offered US$1 million in aid to help resettle the evictees. All the while, however, he maintained that the criticism of his act was ill-founded (*West Africa*, February 28, 1983: 531).

The decision to contravene the spirit of the ECOWAS Protocol and expel the alien workers may have been easier to reconcile in Shagari's mind because of his aversion to the rising signs of disorder and immorality around him. Aluko writes that, as devout Moslems, both Shagari and Alhaji Ali Baba had a distinct distaste for "loose living" and an appreciation for law and order. In December 1982, Alhaji Ali Baba had gone to the National Assembly to seek approval for legislation banning obscene films and imposing censorship on the mass media. Because of Alhaji Ali Baba's almost exclusively business-oriented background, the Minister of Internal Affairs lacked international perspective. Either this handicap or the lack of time to study the implications of the edict resulted in the serious error in judgment represented by the exit order (Aluko, 1985: 542–544).

When the edict was issued, no one seemed to have any realistic idea of the number of aliens affected by the order, whether the aliens would actually leave, or the diplomatic ramifications of the act. Although the order took key departments of the Nigerian government by surprise, in the weeks that followed most of their administrative heads saw fit to offer public support for the act. The Department of Immigration, about to introduce a new alien registration plan, was particularly "left out of the picture" (Gravil, 1985: 526). The Federal Attorney General, Richard Akinjide, stated that Nigeria owed no apology for expelling aliens remaining in the country after the 90-day ECOWAS limit. He said that most crime in Nigeria was committed by aliens, and they dispersed large sums of Nigerian currency abroad (*New Nigerian*, January 30, 1983: 1). Ebun Oyagbola, National Planning Minister, in a January 1983 address, said that despite the international outcry there could be no turning back; she said, "the aliens must go" (*Daily Times*, January 26, 1983: 2).

Top officials of the Ministry of External Affairs were first apprised of the quit order by televised reports. They, having contributed significantly to the establishment of ECOWAS and having worked to enhance Nigeria's status in African affairs, were particularly frustrated by the order. A few of them gave serious consideration to resigning. They felt bypassed as an agency and found the expulsion order incomprehensible given that thousands of Nigerians reside in other West African countries. The Minister of External Affairs, Ishaya Audu, was required, however, to defend the act before the international community. In a February statement, he refuted the charge that the Nigerian order had violated United Nations' human rights provisions (*New Nigerian,* February 5, 1983: 8).

The cabinet as a whole did not ratify the decision until January 18, a day after the public announcement made by the Minister of Internal Affairs. Nigeria's embassies and high commissions abroad received no official notification of the impending act. Afterward they were also dependent on the news media for their information (Gravil, 1985: 527).

SUMMARY

It must be concluded that the 1983 Nigerian expulsion of alien workers in contravention of the spirit of the ECOWAS Protocol on the Free Movement of Persons, Right of Residence, and Establishment well confirms this study's thesis that member-state elites frame their decisions regarding regional initiatives in terms of personal and national loss avoidance. Although Nigeria's leadership publicly voiced consistent support for the community and the protocol, ECOWAS had to that date provided few tangible benefits to the country. On the contrary, the ECOWAS protocol was perceived by many political leaders and the public in general as causing or exacerbating Nigeria's severe economic, social, and political problems.

As described in the segment detailing Nigeria's economic status, the structurally underdeveloped, mismanaged, and corruption-ridden Nigerian economy was suffering the additional negative effects of a glutted global oil market. In 1982, crude oil production was an average 17% lower than 1979 levels, and Nigeria's gross national product had dropped 2% from the previous year. The country experienced high levels of inflation and unemployment and was anticipating difficulties settling its balance of payments.

In addition to economic hardship, religious cleavages and political unrest caused by the upcoming national elections lent an air of crisis to the nation. The fact that the Shagari regime succumbed to a military coup in December of that year provides undeniable evidence that the regime's concerns for its political survival were well founded. Public opinion, as expressed in the nation's leading newspapers, placed responsibility for much of the unemployment, religious and political strife, and social problems such as crime and prostitution on the influx of illegal aliens. Precedents for designating scapegoats for a country's economic, social, and political woes existed throughout West Africa.[13]

It is clear that immediate efforts to cope with the contemporary economic distress and societal and political instability took precedence over the government's commitment to the obligations of the ECOWAS protocol. It is probably immaterial whether Shagari and his Minister of Internal Affairs actually believed the deportation would ameliorate the unemployment, societal unrest, and crime. When faced with the alternatives to sustain compliance with the protocol, which would yield no immediate direct benefits (status benefits had accrued when the country led the fight for promulgation and ratification of the protocol), or to evict the aliens, and at minimum gain political benefit from widespread public antagonism toward the aliens, Nigeria's besieged leadership chose the latter. The decision-making situation must be described as crisis-provoked, capricious, and arbitrary. The decision was taken without intergovernmental or intracommunity study, consultation, or notification. The negative consequences of the quit order in terms of sudden loss of personnel, particularly in the service industries, and the global outcry against the inhuman treatment of the evictees were apparently unanticipated by the decision makers. Short-term elite and national economic, social, and political utilities were not perceived as being served by adhering to the protocol. On the contrary, these interests and those of the community conflicted.

The conflictual framing of the decision scenario may be summarized as shown in Table 4.1. The table shows that there were no areas of congruence between the framework of utilities associated with compliance with the protocol and the way the Shagari government framed its decision to contravene the provision by expelling alien workers. The decision components most responsible for the promulgation of the protocol were expectations of long-term, regional, and national economic gains. However, with their political survival at risk, Shagari government elites acted to avoid immediate, personal and political loss.

The ECOWAS had been operational for almost 8 years at the time of the Nigerian decision to expel alien workers. As previously outlined, it had very few concrete accomplishments to its credit in the several objective areas outlined in its treaty. The member states lagged behind in protocol ratification and program implementation and often failed to meet their annual monetary obligations.

This extended start-up phase by the community, however, is probably no more than might have been predicted. When the large number of

Table 4.1

FRAMING COMPONENT	PROTOCOL ON FREE MOVEMENT OF PERSONS	NIGERIA'S 1983 EXPULSION ORDER
ISSUE CONCEPTUALIZATION	Free movement of productive factors Enhanced economic growth and development	Political instability Unemployment Societal instability
LEVEL OF ASSESSMENT	Regional National	National Personal
GAIN/LOSS	Gain economic growth and development	Loss of political control
PROBABILITY/RISK	Perceived moderate to low probability of economic growth and development	High risk of political loss High risk of societal instability
SURVIVAL	Not applicable	Political survival at risk Potential personal risk
IDEOLOGY	Free trade and integration theories	Not applicable
TIME HORIZON	Long-term	Short-term

members, multiple languages, and diverse political, economic, and social systems inherited from varied colonial pasts are considered in conjunction with their underdeveloped political and economic status, expectation of more than deliberate and halting progress by the community would have been unrealistic. It might be pointed out that the Association of Southeast Asian Nations, a cooperative venture considered by analysts as second only to the European Communities in its (predominately political) achievements, had few solid accomplishments to its credit 8 years into its existence.

The specific, long-term effects of the Nigerian decision on the economic community are difficult to gauge. Most analysts agree that, "Any serious disregard of the concept (of viewing West Africans as a single people), is likely to strike a deep blow at the very foundations of ECOWAS . . . ." (Asante, 1986: 159). Despite the public lamentation over Nigeria's contravention of the spirit of the ECOWAS protocol and its breach of West African unity, the community has persisted in its irresolute course. Pre-1983 progress was so infinitesimal, it would be difficult to identify a loss of momentum. Although trade among ECOWAS members has increased as a result of the conscious effort to foster cooperation, evidence suggests that the trade liberalization program is not making significant progress (Asante, 1986: 100).[14]

There are areas of cooperation among the member states. For example, Benin and Nigeria have begun joint ventures in cement and sugar production in Benin; Guinea and Nigeria are involved in joint venture iron ore mining in Guinea (Nigeria controls 16.2% of the Mifergui project for input into its steel industry); and Nigeria has invested in petroleum refining in Togo and Senegal. It should be noted, however, that these projects are bilateral efforts rather than conforming to the spirit and letter of the ECOWAS treaty (Onyemelukwe, 1984: 205). As previously noted, the Pan African Telecommunications Project is already underway, financed by the ECOWAS Fund and outside resources. As part of the plan to construct the Trans-West Africa Highway extending from Nouakchott, Mauritania, to Lagos, in 1985 the ECOWAS Fund had made loans to Benin to construct two bridges and authorized loans for construction of the Freetown-Monrovia road (Lancaster, 1985: 72).

The Protocol on the Free Movement of Persons, Right of Residence, and Establishment was promulgated and implemented without ECOWAS members fully understanding the potentially negative consequences of the act. One lesson to be learned from the experience by the community is that conscious and systemic education of the general public of ECOWAS's goals, benefits, and costs should be undertaken. A second lesson is that the unrestrained movement of labor in the absence of protective measures against unemployment and crime does not contribute to the member-states' economic well-being. Provisions to deal with the educational, employment, housing, and social service needs of the migrants must accompany freedom-of-movement legislation (Asante, 1986: 160).

Despite the serious and continuous domestic distractions, the leaders of ECOWAS member states, on a rhetorical basis, have not abandoned hope for the community's success. The majority of the member states, in an obvious attempt to shelter the community from negative regional and international fallout from the Nigerian decision, denied the significance of the expulsion as an indicator of a weakened commitment to ECOWAS objectives.

NOTES

1. Although no accurate information is available on the actual number of illegal aliens working in Nigeria that were affected by the expulsion order, most estimates range between 1 and 2 million.

2. Alhaji Ali Baba, Minister of Internal Affairs, "On Aliens Residing in Nigeria . . . ," published in three documents dated January 17 and 25, and February 14, 1983.

3. *The Economist* (February 5, 1983: 49) claimed that no one would ever know the number of persons killed and buried in the bush or on the beaches along the 120-mile journey between Lagos and Accra.

4. *ECOWAS, Treaty of the Economic Community of West African States,* Chapter IV, Article 27, No. 2.

5. *Treaty of ECOWAS* (Lagos, 1975), Article 27 (I).

6. ECOWAS Document ECW/HSG/II.7, Rev. 1.

7. Gravil (1985: 529) comments that, "Many (of the boundaries) were drawn . . . 'with a Frenchman's ruler' and the common view among the Yoruba, for instance, was that Nigeria's western border divided the French from the British, not the Africans from each other."

8. Cape Verde, population 300,000 in 1985, joined the original 15 in 1977 after its 1975 separation from Guinea-Bissau.

9. Political relations among ECOWAS member states immediately after the founding of the organization were turbulent. In January 1977, President Kerekou of Benin accused several states, including *Côte d'Ivoire,* Senegal, and Togo, of involvement in a mercenary attack on his capital. The Benin-Togo border was closed, reopened, and reclosed, deterring the movement of goods and people. This constituted a serious breach of community provisions and resulted in economic hardship for Nigeria. (Goods destined for Nigeria had to be off-loaded in Ghana and sent overland to ease the pressure on the already congested port of Lagos.) Sekou Toure of Guinea, allying himself with Kerekou, accused Senegal and *Côte d'Ivoire* of providing a "spring-board for anti-Guinea activities."

In September 1976, he had accused Guinea-Bissau of similar activities, which resulted in the closure of Guinea-Bissau's embassy. Political difficulties also arose between Nigeria and Togo when the latter offered asylum to General Yakubu Gowan when he fled Nigeria in the wake of the February 1975 coup.

Border disputes characterized relations between several ECOWAS member-states. In 1974–1975, lives were lost in disputes between Mali and Upper Volta. In January 1977, Ghana warned Togo that military action might result from the latter's providing support to the secessionist movement in Ghana's Volta region. Near the end of 1978, disagreements arose between Senegal and Guinea-Bissau over maritime frontiers believed to contain oil resources (Davies, 1983; Gambari, 1991: 36).

10. ECOWAS Documents, ECW/TC/MPC (1) 8, ECW/CM/(1)/9A, Lagos, June 1977.

11. Togo was chosen as headquarters for the fund because of the Fund's shared activities with the Lome Convention. The purpose of the fund is to provide capital for regional development projects and to disburse compensation to member states that suffer as a result of the community's trade liberalization program or location of community enterprises. The Fund began with an authorized capital of US$50 million and called-up capital of US$450 million.

Disputes between the ECOWAS secretariat and the fund over the authority the executive secretary would exercise over the managing director of the fund deterred ECOWAS progress for some years. The issue was resolved when the fund's first managing director was removed and authority clearly delegated to the executive secretary. Outgoing Executive Secretary Aboubakar Diaby-Ouattara expressed concern about the continuing uncertainty in fund-secretariat relations. The quality of interactions between the two bodies remains largely dependent on officials' idiosyncrasies, a less than ideal arrangement (Lancaster, 1985: 70).

12. Shagari also briefly mentioned some of the community's persistent problems: the nonpayment of membership contributions and staffing inadequacies.

13. In the past, Nigerians had been expelled from Zaire, the Congo, Gabon, Equatorial Guinea, and elsewhere. In 1969, the Kofi A. Busia Administration in Ghana in enforcement of the Aliens Compliance Act expelled many Nigerians (the reported numbers vary from 20,000 to 1,000,000) and other aliens without residence permits with the same 2-week warning period. This act was aimed at transferring all foreign-owned businesses, including petty trading, to indigenous Ghanaians. Late in 1976, an additional 500,000 Nigerians were forced out of the country when a new Ghana Investment Policy Decree came into effect (*Nigerian Observer*, July 28, 1973: 3). In December 1982, Sierra Leone expelled from its territory members of the Foulah community (*West Africa*, January 31, 1983: 243). Nigeria's Minister of External Affairs denied that the federal government's actions had anything to do with the earlier expulsions (*West Africa*, February 21, 1983: 471). However, the existing precedent for this response to economic difficulty made the evictions less abhorrent to Nigeria's neighbors and ECOWAS partners.

14. The volume of trade among ECOWAS members in 1973 was 2.1% of total regional international trade. In 1985, that percentage remained below 4% (*West Africa*, 1985: 93).

5 The ASEAN Case: The 1977 Philippine Decision Concerning Sabah

The third and final case of our investigation, the single decision-making scenario in which the member-state leadership elected to pursue policies congruent with the interests of the regional economic organization, focuses on the 1977 Philippine decision to relinquish its claim over Sabah. Sabah had been a source of contention between the Philippines and its Association of Southeast Asian Nations (ASEAN) partner, Malaysia, for more than two decades. Whereas economic duress strongly influenced the decisions in the preceding cases, the Philippine decision, which enhanced regional economic cooperation, derived from its immediate need to avoid domestic political instability.

Philippine President Ferdinand Marcos's stated reason for dropping the claim to Sabah was "to eliminate one of the burdens of ASEAN," and to make "a permanent contribution to the unity, the strength and prosperity of all of ASEAN" (Marcos, 1977: 308–310). As will be demonstrated, this announcement resulted from the Philippines' immediate need to deal with the internal threat posed by Islamic insurgents in its southern islands. Philippine officials elected to give up the long-term territorial claim, because eliminating this issue of contention with Malaysia was seen as a way to assure its assistance in squelching the rebellion in the south. Of secondary importance was the Philippine belief that potential long-term benefits were forthcoming from ASEAN participation in the areas of regional security and economic development. A stronger ASEAN was perceived as a means to fill the power vacuum emerging in the wake of decreased British and US involvement in the region and to facilitate economic development.

It may be argued that Marcos' 1977 renunciation of the Sabah claim cannot be considered a decision in the strictest sense because the policy announcement was never implemented. No constitutional amendment or legislation was enacted to alter the Philippines' delineated "historic right" to Sabah or the Philippine Base Line Act (1968), which states that the Philippines has acquired "dominion and sovereignty" over the territory. The nonimplementation of the 1977 decision, however, effectively underscores the difficulties encountered by developing countries in following through with decisions that are congruent with long-term objectives. The Marcos government ostensibly elected to drop the Sabah claim to facilitate cooperation within the regional economic organization. In the wake of the 1977 announcement, however, other short-term considerations, specifically nationalism and the demands of domestic Muslim politics, prevented the Marcos and subsequent regimes from implementing the decision (Weatherbee, 1987: 1232, 1235). We begin our study of decision making regarding these complex issues by taking a look at the historical context of the Sabah controversy and the Philippines' record of participation in regional cooperation efforts.

THE SABAH CONTROVERSY

Sabah, formerly British North Borneo, is a 29,000-square-mile tract of territory that presently constitutes the northeastern tip of Malaysia. It is a valuable property, rich in oil, hemp, timber, rubber, tobacco, and fishery resources. A 1963 census put Sabah's population at 809,737.[1]

The origins of Philippine and Malaysian claims over Sabah lie in the colonial past of the territory and feature a cast of colorful characters. The dispute has unfolded with a minimal amount of bloodshed but, as Jorgensen-Dahl (1982: 190) allows, has ". . . posed a very real threat to the existence of two different regional organizations . . . ."

In 1877, Baron de Overbeck, the Austrian Consul General in Hong Kong, operating as an agent of the British firm of Dent Brothers, concluded an agreement with the Sultan of Brunei granting Dent Brothers a portion of North Borneo. Shortly thereafter, de Overbeck learned that the land had been ceded in 1704 to the Sultan Mohamet Jamal Al Alam of Sulu, and in January 1878, de Overbeck reached an agreement with him to gain clear title to the territory. In 1881, Dent Brothers and de Overbeck received a royal charter, and in March 1882, the British North Borneo Company was formed. The company sold its interest in the territory to the British government in 1946, and North Borneo became a Crown Colony (Meadows, 1962: 327). The Philippines claims to have been granted sovereignty over the territory by the heirs of the Sultan of Sulu.

The source of dispute over whether the United Kingdom and then Malaysia or the Philippines most legitimately can claim Sabah rests in the translation of a single word in the January 1878 agreement: *padjak.*[2] The Philippines claims that the agreement only leased the territory, with an annual payment of 5,000 Malayan dollars (US$2,340) to the Sultan of Sulu and his heirs, whereas the British and Malaysians insist that the document represents a transfer of sovereignty from the Sultan of Sulu to de Overbeck and later Britain and Malaysia.

The Philippine claim to North Borneo lay dormant for many years. Future Philippine President Diosdado Macapagal became acquainted with the Sabah issue in 1948 when, as a division chief within the Department of Foreign Affairs, he was assigned to negotiate the return of the Turtle Islands, located near North Borneo, from British control. Upon his subsequent election to Congress, he introduced a resolution in 1950 urging the government to press the Sabah claim. There was very little interest in the issue at the time; although the House of Representatives adopted the resolution on April 20, 1950, the resolution failed to win Senate approval. In 1957, a Muslim delegation from Mindanao appealed to Macapagal to recover that part of Sabah that had originally belonged to the Sultan of Sulu (Hanna, 3–5).

In January 1962, shortly after Macapagal was elected President, a series of articles entitled "North Borneo is Ours!", authored by Napoleon G. Rama, appeared in the *Philippine Free Press*. As the title suggests, the articles asserted that North Borneo belonged to the Philippines. During an Association of Southeast Asia (ASA) conference, April 1962, at Cameron Highlands in Malaya, Vice President Emmanual Pelaez (who hailed from Mindanao) discussed the Philippine claim with the Malayan Prime Minister, Tunku Abdul Rahman. Tunku indicated that the matter should be resolved by the Philippines and Great Britain as soon as possible. On April 24, 1962, the House of Representatives passed a resolution encouraging President Macapagal to take the necessary steps to "recover" North Borneo. On April 29, a new Sultan of Sulu "ceded sovereignty over the territory of North Borneo to the Philippines without prejudice to its own proprietary holdings" (Ortiz, 1963: 52). On June 22, a note was handed to the British government announcing the Philippines' intent to claim North Borneo as successor to the Sultan of Sulu.

Simultaneous to Macapagal's quest to regain control of Sabah, British plans progressed to transfer sovereignty over its territory to the nascent Malaysian Federation. President Macapagal countered with his own confederation proposal: the uniting of Malaya, the Philippines, Singapore, Sarawak, Brunei, and North Borneo into a "Greater Malay Confederation," later dubbed "Maphilindo" by Indonesia's Foreign Minister Subandrio. As will be discussed, this scheme, reflecting Philippine anti-British and pan-Malay sentiment, was designed to deter the establishment of the Malaysia Federation and preserve an avenue for continued pursuit of the Sabah claim.

Marcos was elected president of the Philippines in late 1965 and normalized relations with the new state of Malaysia without abandoning the claim to Sabah. For a time so little was heard about the issue that some assumed that it had died a silent death. On August 8, 1967, the Philippines and Malaysia were among the original five signatories of the Bangkok Declaration establishing the new Association of Southeast Asian Nations. A month later Malaysia and the Philippines concluded an agreement of substantial benefit to the Philippines, which dealt with smuggling and border traffic in the Sabah area. In January 1968, Marcos paid a state visit to the Malaysian capital, during which it was announced that the long-delayed conference on Sabah would be convened in Bangkok in June.

However, in March 1968, the Corregidor Affair erupted into the public arena, bringing further confusion and discord into the controversy. Manila newspapers reported that a battered young Muslim paramilitary recruit, Jibin Arula, claimed to have barely survived an uprising among trainees in a secret army of about 150 Sulu youths being prepared on Corregidor for "Operation Merdeka," a scheme to invade Sabah. The Philippine government immediately disavowed this charge, but a congressional investigation was initiated to ascertain the facts.

Air Force Major Eduardo Martelino, the officer in charge of the camp, told the congressional committee the operation had been undertaken in response to intelligence reports that private army and guerrilla groups were forming in the southern Philippines to invade Malaysia in support of the Sultan of Sulu's claim. He stated that the project's goal was to preclude "any attempt by Filipinos to invade Sabah" which "would embarrass the Government and create an international crisis" (*Manila Times,* March 30, 1968).

Malaysia sent a note of protest on March 23 against these proceedings, but the Philippines steadfastly maintained that the incident was a domestic matter. When some Filipino Muslims asked for permission to liberate Sabah by force, Marcos instructed the Defense Department to prevent their crossing. This did not satisfy Malaysia. Foreign Minister Tun Abdul Razak demanded an explanation from the Philippine government. As many as 26 armed Filipinos were arrested in Sabah; 17 of them allegedly had been trained in the Philippines (*Straits Times,* April 4, 1968).

Other incidents occurred. Malaysia detained a Philippine boat during a routine check (*Manila Times,* April 11, 1968). It was reported that two Malaysian gunboats and an aircraft invaded Philippine territory (*Far Eastern Economic Review,* June 13, 1968: 544). The Philippine military made preparations to deal with any security threat. On July 1, the Philippine Navy was placed on 24-hour alert in Sulu "in case of any incident with Malaysia" (*Far Eastern Economic Review,* July 11, 1968: 1001).

As planned, Philippine and Malaysian officials met in Bangkok, June 16 through July 17, with disastrous results. Marcos' state visit to Malaysia in January convinced Malaysian officials that he regarded the Sabah claim as an unwanted legacy of the preceding Macapagal administration, and that he would seek a dignified means to bury the issue. However, the Philippine delegation arrived at the meetings determined to press for resolution of the claim by referring it to the World Court (Hanna, 17). After a month of rhetoric, interruptions, and adjournments, the Malaysian delegation rejected the Philippine proposal and walked out. Tan Sri Ghazali bin Shafie, the chief Malaysian representative at the talks stated: "We believe the Philippine claim to Sabah is founded neither in legal nor in political terms. We are fully aware that you have a number of problems uppermost in the minds of your government, in the economic as well as the security sphere, which we believe are the motivations of your persistent pursuit of your claim to Sabah." (*The London Times,* July 16, 1968). On July 21, Marcos recalled the Philippine ambassador to Malaysia and most of his staff, virtually cutting off relations with Kuala Lumpur. At the August ASEAN Foreign Ministers conference in Jakarta, Tun Razak and Narcisco Ramos agreed to a "cooling-off" period between the two countries, to be followed by talks for improving relations.

Philippine congressional action was the impetus for the official break in diplomatic relations between the two countries in September. On August 25, in response to a United Nations request that member states provide documents pertaining to the delimination and control of the territorial seas, contiguous zones, and continental shelf, the Philippine Senate passed Bill No. 954, An Act to Define the Baselines of the Territorial Seas of the Philippines. Section 2 of the bill read: "The definition of the baselines of the territorial sea of the Philippines archipelago as provided in the Act is without prejudice to the delineation of the baselines of the territorial sea around the territory of Sabah situated in North Borneo, over which the Republic of Philippines has acquired dominion and sovereignty." This amendment was contrary, of course, to the Philippine Constitution, Article 1, Section 1, which stated that the Philippines comprised all territories ceded to the United States by Spain in the Treaty of Paris, which ended the Spanish-American War. When signing Bill No. 954 on September 18, Marcos insisted that the law did not signify Philippine intent to physically incorporate Sabah into the country. Nevertheless, the legislation precipitated a break in diplomatic relations with Malaysia and abrogated the antismuggling act signed by the two countries the year before (*Asian Almanac,* January 11, 1969: 3120). Effigies of Marcos were burned in Sabah, and on September 21, demonstrators seized the Philippine embassy in Kuala Lumpur and pulled down and trampled the Philippine flag (*Far Eastern Economic Review,* October 3, 1968: 4).

In October, the Philippines reiterated their demand that the territorial claims be argued before the World Court. In November, because of violent mass demonstrations in Manila, Kuala Lumpur withdrew its entire diplomatic staff. At an informal meeting of ASEAN Foreign Ministers in Manila in December, another cooling-off period was arranged. Resumption of full diplomatic relations was announced at the opening session of the third annual Foreign Ministers conference that same month.

Between 1969 and 1977, the Sabah issue arose periodically, but these occasions lacked the intensity of earlier exchanges. In fall 1970, the Philippines renewed its appeal that the issue be taken to the World Court. At a May 1971 meeting of the Southeast Asian Treaty Organization in London, the Philippines sought and received assurances from Australia, New Zealand, and the United Kingdom that no secret clauses were attached to the newly concluded Five-Power Defense Arrangement, among them, Malaysia, and Singapore, presumably to preclude their collusion against the Philippines on the Sabah issue.

In 1973, although a committee of senior ASEAN officials agreed in principle that the regional partners should intervene to ameliorate disputes between member states, Malaysia and the Philippines could not agree on the details of implementation. The Philippines wanted an ASEAN mechanism that would permit member states to intervene into disputes in which they were not parties, with or without the invitation of the disputees. Malaysia, suspecting that the Philippines wished to induce others to intervene in the Sabah controversy, insisted that the ASEAN procedure should permit mediation by third parties only if both sides to the dispute consented.

In August 1975, Philippine Foreign Minister Carlos Romulo announced that Malaysia and the Philippines agreed to "put into the background" his government's claim to Sabah for the sake of regional cooperation. He acknowledged that the issue had been detrimental to ASEAN progress. At the same time, he expressed concern that Sabah's chief minister, Tun Mustapha, was aiding Muslim rebels in southern Mindanao. Unconfirmed reports in Manila suggested that Tun Mustapha wished to create a separate state consisting of Mindanao, Palawan, Sulu, Tawitawi, and Basilan in the Philippines and Sabah in Malaysia. It was widely believed that Sabah was being used as a training ground and entry point for weapons for Filipino rebels in Mindanao (Vreeland et al., 1976: 243–244).

Intense negotiations and heavy pressure to arrive at a consensus on restructuring ASEAN forced residual Sabah concerns off the agenda of the February 1976 Bali summit. Datuk Harris Salleh, Sabah's new chief minister, visited Manila in early July 1977, and it was announced that Marcos would reciprocate with a visit to Sabah enroute home from the upcoming Kuala Lumpur ASEAN summit. Foreign Minister Romulo was quoted as saying that Marcos was "taking the pulse of the Filipino people" with regard to the territorial claim, and would make a decision on the basis of his findings (*Daily Express,* August 1, 1977: 1). In late July, the National Security Council met in a closed-door session, and several public hearings were held to discuss a course of action on the Sabah issue.

At the Kuala Lumpur summit in August 1977, Marcos announced: "the Government of the Republic of the Philippines is . . . taking definite steps to eliminate one of the burdens of ASEAN, the claim of the Philippines Republic to Sabah. It is our hope that this will be a permanent contribution to the unity, the strength, and prosperity of all of ASEAN." (Marcos, 1977: 308–310). It was assumed that the decades-long dispute was over. Upon his return to Manila, Marcos met with the *Batasang Bayan* (the legislative advisory council) and the Cabinet to formulate the steps necessary to withdraw the Philippine claim to Sabah. There was even talk of holding a national referendum on the subject (*Daily Express,* August 11, 1977: 1) However, the claim was never officially and unequivocally dropped (Jorgensen-Dahl, 1982: 193–209). The issue will not be legally laid to rest until the Philippine constitution is amended or counteractive legislation is enacted. The Philipines' official explanation for the rhetorical dropping of the Sabah claim was its desire to facilitate regional cooperation. The extent to which this explanation is complete must be examined in the context of the Philippines' historical commitment to regional cooperation.

THE PHILIPPINES AND REGIONAL ECONOMIC COOPERATION

As the state with the longest history of political independence in the region, the Philippines sought to provide leadership in early regional economic cooperative efforts, a role not enthusiastically acknowledged by other countries in the region. Consequently, the early course of Philippine participation in regional cooperation might best be described as strong in rhetoric and on paper, yet weak in substance.

In January 1949, several Asian nations met in New Delhi to discuss the Dutch presence in Indonesia. Carlos P. Romulo, the Philippine representative, was instructed to sound out his Asian colleagues on the possibility of establishing a permanent organization of all Asian nations, regardless of ideology, for economic, political, cultural, and military cooperation. This suggestion was received without much enthusiasm.

In May 1950, Philippine President Elpidio Quirino convened a conference in the mountain resort of Baguio, which was attended by Australia, Ceylon, India, Indonesia, Pakistan, and Thailand. Nationalist China,

South Korea, and other Indochinese states were not invited. The gathering yielded a single resolution calling for cultural, commercial, and financial cooperation (Buss, 1977: 28).

The first significant institutionalized effort at regional economic cooperation was the Association of Southeast Asia (ASA) established by Malaya, the Philippines, and Thailand in Bangkok on July 31, 1961. The initial proposal for ASA was agreed on by Philippine President Carlos P. Garcia and Malayan Prime Minister Tunku Abdul Rahman in January 1959. ASA's stated objectives were cooperation in the economic, social, cultural, scientific, and administrative spheres. However, the association was handicapped from the beginning by its limited size and lack of specific objectives. Although it attempted to maintain a low profile politically, detractors viewed the group as pro-Western and anticommunist in focus. ASA convened three meetings at the Foreign Ministers' level in Bangkok (1961), Kuala Lumpur (1962), and Manila (1963) (Kaul, 1978: 159). Activities of the association were brought to a standstill when the Philippines suspended diplomatic relations with Malaya during the first Sabah confrontation (Roger Irvine, 1982: 9). It must be inferred that in the early 1960s, the Philippines considered its claim on Sabah of higher priority than sustaining the nascent regional cooperative effort. Although Garcia had been instrumental in the formation of the association, his successor, Diosdado Macapagal, was less interested in assuring its success. (Garcia and Macapagal represented the Nacionalista and Liberal parties, respectively.)

A second, even more ephemeral, effort at regional integration was undertaken in 1963, the Greater Malay Confederation, or "Maphilindo." Maphilindo evolved during discussions among Indonesia, Malaya, and the Philippines in Manila in July and August 1963, centering on the nations' differences over the founding of Malaysia. The Maphilindo proposal was promoted by Philippine President Macapagal to sidetrack the planned Federation of Malaysia and to keep alive the Philippine claim over North Borneo. Indonesia and Malaya raised no objections to the proposal primarily to gloss over the serious differences among the three countries.

The Manila talks yielded three documents of long-term significance to regional relations: the Manila Accord (accepted July 31) and the Manila Declaration and Joint Statement (approved August 5). In these treaties, Indonesia and the Philippines agreed to welcome the creation of Malaysia if it was determined by the United Nations Secretary General that the people of Sarawak and North Borneo favored the formation of the Federation. The Manila Accord also stipulated that the incorporation of North Borneo into the Malaysian Federation would not prejudice the right of the Philippines to pursue its claim to the territory (Fifield, 1979: 5). Heralded in Manila as the Philippines' "greatest achievement in

1963," the Maphilindo concept never assumed a prominent role in regional affairs.

Denouncing the proposed Malaysia Federation as a vehicle for perpetuating British military presence and colonialism in Southeast Asia, Sukarno of Indonesia launched a "Crush Malaysia" campaign, often referred to as the "Confrontation." His goal was to incorporate Malaya into a "greater Indonesia." Suspicion in Malaya and the Philippines that Sukarno was warming up to the People's Republic of China and "leaning towards communism" did little to make credible the Maphilindo scheme (Roger Irvine, 1982: 9–10). An ill-fated coup attempt on September 30, 1965, removed Sukarno from power and brought an end to the Confrontation. Indonesia, under the new leadership of Suharto, normalized relations with Malaysia in August 1966. The 1965 election of President Ferdinand Marcos in the Philippines resulted in the temporary soft-pedaling of the the Sabah claim. The end of the Confrontation and the temporary cessation of hostility over Sabah paved the way for a new regional economic cooperation effort (Vreeland et al., 1976: 234, 242).

Formal talks were held May 29 and June 1, 1966, in Bangkok among Indonesian Foreign Minister Adam Malik, Malaysian Deputy Prime Minister Tun Abdul Razak, and Thai Foreign Minister Thanat Khoman concerning the establishment of a new regional economic organization. Malik remained, with active support from Thanat, at the forefront of subsequent diplomatic endeavors to establish a new regional grouping. Membership was declared open to all states in the Southeast Asia region that subscribed to its projected principles and objectives. Malik attempted unsuccessfully to induce Burma and Cambodia to join. Roger Irvine contends that Malik's goal seemed to be to establish peaceful and cooperative regional relations within an organizational context that would allow Indonesia to assume a leadership role.

Late in 1966, Thanat is believed to have circulated a "Draft Joint Declaration" providing for the establishment of a "Southeast Asian Association for Regional Cooperation (SEAARC)." The draft's preambular statement of principles drew heavily on the Manila agreements of July and August 1963 which, among other things, endorsed the concept of Maphilindo. The proposed organization possessed strong similarities with ASA. Again, cooperation was to be promoted in the social and cultural spheres. However, economic cooperation, regarded as the precondition for achievement in other areas, was designated the organization's primary focus.

ASEAN was born during a period of great political and military significance in Southeast Asia. In July 1967, the United Kingdom announced the planned withdrawal of all of its forces east of the Suez by the mid-1970s. China was in the throes of the Cultural Revolution, and United States' involvement in Vietnam was escalating at an alarming pace. Cooperation within ASEAN provided the five developing countries a means of dealing with the uncertainties generated by these events. Outsiders speculated that the embryonic organization could not avoid serving as an anticommunist mechanism, a charge vocalized by the Soviet Union and China (Roger Irvine, 1982: 10–15).

In August 1967, Thailand invited the foreign ministers of all Southeast Asian nations to a conference to discuss finalization of a regional economic cooperation agreement. Four nations responded: the original nations of ASA and Maphilindo and the newly independent Singapore. On August 8, after 3 days of talks in the seaside resort of Bangsaen, the five signed the Bangkok Declaration, thereby bringing into existence a new Association of Southeast Asian Nations.

The Bangkok Declaration established seven goals for the new association: (1) accelerate economic growth, social progress and cultural development; (2) promote regional peace and stability; (3) promote collaboration on matters of common interest; (4) provide assistance in training and research facilities; (5) encourage greater use of agriculture and industry, expansion of trade, and improvement of transportation and communication facilities; (6) promote Southeast Asian studies; and (7) promote closer ties with other regional organizations with similar purposes.

An annual meeting of foreign ministers (rotating among the members' capitals) was made the primary policy-making organ. A Standing Committee (consisting of the foreign minister of the host country, the ambassadors of the other member states, and the Directors-General) was established as the executive organ. The Standing Committee met once a month in the capital of the member hosting the annual meeting. Routine and urgent matters were the responsibility of the Standing Committee, as well as oversight of nine permanent and seven *ad hoc* committees. As might be expected, the committee structure expanded over time. A secretariat in each member country coordinated the member's response to ASEAN decisions (Taylor, 1984: 73–76).

The new regional association did not lack for human or natural resources. In 1975, the region exported 83% of the world's natural rubber and abaco fiber, 84% of its palm oil, 73% of the tin, and 76% of the world's coconut products, in addition to other mining and agricultural products. Although rich in resources, the new economic organization suffered many limitations common to economic cooperation schemes among developing countries. The *New York Times* (January 19, 1968: 60:3) pessimistically pointed out that the member-states' economies were competitive rather than complementary, were overly dependent on primary commodity exports, and had nonconvertible currencies. At the time of their union, less then 21% of the ASEAN countries' trade was among each other. In addition, association members lacked a common language.

Early on, the Philippines under Marcos was a less than enthusiastic participant in ASEAN. Although his political predecessors played important roles in earlier regional efforts (Garcia in ASA and Macapagal in Maphilindo), Marcos was not a primary architect of the new ASEAN and had no desire to ally himself closely with policies of his immediate predecessor and political rival, Macapagal. When the new association was established, the Philippines had not completely given up on the usefulness of ASA as a means of achieving regional cooperation and economic gain.[3] Fifield (1979: 9–10) comments: "Of the participants, its (the Philippines') commitment in 1967 was the most questionable."

ASEAN activities had been underway only 8 months when the Corregidor Affair erupted in March 1968; thereafter relations between Malaysia and the Philippines rapidly deteriorated. Malaysia and the Philippines severed diplomatic relations, and ASEAN activities were suspended beginning in October 1968 and only resumed in May 1969 (Roger Irvine, 1982: 16–19). Jorgensen-Dahl (1982: 199) comments on the Philippine revival of the Sabah claim in the midst of the Corregidor Affair: "—the reactivation appeared to be a sign that the Marcos administration put less value on relations with Malaysia and the membership of ASEAN than on the territorial claim."

Some Philippine government spokespersons claimed that the Sabah issue need not lead to the collapse of ASEAN; they contended that the Sabah question and ASEAN cooperation could be dealt with separately. But Malaysia, from the outset, insisted that ASEAN and the Sabah issue were closely linked. Malaysia's Prime Minister Tunku and Minister of Finance Tan Siew Sin accused the Philippines of destroying the prospects for an ASEAN common market (*Straits Times*, June 8, 1968; July 11, 1968).

At ASEAN's second Ministerial Meeting in August 1968, Tun Razak of Malaysia and Narcisco Ramos of the Philippines agreed to Indonesia's call for a "cooling-off period." However, during a meeting of the ASEAN Permanent Committee on Commerce and Industry, September 30–October 5, 1968, in Manila, the Philippines questioned the Malaysian delegation's competence to represent Sabah on the issues under consideration. Malaysia responded that it would not participate in further ASEAN meetings until the Philippines withdrew its reservation. Malaysia made it a condition of its participation in ASEAN gatherings that the Sabah issue not be raised (Jorgensen-Dahl, 1982: 206–207).

Another incident arose during this period to further strain ASEAN relations. In October 1968, Singapore executed two Indonesian marines found guilty of committing sabotage and murder during the Confrontation. The Indonesian public reacted angrily, but the government responded with relatively mild reprisals and expressed the desire to maintain good relations with Singapore (Roger Irvine, 1982: 20).

At a Tokyo news conference in early November, Philippine Foreign Minister Ramos commented on the problems besetting ASEAN: "ASEAN is in great difficulty. Unless we do something quickly, ASEAN may fall apart. Certainly we are able to do nothing about things like an ASEAN common market until we settle these disputes." Indonesia's Foreign Minister Malik was more optimistic about ASEAN's future: "I admit it's hard to concentrate on political and economic cooperation when the members are at each other's throats, but I think ASEAN will survive." He continued: "The organization at the moment is like a baby cutting teeth. It hurts for a while, but you don't kill the baby to make the pain go away."

Diplomatic efforts by other association members to resolve the Malaysia-Philippine conflict continued until the spring of 1969 when Manila agreed not to raise the Sabah issue at the May ASEAN meeting. At the third Ministerial Meeting of the Association in December 1969, Malaysia and the Philippines announced the normalization of diplomatic relations, evidence of, according to the Malaysian Prime Minister, "the great value we place on ASEAN." ASEAN, unlike ASA, had not succumbed to the Sabah dispute (Fifield, 1979: 12).

On January 2, 1969, Philippine Foreign Minister Ramos was replaced by veteran statesman Carlos P. Romulo. Romulo announced that the Philippines would undertake a New Developmental Diplomacy designed to address economic and social development needs and reduce its excessive reliance on the United States. A summary of the foci of the policy released by the Office of the President on May 23, 1975, listed the intensification of ASEAN participation "along a broader field" as the first priority of the new policy. Marcos also became a vocal proponent of the establishment of an Asian Forum to settle Asian issues and an ASEAN constitution (Fifield, 1979: 43).

In 1975, Marcos proclaimed August 1–8 and every first week in August thereafter "ASEAN Week" to dramatize ASEAN's importance. When issuing Proclamation No. 1473, Marcos stated that ASEAN always had been a cornerstone in Philippine foreign policy to meet the challenge of economic development (*Asian Almanac,* January 3, 1976: 7396B).

The February 23–24, 1976, Bali summit is recognized as a watershed in ASEAN history. The chief executives of the five member states signed a Treaty of Amity and Cooperation in Southeast Asia renouncing the use of force as an instrument for settling disputes among themselves. A Program of Action was signed as part of the Declaration of ASEAN Accord. The phrasing of the Treaty of Amity and Cooperation made it difficult for the Philippines to revive its claim on Sabah. Article 10 prohibited participation "in any activity which would constitute a threat to the political and economic stability, sovereignty or territorial integrity of another High Contracting Party." The Declaration demanded the "settlement of intraregional disputes by peaceful means as soon as possible."[4] Despite the increasing evidence of association success and usefulness, short-term, domestic concerns were the most important impetus for the Philippines' 1977 decision to forego its Sabah claim.

NATIONAL SHORT-TERM POLITICAL STABILITY NEEDS

During the mid-1970s, the Sabah claim became increasingly affected by the Muslim insurgency in the south.[5] For decades, Muslims were treated as second-class citizens by the Philippine political and social elite who are Christians. This alienation was exacerbated by fears of being overrun by the influx of Christians from the north, land tenure disputes, official neglect, and governmental and private exploitation. Decades of migration by Christian settlers from the north, and the intrusion of Filipino and foreign corporations seeking gold mining, logging, and agribusiness profits displaced hundreds of thousands of Muslims in Mindanao.

When Malaysia was founded, some Philippine political leaders feared that the new federation would encourage Muslims in Mindanao, Sulu, and Palawan to form a secessionist movement. Then-Philippine President Macapagal's decision to claim Sabah as Philippine territory derived in part from the desire to deter such a move (*Asian Almanac,* 1968: 2918). Filipinos claimed to have captured a letter from the Malay Chief Minister of Sabah, Tun Mustapha, exhorting Muslims in the southern Philippines to secede and join their Muslim brothers. Filipinos even harbored fears of a pan-Muslim conspiracy between Malaysia and Indonesia on the Sabah issue (*The Economist,* June 2, 1968: 30).

When Marcos assumed power, he sold off land and resources in Mindanao to his cronies and foreign firms. Whereas in 1913, Muslims made up 98% of Mindanao's population, by 1976 they represented 40% of the population and owned only 17% of the land. In the late 1960s, Muslim communities experienced widespread terrorism by paramilitary groups, financed, it was assumed, by individuals and companies wishing to expropriate Mindanao's remaining resources. As no protection was afforded by Christian governors and mayors, Muslims, in 1968, founded the Muslim Independence Movement. The Moro National Liberation Front (MNLF) and its military arm, the Bangsa Moro Army, were operational within 2 years. Their goal was secession. During the military training stage of the movement, Nur(ralaji) Misuari, a 27-year-old political science professor at the University of the Philippines, was elected chairman of the MNLF.[6]

By 1971 an estimated 800,000 Muslims had been evicted from their lands. And 2,000 persons had been killed during 18 months of regular fighting between armed groups from the two communities. When Marcos declared martial law in 1972, more than a quarter-million refugees fled to Malaysia. At the March 1973 Fourth Islamic Foreign Ministers' Conference in Benghazi, Libya, Muammar Khaddafy accused the Marcos administration of genocide and oppression of Filipino Muslims. He announced: "Libya is extending assistance to several peoples fighting for their freedom in Northern Ireland, the Philippines, the heart of Africa and the two Americas." (Lin, 1974: 184) Marcos mounted an aggressive diplomatic effort to convince moderate Muslim states of his government's willingness to address the political, economic, and social concerns of its Muslim population, and to reach a negotiated settlement with the rebel leaders. Several Muslim missions from abroad toured the troubled areas, including, in March 1974, Saudi Arabia's Minister of State for Foreign Affairs, Omar Sakaff.

Widespread violence in the Philippines preceded the convening of the Fifth Islamic Foreign Ministers' Conference in Kuala Lumpur, June 20–24, 1974. Jolo (Sulu Province), Upi (North Cotabato), and Balabagan (Lanao del Sur) were virtually destroyed. It was commonly assumed that the Muslim rebels wished to draw the attention of the Islamic leaders to their struggle. In Resolution No. 18, the conference urged the Philippine government "to find a political and peaceful solution through negotiation with Muslim leaders and particularly with representatives of the Moro National Liberation Front (MNLF) in order to arrive at a just solution to the plight of the Filipino Muslims within the framework of the national sovereignty and territorial integrity of the Philippines" (Lin, 1975: 121). Aid was offered by the Foreign Ministers in the form of the "Filipino Muslim Welfare and Relief Agency."

By 1975, the MNLF emerged as the driving force behind the insurgency. A sophisticated organizational structure evolved, which included 8,000–16,000 armed regulars and between 20,000 and 30,000 active supporters (Vreeland et al., 1976: 378–379). Sporadic warfare in the south resulted in the displacement of 1.5 million Muslims and Christians and thousands of deaths. Brutalities were reported by both sides, and government resources went into fighting the insurgency that might otherwise have been used in economic developmental efforts.

Mohammed Hassan Al-Tohamy, the Egyptian Secretary-General of the Islamic Secretariat, was credited with laying the groundwork for a dialogue between the Muslim rebels and the Philippine government. In mid-January 1975, Marcos' Executive Secretary, Alejandro Melchor, flew to Jiddah to meet with MNLF leaders, but the talks yielded no positive results. During the Jiddah negotiations, Melchor traveled to Libya and Egypt to present the Philippine government's case. Imelda Marcos also visited Algeria, Egypt, and Saudi Arabia during this period.

In July, Al-Tohamy sent a proposed agenda to the Philippine government to provide a basis for resumption of peace talks between the government and the MNLF. The government presented the proposal to 250 delegates gathered in Zamboango City representing rebel groups who did not acknowledge Misuari as their leader. This group rejected Al-Tohamy's proposals outright (Rajaretnam, 1976: 256).

The threat of an Arab oil boycott encouraged the Marcos government to sue for peace. In November 1976, Imelda Marcos was dispatched to Tripoli to negotiate a cease-fire and compromise agreement with Khaddafy under the sponsorship of the Organization of the Islamic Conference. In December, a tentative agreement and cease-fire were announced. By 1977, pressure from revolutionary groups in the south had heightened considerably. Talks resumed in February 1977 but broke down as each side sought to revise the terms of the Tripoli Agreement and the territory to which it applied. In March 1977, as negotiations continued, Saudi Arabia announced the extension of a US$19.5 million loan for an electrification project in Cotabato province, and the Arab Economic Development Fund provided a loan of US$12.3 million to bring power to Zamboanga. In April, Imelda Marcos journeyed again to Libya to sign the Tripoli Agreement, a plan calling for the establishment of an autonomous region of 13 provinces comprising Mindanao, the Sulu Archipelago, and Palawan Island. The provinces were to exercise power over local administration, finances, and education, and the *Sharia* was to be the basis of the legal system. Marcos later reneged on the agreement, insisting that a plebiscite was required for its implementation. The MNLF boycotted the plebiscite. Although it seems that Libyan support for the rebels decreased, the cease-fire ended, and diplomatic acrimony between Marcos and the MNLF resumed.

The decision to renounce the Philippine claim on Sabah coincided with this resumption of hostilities. During the 1970s, the insurgency claimed approximately 60,000 lives. Marcos was anxious to arrange a summit meeting of ASEAN officials to discuss with Malaysian Premier Tun Abdul Razak Sabah's role in the rebellion. Kuala Lumpur steadfastly maintained that the Malaysian government provided no aid to the Philippine rebels. This was technically correct, but Filipino rebels received aid in, from, and through Sabah.

Manila registered a secret protest with Kuala Lumpur in July complaining that two battalions of between 1,600 and 1,800 MNLF troops had been trained in a camp in an isolated part of eastern Sabah. Word of the protest leaked to the press, and Malaysian Deputy Prime Minister Mahithir Mohamad publicly denied the charge (*Far Eastern Economic Review,* August 5, 1978: 27). That same month, Marcos was quoted as saying that had the Philippines not pursued the Sabah claim, fighting in the south might never have happened. He also said: "I am convinced that so long as the claim to Sabah remains, fighting and violence will prevail supreme in the southern part of the Philippines." (*Daily Express,* July 17, 1978: 8).

Arturo R. Tanco, Jr., then-Philippine Secretary of Agriculture, was one of two cabinet officers assigned in 1977 to deal directly with Datuk Harris Salleh, the Chief Minister of Sabah, regarding the Philippine-Sabah issue. In a January 1978 seminar conducted by the Institute of Southeast Asian Studies (Singapore), he offered this assessment of the overall importance of the rebellion to Marcos' decision to drop the Sabah claim:

Sabah was an important conduit of arms of the M.N.L.F. Although Harris Salleh says that this was not condoned officially, still there is considerable evidence to indicate that there was not very strict surveillance imposed. Therefore as people have been doing for centuries, goods moved through the Sabah connection. Because of the proximity of the Sulu Archipelago to the Sabah coast, it is impossible to police this area effectively. So one of the conscious reasons for dropping the claim was to improve relations with Malaysia so that we could then talk about instituting border patrols which would be more efficient. With our 7,000 odd islands it was not contemplated that we would be able to plug the conduit effectively but certainly we hope that it would be more difficult for the M.N.L.F. to use it. This was certainly a conscious aspect of our discussions on the issue (Rajaretnam, 1978: 158).

It must therefore be concluded that the Philippines' immediate need to secure Malaysian assistance in dealing with the Muslim rebellion in the south was the single most important factor in determining the Philippine decision to forego the claim on Sabah. Although it is clear that domestic security concerns alone were sufficient to induce the Philippines to drop the claim, ASEAN also offered the Philippines potential benefits in the areas of national security and economic development.

POTENTIAL LONG-TERM NATIONAL SECURITY BENEFITS FROM REGIONAL COOPERATION

Ferdinand Marcos' August 1977 announcement, which ostensibly relinquished the Philippines' claim on Sabah and removed it as an impediment to ASEAN progress, also might be examined within the context of change in the Southeast Asian political/strategic environment. The latter half of the 1960s and the decade of the 1970s brought the potential for a rearrangement of the primary power relationships in Southeast Asia.

The Viet Cong's psychological victory in the 1968 Tet Offensive, and the March 31 announcement by US President Lyndon B. Johnson that he would not seek reelection, signaled that change in US policy toward Vietnam and possibly all of Asia was inevitable. Upon assuming office, the new US President, Richard M. Nixon, announced plans to "Vietnamize" the war. American servicemen were to be withdrawn from Vietnam on a gradual basis, and the South Vietnamese army was to be responsible for security in the south. During a brief visit to Manila in 1969, Nixon made clear to Philippine leaders what shortly thereafter was enunciated as the Nixon (Guam) Doctrine. The United States would keep its treaty commitments including providing a nuclear shield if a nuclear power threatened the freedom of an ally or nation whose security was vital to the United States. Conventional defense, however, would be the responsibility of the country directly involved, with the United States offering assistance when asked and where its interests were at stake. Insurgencies were to be dealt with by the threatened governments by means of police and paramilitary action and economic and social reforms (Buss, 1977: 109).

In mid-1970, the United States announced plans to reduce its troop strength in the Philippines from 28,000 to 18,900 within the next year. In 1968, the British also had announced the cessation of military commitments east of the Suez Canal. In 1971, with Nixon's surprise trip to Beijing and the normalization of relations between the United States and the People's Republic of China, it became clear to the leaders of the ASEAN states that the US role in Southeast Asia was changing and that a decrease in US military presence was in the offing.

Between 1969 and 1975, the United States withdrew more than 600,000 men from various military posts throughout the region. Cambodia, Laos, and Vietnam fell to the communists in 1975. Bases in Thailand were closed at the end of 1976, and troop levels were drawn down in Korea (Vreeland et al., 1976: 235). The Southeast Asia Treaty Organization resolved in 1975 that, in light of the changing climate in the region, its mandate was obsolete; by 1977, it was disbanded.

Although the Philippines continued to be described in policy pronouncements as "an important ally of the United States in Asia," at a meeting of the Asia Society in New York on June 18, 1975, US Secretary of State Henry Kissinger explained that Japanese security was the only vital US interest in Asia. He stated that the US-Japanese alliance was the cornerstone of US policy in that region (Buss, 1977: 109). The Marcos administration was unsettled by the heated and ongoing debates in the United States government over the future of US commitments worldwide.[7] This uncertainty continued throughout the 1970s as the Philippines, under martial law, was uncomfortable with the Carter administration's emphasis on human rights, and, with its Southeast Asian neighbors, questioned US resolve to parry Soviet ventures in the developing world.

The Marcos government was not reticent to express its concerns:

The refusal of the United States Congress to extend further assistance to Indochina suggests strongly that in its new assessment of Indochina, and by extension, Southeast Asia, which includes the Philippines, is no longer an area of vital interest to the United States.

To say that we in the Philippines are concerned about these new developments is to state the obvious. We are directly affected by these policy oscillations because they concern our security, because they concern our plans for economic and social development, and because they concern our very life and our survival (Marcos quoted in Fernandez, 1977: 26).

Concern about the potential retraction of US involvement was not limited to Southeast Asia. In a *Foreign Affairs* article, in 1971, Hedley Bull (1971: 669) predicted: "It now seems likely that the U.S., convinced that the global balance of power is at stake, will be prepared to allow aggression to succeed and communism to expand, in Indochina and possibly in other areas of Asia and the Pacific, rather than intervene directly to prevent it."

The Marcos regime responded to these uncertainties with an increased emphasis on regional relations and a diversification of contacts worldwide. Foreign Minister Romulo announced that the administration would undertake a "New Developmental Diplomacy" designed to meet Philippine needs for economic and social development, and to reduce its reliance on the United States. A summary of the foci of the "new" policy released by the Office of the President began: "First, to intensify, along a broader field, our relations with the members of ASEAN . . . . " Marcos proposed an ASEAN summit, reasoning that the ASEAN leadership should take stock of its situation in light of the changing strategic relationship among the powers of the western Pacific.

At the ASEAN Foreign Ministers Conference in November 1971, the Philippines joined other members in signing the Kuala Lumpur Declaration, which designated Southeast Asia "a zone of peace, freedom, and neutrality," and appealed to the United States, the Soviet Union, and the People's Republic of China to guarantee the neutrality of the region (Bull, 1971: 669). The ministers asserted their nations' determination "to exert initially necessary efforts to secure the recognition of, and respect for, Southeast Asia as a zone of peace, freedom, and neutrality, free from any form or manner of interference by outside powers." (*FBIS Daily Report, Asia and Pacific,* November 29, 1971: 0–2). Malik of Indonesia stated: "It is only through developing among ourselves an area of internal cohesion and stability, based on indigenous socio-political and economic strength, that we can ever hope to assist in the early stabilization of a new equilibrium in the region that would not be the exclusive diktat of the major powers." (*Far Eastern Economic Review,* September 26, 1971: 32).

At a *Financial Times* conference in 1976, Philippine Foreign Minister

Carlos P. Romulo summarized the concerns expressed earlier by Marcos:

The fall of Saigon and Phnom Penh dramatized the urgent need for the countries of Southeast Asia to reassess their roles and relationships in the post-Vietnam world. Never in the history of these young nations have they been placed in this situation where each is compelled by necessity to forge a redefined system of interaction for achieving and strengthening regional peace, cooperation and development.

Galbonton, in the *Fookien Times Yearbook* (1976: 51), wrote that Marcos hoped that politically ASEAN "could be the indigenous counterpoise to big-power rivalry in the region . . . . " The domestic interests that prompted earlier Philippine intransigence on the Sabah issue to the detriment of ASEAN relations now assumed a back seat to a new foreign policy focus on regionalism.

POTENTIAL LONG-TERM NATIONAL ECONOMIC BENEFITS FROM REGIONAL COOPERATION

Although Marcos partially justified his relinquishing the Sabah claim on the grounds that ASEAN had always been a "cornerstone in Philippine foreign policy to meet the challenge of economic development" (*Asian Almanac,* January 3, 1976: 7396B), when the 1977 decision was made, ASEAN was only "trembling on the brink" of making a significant contribution to the developmental progress of the Southeast Asian partners. Although the stated purpose of the association was trade and industrial cooperation, very little was accomplished in these areas during the first decade of its existence. In November 1975, the economic and planning ministers met for the first time. They decreed that meetings be held at least twice yearly, attended by all officials involved in economic matters: planning, trade, industry, finance, agriculture, transportation, communications, etc. The labor ministers convened separately, a move soon duplicated by other ministers. Decisions reached in these separate sessions required ratification in the economic ministers' meetings. Five economic committees to foster cooperation were also established in 1975: the Committee on Food, Agriculture, and Forestry (headquartered in Indonesia), the Committee on Transportation and Communication (headquartered in Malaysia), the Committee on Industry, Minerals, and Energy (headquartered in the Philippines and chaired by Philippine Industry Secretary Vicente Paterno), the Committee on Trade and Tourism (headquartered in Singapore), and the Committee on Finance and Banking (headquartered in Thailand).[8]

Formal relations—"dialogues"—were established with the European

Community, the General Agreement on Tariffs and Trade, Japan, Australia, New Zealand, and Canada to address mutual economic concerns. David Irvine (1982: 37) writes that the most concrete consequence of 10 years of interaction was that time was provided for the concept of regionalism to embed itself within the strongly nationalistic cognitive processes of the leadership. A consultation mechanism was created. A decade of interaction fostered a deeper understanding of the partners' points of view and the problems confronting them.

At the opening of the fourth Ministerial Meeting in Manila, March 12–13, 1971, President Marcos proposed that the ultimate goal of ASEAN be the establishment of a common market. He urged that a limited free trade zone be set up for selected commodities, and a regional investment bank and payments union be established (Roger Irvine, 1982: 22). At the February 23–24, 1976, Bali summit, limited progress toward the creation of a free trade zone was made. A central secretariat was established in Jakarta, and the administrative structure of the association was redesigned to more efficiently undertake new initiatives.

Philippine trade with its ASEAN partners totaled US$261 million in 1976. Its leading trading partner within ASEAN, Indonesia, alone represented US$97.5 million. Singapore also provided a ready market for Philippine goods; trade with this partner totaled US$60 million (*Asian Almanac*, XIV, No. 1, January 3, 1976). These sums represented, however, only a small percentage of overall Philippine trade. Although Philippine exports to ASEAN partners more than tripled between 1970 and 1977, ASEAN countries received only 4% of total exports.[9] An association-wide Preferential Trading Arrangements (PTA) agreement was hammered out during 1976 and initialed by the economic ministers at their third meeting in Manila, January 20–22, 1977. The PTA was signed by the foreign ministers in Manila on February 24, 1977, and subsequently ratified by the individual members. Tariff reductions were to be negotiated at quarterly roundtable sessions on a commodity-by-commodity basis.[10] It was estimated that upon the PTA's implementation, the direct effect of a 10% across-the-board tariff cut on Philippine imports from ASEAN would increase Philippine intra-ASEAN imports only 2.5% (Armas, 1978). In January 1977, the Philippines signed a tariff reduction agreement with Singapore. The ASEAN partners also agreed in principle to an emergency sharing scheme in crude oil and/or oil products, and on mutual assistance in times of shortage or excess in rice production.

In 1968, an ASEAN fund was established to finance projects approved by the foreign ministers. Industrial cooperation schemes in the production of key commodities were called for. By August 1977, the feasibility study for Indonesia's industrial project in urea fertilizer was completed, and studies for production of diesel engines in Singapore, soda ash in

Thailand, superphosphates in the Philippines, and urea fertilizer in Malaysia were in progress.[11]

The stimulus for efforts toward industrial complementarity came mainly from the private sector and was organized on a regional basis as the ASEAN Chamber of Commerce and Industry (ASEAN-CCI). The ASEAN-CCI, founded in Jakarta in 1971, developed an array of committees and working groups distinct from but paralleling those in the governmental sector. During the August 1977 Kuala Lumpur meeting, ASEAN-CCI was granted sole consultative status within ASEAN.

An ASEAN Bankers' Council existed even before the ASEAN-CCI, and there were an ASEAN Shippers Council, an ASEAN Tourism Association, etc. The ASEAN Natural Rubber Producers' Association was an early success and paved the way for similar cooperation across a range of products (David Irvine, 1982: 44). By 1977, seven "industry clubs" had held at least one organizational meeting, and five others were being organized. Their objective was to identify products within their respective industries that could be exchanged through industrial complementary programs among the countries. New commodity clubs were planned to submit lists of commodities to be considered for possible preferential trading benefits. The appearance of these groups outside of the member-governments' apparatus was evidence of the gradual "Aseanisation" of the nongovernmental community. A sense of regional identify blossomed among relevant elites, further legitimizing the concept of regional cooperation (David Irvine, 1982: 62–63).

Between 1974 and 1977, cumulative investment in the Philippines from ASEAN countries averaged only 0.30% annually. In 1976, Australia, New Zealand, and Japan expressed a willingness to provide financial assistance for ASEAN industrial projects deemed creditworthy by their economic analysts. After the August 4–5, 1977, Kuala Lumpur summit, the prime ministers of Japan, Australia, and New Zealand joined ASEAN leaders August 6–8 to discuss aid. Prime Minister Takeo Fukuda of Japan offered his country's assistance in the form of US$1 billion credit for five proposed industrial projects on the condition that Japanese economic advisors could be convinced of the projects' viability. Australia and New Zealand's Prime Ministers also agreed to step up aid to the association. It was at the beginning of these Kuala Lumpur meetings that Marcos of the Philippines publicly indicated that he was willing to drop the Sabah claim (Fifield, 1979: 15–18).

It must be concluded, therefore, that in 1977 only the outline of a developmental framework within ASEAN was clearly visible; concrete economic benefits had yet to be realized from cooperation. Throughout the region, however, a consensus had emerged that the member-states' economic potential could best be actualized through ASEAN. This anticipation of ASEAN's utility in meeting long-term economic needs did not, however, supersede in importance the Philippines' immediate political security needs in affecting the decision to relinquish the claim over Sabah.

SUMMARY

The 1977 announcement by President Ferdinand Marcos that the Philippines would forgo its sovereignty claim over Sabah to facilitate cooperation within ASEAN is our single case in which regional cooperation obtained despite the fact that the Marcos government's framing of the decision contrasted with the framework of benefits implied by the regional cooperative efforts. In effect, the Philippine government made the "right" decision, to facilitate regional cooperation, for the "wrong" reason—to avoid immediate national political instability. As with the two preceding studies, this case confirms the thesis of this study that developing country elites frame decisions regarding participation in their respective regional economic organizations in terms of short-term national and personal loss avoidance. Alternative ways the decision may have been framed are summarized in Table 5.1.

This case points up the fact, however, that incongruence between the framework of long-term, collective, economic gains offered by regional cooperation and the way developing country elites frame their participa-

Table 5.1

FRAMING COMPONENT	COOPERATION WITHIN ASEAN	THE 1977 SABAH DECISION
ISSUE CONCEPTUALIZATION	Enhanced economic development and growth	Need to secure Malaysian assistance re. insurgency
LEVEL OF ASSESSMENT	Regional National	National Regional
GAIN/LOSS	Economic gain	Loss of political control
PROBABILITY/RISK	Moderate probability of economic gain	High risk of armed conflict
SURVIVAL	Not applicable	Low-level threat to regime's survival
IDEOLOGY	Free trade, customs union, and integration theories	Nationalism
TIME HORIZON	Moderate-->long-term economic gains	Immediate

tion decisions does not *always* yield incompatible outcomes. Cooperation is facilitated when regional cooperation schemes contribute to short-term national and personal loss avoidance. In this case, immediate national needs coincided with the objectives of the regional economic organization.

As noted, Sabah served as a sanctuary and training site for the MNLF and conduit for arms from various foreign Muslim supporters including Libya. Marcos hoped that dropping the Sabah claim would elicit Malaysian cooperation in more careful patroling of the extremely porous southern perimeter and the elimination of Sabah as a source of rebel training and weapons. The Philippines' immediate need to deal with domestic political instability was sufficient reason for Marcos' decision to relinquish the Sabah claim. However, ASEAN also offered potential long-term gains in the form of providing an indigenous response to changes in major power relations in Southeast Asia and a means of enhanced economic development.

With the 1968 announcement of the withdrawal of British forces from the area by the mid-1970s, the enunciation of the Nixon (Guam) doctrine in 1969, and the 1975 fall of Saigon and Phnom Penh to communism, the Marcos administration (and its western Pacific neighbors) became aware that it could no longer rely on traditional allies for protection. The rise of neo-isolationist sentiment and the pronouncement of the Nixon Doctrine suggested that in the immediately foreseeable future, US ground troops no longer would be available to provide indiscriminate assistance to allies around the world. Furthermore, the policy specifically stated that internal problems experienced by US Southeast Asian allies must be addressed by the countries involved. The Philippines always had harbored concerns that the 1951 Mutual Defense Treaty lacked provisions for automatic assistance in the event of external or internal threat such as those embodied in the North Atlantic Treaty Organization Treaty. The Southeast Asia Treaty Organization had proved to be of little value in dealing with indigenous communism and on September 23, 1975, was voted out of existence by its Council of Ministers. It was clear that new arrangements were needed to assure Philippine security.

ASEAN was perceived as a potential indigenous alternative to the superpowers' presence in the area. The Philippine leadership hoped that the five noncommunist members of ASEAN, buoyed by association-induced solidarity and the potential for economic development, might resist the introduction of new hegemons into the area. The association sought guarantees from the People's Republic of China, the Soviet Union, and the United States of the neutral status of the area.

Economic development was the final long-term need expected to be addressed by Filipino cooperation within ASEAN. Marcos was the most vocal proponent within ASEAN for the establishment of a common market, payments union, and regional investment bank. In January 1977, a tariff reduction agreement was signed with Singapore, and in February, association-wide preferential trading arrangements were signed. By the time of the August announcement to drop the claim, a feasibility study on producing superphosphates had been completed, the Philippines' initial allocation in ASEAN's industrial projects. It seemed that developmental assistance from Australia, New Zealand, and Japan would be forthcoming via the association. To Marcos, ASEAN offered the potential for economic development independent of US control.

From the time of the watershed 1976 Bali Summit and the 1977 Kuala Lumpur Summit, where Marcos formally renounced Philippine intentions to pursue the Sabah claim, ASEAN's progress, achieved in small and gradual steps, has continued. Taylor (1984: 78) contends that most progress has been achieved "within the member-states collective zone of indifference." Although the areas of association accomplishment may be better characterized as increasing in scope rather than depth, no one questions ASEAN's usefulness as a mechanism for resolving differences among its members, or as a coalition for dealing with the outside world on both security and economic issues. Brunei joined the original five members of the association shortly after it achieved full independence in late 1983.

The benefits of ASEAN are so widely acknowledged that it is unlikely that regime change within a member state will affect the members' commitment to ASEAN. Continued Filipino participation in ASEAN was not a subject of debate when Corazon Aquino assumed office in the February 1986 People's Revolution. ASEAN is without question a political success; it remains to be seen if this political achievement can provide impetus for further economic cooperation to facilitate development in the resource-rich economies. This latter objective is, of course, the primary stated purpose of ASEAN.

NOTES

1. Between 25,000 and 50,000 people in the territory were Filipino citizens or of Philippine origin. Approximately 100,000 Chinese constituted the commercial class (*New York Times*, September 28, 1968: 3:2).

2. *Padjak* describes the payment arrangements between de Overbeck and the Sultan (and his heirs). Filipino experts claim that the word in the original document, written in the Sultan's Malay-Arabic language, implied a routine rental agreement. They insist that the validity of this claim is not weakened by the fact that the long-accepted English translation of the document uses the word *cede* to describe the transaction. The original Malay-Arabic document has long since disappeared. The Philippines claims that British agents stole it from Sultan Jamalul Kiram II when he visited Singapore to renegotiate the payments. The British thereafter ignored all requests for a copy of the document, but a valid copy was

located in the Washington, DC, National Archives in 1946 with the word *padjak* distinctly inscribed (Hanna, 3–5).

3. The ASA was formally dissolved August 29, 1967.

4. Section A, clause 3 of the Program of Action.

5. At approximately 2,100,000 of a total population of 38,000,000 by the 1970 census, Muslims constituted the second largest religious group in the predominantly Catholic country.

6. The activities of two additional Muslim factions contributed to Philippine political instability. Hashim Salamat, who at one time had been Misuari's number two, headed the Moro Islamic Liberation Front and the MNLF Reformist Faction was led by Dimas Pundato. Although these two groups advocated political autonomy rather than secession, ethnicity was the major difference among the three groups (Komisar, 1987: 166–167).

7. A Mutual Defense Treaty with the United States was signed by the Elpido Quirino Administration in 1951. In the event of an attack, the treaty committed the parties to act to meet the common threat in accordance with their respective constitutional processes. There was no provision for automatic US assistance to the Philippines in the event of external or internal danger such as that guaranteed in North Atlantic Treaty Organization documents. Critics of the Mutual Defense Treaty (Nacionalista Senator Clara Recto was among the most vocal) claimed that its provisions were vague and questioned the steadfastness of US commitment to the Philippines' defense (Vreeland et al., 1976: 234).

8. The host country was to designate a chairperson for the committee, provide a technical secretariat, and convene meetings at least twice yearly. The committees were served by subcommittees, technical experts, and *ad hoc* and subsidiary bodies (Castro, 1982: 77–79).

9. Philippine exports to ASEAN countries as a pecentage of total exports beginning the year of ASEAN's founding were as follows:

1967	1.4%	1973	1.4%
1968	1.8%	1974	2.1%
1969	1.2%	1975	2.7%
1970	1.2%	1976	3.2%
1971	1.2%	1977	4.0%
1972	2.2%		

1977 figures represent 5.6% of total transactions (*UN Yearbook of International Trade Statistics,* 1967–1977, New York).

10. The PTA provides for trade preferences to be granted via long-term quantity contracts, purchase finance support at preferential interest rates, preference in procurement by government agencies, extension of tariff preferences, and liberalization of nontariff barriers on a preferential basis. Negotiations for tariff preferences are conducted quarterly in the Trade Preferences Negotiating Group of the Committee on Trade and Tourism (COTT). COTT makes the final recommendations to the economic ministers. If approved, the preferences are effective on a date set by the economic ministers, usually 90 days after their approval to enable participating countries to implement national procedures. Preferences

also may be negotiated bilaterally or implemented on a unilateral, voluntary basis. The first series of offers, accepted June 1977, placed 71 commodities under the PTA. It was agreed that each member would offer a minimum of 50 items at each quarterly negotiating session. This minimum was later raised to 150 and then 750 preferences per quarter, both negotiated and voluntary. By 1980, there were 6,000 items covered by the PTA, reducing tariffs on intra-ASEAN trade by 20% (David Irvine, 1982: 61; Castro, 1982: 82–83).

11. The ASEAN Fertilizer Industry Authority was chaired by Philippine Secretary of Agriculture, Arturo R. Tanco, Jr.

6 Conclusions and Policy Recommendations

It is the thesis of this study that developing country elites frame their decisions to cooperate or not to cooperate with initiatives of their respective regional economic organizations in terms of short-term national and personal loss avoidance. Although developing countries are, by definition, economically disadvantaged, concurrent political and societal instability often result in risk avoidance and political and personal survival needs dominating elites' decision making regarding regional participation.

The primary benefits of regional economic integration schemes, however, are long-term and collective in nature. Free trade, customs union, and regional integration theories assert that these utilities derive from enlarged markets, a reduction of trade barriers including tariffs, productive specialization and the achievement of economies of scale, and the rationalization and enhancement of regional infrastructure.

The discrepancies between the framing of utilities associated with questions of regional economic cooperation yield a noncooperative decision in most instances. However, as illustrated in the 1977 Philippine decision to relinquish its territorial claim over Sabah, national and regional interests are not always contradictory. After discussing the conclusions we draw from these cases of developing country elites' decision framing regarding participation in regional economic organizations, we will return to the theoretical literature to ascertain how institutional policies and regional political leadership and entrepreneurship may ameliorate the problem of contradictory framing and ultimately alter the way developing country elites frame their decisions.

DIVERGENT DECISION FRAMING

Discrepancies between the benefits offered in regional cooperation schemes and the way developing country elites frame cooperation utilities were clear in each case. In the Andean case, the primary utility associated with compliance with the pact's Decision 24 (D24) was medium- to long-term member-states' control over their developmental futures. Regional policy makers wished to decrease foreign dependence by gradually reducing the foreign equity content of direct foreign investment ventures. Restrictions on profit remittances were designed to prevent decapitalization and enhance member-states' balance of payments. Ideology dominated the way Chilean Junta elites assessed D24. Their commitment to Friedmanite prescriptions for economic recovery and growth convinced them that D24 would be detrimental to attracting direct foreign investment and to their overall plans for economic recovery and growth.

In the Economic Community of West African States (ECOWAS) case, according to liberal economics, long-term regional and national economic gains would result from the rationalization of the labor market resulting from implementation of the Protocol on the Free Movement of Persons, Right of Residence, and Establishment. Nigeria's beseiged government's 1983 decision to expel approximately 2 million alien workers, which contravened the protocol, was dominated by immediate personal and political survival needs.

The Philippine-Association of Southeast Asian Nations (ASEAN) case is perhaps the most interesting and optimistic in that, although it confirms the incongruity between the way utilities are framed in regional integration schemes and the way developing country elites frame issue-specific decisions, it also provides evidence that these disparities do not necessarily result in decisions detrimental to regional cooperation. The Marcos government's 1977 decision to relinquish the Philippine claim on Sabah, which had bedeviled Malaysian-Philippine relations and regional cooperation for more than a decade, was made on the basis of an immediate, national need to avoid political instability and warfare in the country's southern region. However, the consequences of this decision facilitated long-term regional economic cooperation. Therefore, this case suggests that short-term national loss-avoidance strategies are not always incongruous with policies designed to secure the long-term regional benefits of economic cooperation. The challenge to regional organization and national leadership is to identify areas of congruence and cultivate policies that address member-states' short-term need to avoid loss and long-term regional economic objectives. The following segment will summarize the study's findings regarding the propositions found in the literature pertaining to the specific components of cognitive framing.

A COGNITIVE FRAMING MODEL

1. Issue Conceptualization

In each decision scenario of this study, regional and member-state decision makers conceptualized the policy question in disparate ways. Andean Pact policy makers enacted Decision 24, which required a gradual indigenization of ownership and limited profit repatriation by foreign transnational corporations to assert control over the path of economic development in the region and reduce foreign dependence. In contrast, Friedmanite ideology led Chilean economic leaders to assume that D24 would result in loss of direct foreign investment and the economic benefits of imported capital, technology, and expertise.

In the ECOWAS case, regional leadership, acting more out of liberal economic theoretical assumptions regarding the benefits of free movement of productive factors than an immediate regional imperative for liberalization of immigration restrictions, enacted the Protocol on the Free Movement of Persons to facilitate long-term regional economic development and growth. However, in January 1983, when faced with immediate political, social, and economic disorder, Nigeria's Shagari regime decided to expel 2 million alien workers in a futile attempt to avoid the political and social disorder that precipitated a *coup d'etat* the following December.

In the Philippine case, cooperation within ASEAN presented opportunities for long-term enhancement of economic development and growth. In contrast, although Marcos explained his country's ostensible relinquishment of the claim on Sabah as motivated by the desire to remove the issue as an impediment to ASEAN's progress, Philippine policy makers conceptualized the issue in terms of the government's immediate need to ameliorate political instability posed by Muslim insurgents in the south. Proposition I, *Divergence may obtain between the regional economic organization and member-state elites' conceptualization of the substantive content of the policy question,* is confirmed in each of the three cases. In two of the three cases, disparity between the way national and regional decision makers conceptualized the policy issue was sufficient to yield noncooperation. However, the Philippine case provides evidence that a cooperative outcome may be forthcoming despite disparate regional and national conceptualization of the issue.

2. The Level of Utility Assessment

In all three cases, incongruity prevailed between the level of potential benefits sought in the promulgation of regional initiatives and the level on which national elites framed their policy decisions. Regional economic integration initiatives were framed in terms of providing regional/collective and national benefits. Invariably, developing country elites framed their policy decisions in terms of national and/or even personal needs. The Andean Pact's D24 was intended to facilitate regional control over the activities of direct foreign investors and to avoid counterproductive competition for foreign investment among the regional partners, whereas Chile's economic leadership sought to avoid the loss of these foreign inputs into the national economy. In promulgating the Protocol on Free Movement of Persons, ECOWAS leaders wished to rationalize labor resources on a regional basis to facilitate economic development and growth. Nigeria's Shagari government acted to contravene the regional initiative to avoid personal political loss and national political and societal instability. The primary benefits of cooperation within ASEAN were regional in focus, whereas the Marcos government's decision to forgo the territorial claim on Sabah derived from an immediate national need to stem the flow of assistance to Muslim insurgents in the south. Propositions II, *Regional decision makers formulate policy to maximize* regional and national *gains,* and III, *Member-state elites assess the utilities of regional cooperative schemes on* personal, national, and regional *bases,* consecutively, are confirmed.

The policy implications of this finding of incongruence between the levels on which utilities are framed by regional cooperative initiatives and developing country elites is that regional policy must be designed to address immediate national concerns, perhaps even the personal political concerns of member-state elites, if it is ultimately to generate regional/collective benefits. Among the policy recommendations to follow is the suggestion that developing country elites be educated or socialized to anticipate enhanced economic benefits from policy collaboration, to establish a commitment to regional cooperation. Close examination of the level of utility assessment of developing country elites suggests that if their national and personal political concerns are not addressed by regional policy makers, there may be no subsequent opportunity to cultivate understandings of the enhanced benefits offered by regional cooperation, or to generate a commitment to regional goals.

3. Association of the Issue with Gain or Loss

It is a significant finding of this study that in each of the three cases of the investigation, developing country elites framed their decisions with regard to cooperation with the regional initiative in terms of loss avoidance rather than the maximization of gain. The Andean Pact, ECOWAS, and ASEAN initiatives were designed to increase indigenous control over investment enterprises and to facilitate economic development and growth through enhanced labor mobility and regional economic integration, respectively. The policies of these undertakings were framed in terms of enhancing the collective prospects of the member states. In stark contrast, developing country elites framed their decisions in terms of loss avoidance. Chilean economic decision makers wished to avoid the loss of direct foreign investment they believed a sure consequence of compliance with the Andean Pact's D24. Facing immediate societal, political, and economic instability, Nigeria's Shagari government sought to forestall loss of political control. Similarly, in ostensibly giving up its territorial claim on Sabah, Marcos' government wished to put an end to the trafficking in arms and personnel to Muslim insurgents in its southern islands.

Proposition IV is confirmed by the cases of this study: *Certain or potential losses are more highly weighted than those associated with gain in member-state elites' decision making.* Developing country elites framed their policy decisions more in terms of loss avoidance then welfare maximization. Proposition V, *Certain or potential loss very near the decision maker's primary point of reference may induce risk-acceptant behavior,* however, was not confirmed. The threat of loss very close to the decision makers' primary point of reference did not induce risky behavior. The explanation for this negation is that, at least in the Nigerian case, political survival was the primary point of reference. This component exercised lexicographic influence on the framing of utilities. The desire to avoid loss exerts significant influence on the decision outcome of these three cases. In each of the three cases, the regional economic organization offers long-term potential collective economic gains, whereas developing country elites frame their decision making in terms of immediate national and personal loss avoidance.

4. The Influence of Perceived Probability and/or Risk on Utility Assessment

The psychological literature suggests that it is very difficult for the individual policy maker to accurately assess probability and risk components of a decision question. Policy options with very high loss outcome probabilities may be discounted altogether. Options with high probability of risk are likely to be more highly weighted than probabilities associated with positive options. The literature suggests, however, that decision makers may be more willing to tolerate risk to avoid loss.

In each case of our study, the long-term economic gains associated with regional cooperation involved, at best, medium to low probability of gains. Because the record of benefits forthcoming from regional integration efforts among developing countries was not strong, and those benefits were often inequitably distributed, developing country elites' assessment of the probability of gains had to be based on some faith in the theoretical benefits of free trade and customs union theory. In contrast, the risk component of the decisions of developing country elites was overwhelmingly immediate and specific. If D24 was implemented, the Chilean economy faced the immediate risk of losing direct foreign investment. Without successful political frustration reduction strategies, the survival of Nigeria's Shagari government faced immediate risk. Sixty thousand lives had been lost during the 1970s to Muslim insurgency in the south of the Philippines. There were guns and personnel flowing to the insurgents from Sabah. Marcos' decision regarding the claim on Sabah was framed in terms of the palpable risk of political and societal disorder.

These cases confirm that risk components are more highly weighted in the framing of developing country elites' decisions than are the probabilities of gain. There is no evidence that the possibility of loss increased the decision makers' risk tolerance. This latter finding may be explained, in part, by the fact that survival concerns dominated the framing of the decisions in at least two of the three cases.

5. Association of the Issue with the Need for Political, Economic, or Personal Survival

Proposition XIII granted that in the event that developing country elites framed their regional cooperation decision in terms of national or personal survival, it was likely that this utility would dominate policy assessments. As a matter of fact, it was postulated that the satisfaction of the survival need would precede all other utility assessments. As previously noted, each of our three decision scenarios involved loss avoidance under perceived conditions of high risk to certain loss on the part of developing country elites. It is likely that only Nigeria's leadership, the Shagari government, accurately adjudged its personal political (and possibly economic) survival at stake. The fact that the government succumbed to a *coup d'état* led by Muhammadu Buhari on December 31 of that same year validates its survival concerns. Developing country elites faced with the possibility of a *coup d'état* rightly fear for their personal safety, the safety of their families, and their personal fortunes. At minimum, a *coup d'état* will preclude further participation in the political future of their countries, and may result in a life of exile for them, their families, and closest supporters. The ultimate costs of these outcomes are extremely difficult to estimate, and therefore all effort must be expended to avoid them.[1]

Arguments may be advanced that the Chilean and Philippine leadership also framed their decisions in terms of survival. The Marcos government did not underweight the threat posed by armed insurgents receiving assistance from external agents. And the Chilean economy was in dire straits. The Muslim insurgency in the south of the Philippines was, however, a chronic problem. Although it had claimed 60,000 lives during the 1970s, the Marcos government did not regard it as an immediate threat to the government's survival. Mindanao was many miles from Manila, and Philippine governments were accustomed to challenges to societal stability from the left in the form of the New People's Army as well as Muslim secessionists. Similarly, despite the desperate condition of the Chilean economy, Junta leaders did not see compliance with the Andean Pact's D24 as a direct threat to their personal and economic existence. Ideology rather than political and economic survival needs exerted lexicographic influence over the Chilean elites' framing of the decision to withdraw from the Andean Pact. Therefore, Proposition VIII, *Political, economic, and/or personal survival is given preeminent weight by member-state elites in utility assessment; other policy objectives are considered only after these objectives are attained,* is relevant only to the Nigerian case.

6. The Influence of Ideology on Utility Assessment

Proposition IX, which posits that ideology may dominate, to the virtual exclusion of most other factors, the way developing country elites frame their decisions, is only supported in the Chilean decision-making scenario. It is likely that a general ideological adherence to free trade and customs union theory and a subscription to the policy recommendations of dependency theory framed developing country elites' initial commitment to the establishment of regional integration organizations. However, when faced with more immediate national and personal needs, these philosophical tenets did not figure prominently in the way Chilean, Nigerian, and Philippine government leaders assessed their utilities. In each of the three countries of the investigation, the leaders responsible for the original commitment of their country to regional cooperation had passed from their executive-level posts. The subsequent leadership undertaking utility assessment with regard to the specific issues of this study demonstrated less ideological and theoretical commitment to regional economic integration. The most salient example provided of the level of original ideological commitment by the organization founders was the rearguard action against Chile's withdrawal from the pact by former Christian Democratic President Eduardo Frei. Frei, the Latin American statesman most impressed with the potentialities represented by regional integration, had spearheaded the establishment of the Andean Pact in frustration with the lack of progress toward the achievement of the Latin American Free Trade Association's objectives.

Despite the explicit dangers of political opposition to Junta policies, Frei fought by all means available to him against the Junta's decision to withdraw from Andean Pact membership.

Political-economic ideology among the Chilean leadership was strikingly polarized. The Allende regime, which preceded Pinochet's Junta, had been radically socialist in its approach to meeting Chile's desperate economic needs. The Junta's economic leadership, in most cases having in their educational background a stint at the University of Chicago, was equally committed to the radical Friedmanite version of free trade ideology. The fact that Christian Democratic and Socialist leadership turned to regional cooperation as a solution to their problems, whereas Junta leadership, facing virtually the same economic conditions, was unequivocally committed to abrogating D24, provides persuasive evidence of the dominance of the ideological component in Junta leaders' framing of policy decisions. However, this case is the only one among the three in which ideology dominated framing of the decision.

7. The Influence of the Time Horizon on Utility Assessment

The time horizon in which member-state elites frame their decisions to cooperate is highly significant in each of these three cases. Proposition X, *Developing-country elites act to maximize immediate payoffs at the expense of future ones,* was well confirmed. In each instance, the economic benefits of regional economic cooperation were perceived as forthcoming in the moderate to distant future. Control over the member-states' economic destiny and the concurrent reduction of dependency on foreign sources of capital, technology, and expertise were the medium-to long-term benefits to be derived from implementation of the Andean Pact's D24. Abolishing restrictions on worker mobility and, thus, the rationalization of the labor market were conceived as a means to long-term economic progress in the ECOWAS member states. And, as with all regional integration efforts among developing countries, the potential for economic benefits from cooperation within the ASEAN was only vaguely discernible after a decade of existence. Thus, any decision to cooperate within these regional integration organizations remained an exercise of faith or commitment to integration theory.

However, a long-term theoretical commitment to regional integration was not the primary consideration of developing country elites as they were confronted with regional cooperation decisions. Instead, immediate or short-term needs dominated their decision making. Chilean Junta elites feared an immediate loss of direct foreign investment if D24 was implemented; Nigeria's leadership faced an immediate threat to its political survival; and the Philippines' government was engaged in armed conflict in the southern islands. In each of these cases, member-state elites could not afford the luxury of choices that maximized long-term economic gains, even if those benefits might have been sizable. In effect, the political, societal, and economic instability endemic to developing countries preclude their elites' taking the long-term view. They must frame their decisions to maximize risk avoidance and survival. With the history of political upheaval in each of these countries, the regimes could not be assured of reaping the long-term benefits from regional economic cooperation.

To reiterate, the incongruity between the potential long-term regional economic benefits offered by the policy initiatives of regional integration organizations and the decision framework out of which development country elites take their foreign economic policy decisions does not necessarily consign regional economic organizations to failure. It does, however, provide strong evidence that: (1) institutional policies must be designed to compensate for this divergence in utility framing; and (2) it is imperative that regional elites exercise political leadership and entrepreneurship to educate and socialize member-state elites as to how regional policies may assist them in avoiding short-term national loss. The literature on effective institutions and political leadership sheds some theoretical light on how these imperatives might be undertaken.

EFFECTIVE INSTITUTIONS—A SOLUTION TO INCONGRUENT PAYOFF STRUCTURES

Effective institutions[2] may act as intervening variables to alter the way national decision makers frame the issues and assess the utilities of regional cooperation. Institutions are "persistent and connected sets of rules (formal and informal) that prescribe behavioral roles, constrain activity, and shape expectations." In contrast to regimes which are issue-specific, institutions have multi-issue agendas (Keohane, 1989: 3–4). Creating and maintaining effective institutions may be the solution to conflicting payoff structures offered by regional economic cooperation and the cognitive framework out of which the developing country elites make decisions. Regional economic cooperation offers potential, long-term, collective and national gains, whereas the cognitive frameworks of developing country elites' focus on avoiding highly probable, immediate, political, economic, and personal losses. To the extent that their activities and policies reduce uncertainty and risk, lengthen the shadow of the future, and educate and socialize decision makers to believe that a larger pool of resources is available to address personal and national goals through collective action, institutions can bridge the gap between these two payoff structures.

The institutionalization of interactions among regional partners will reduce the level of uncertainty associated with future collective benefits to be derived from cooperation. The prospect of future collective benefits is made more tangible in the minds of decision makers by repeated interaction on policy issues. Routinized interaction permits and encourages government leaders to consider policy issues in terms of collective gains in addition to their inevitable preoccupation with personal and national utilities.

The codification of rules, norms, and decision-making procedures limits the ambiguity and uncertainty experienced by members. The very act of clarifying standards of conduct renders more transparent members' intentions and behavior. Defining what is regarded as cooperative and uncooperative behavior facilitates monitoring and surveillance functions, makes breaches of policy implementation and compliance less ambiguous, and provides a basis for undertaking immediate proactive or subsequent remedial action should there be lapses in cooperation.

Developing countries are seriously handicapped in their ability to gather information. To the extent that institutionalization involves formalizing procedures to publicize the goals, activities, and benefits of the organization and the record of member-states' compliance, access to information is enhanced and uncertainty reduced (Stein, 1992: 207). Haas (1983) points out that information generated by regimes may alter states' understanding of their interests. Regional organizations may gather and distribute information that highlights policy values and beliefs, including previously unconsidered cause-and-effect relationships, that change decision-makers' utility calculations and their perceptions of their interests.

The fostering of common expectations and norms reduces uncertainty and perceived risk. Norms generated by the institution may be internalized by the member-state elites, altering the way that they frame cooperation questions and calculate payoffs (Oye, 1985: 9, 16–17). Internalized norms acquire a "life of their own," an influence independent of the conditions of their original adoption. For example, justice is, for many, a value to be served without respect to personal consequences. Participation or cooperation may acquire intrinsic value without requiring a constant recalculation of its merit by developing country elites. Establishing or maintaining a reputation as a cooperative player or occupying a leadership role may acquire a similar independent value.[3]

Young (1989: 20) contends that there is no basis for assuming that international actors make multiple discrete cost and benefit calculations regarding compliance with the provisions of regimes. When member states collaborate over time to develop common rules, procedures, and policies, it is reasonable to expect the evolution of some sense of collective identity and socialization that assigns value to the collective enterprise. These rather difficult to analyze processes of acculturation likely will engender feelings of commitment and obligation which encourage compliance with regional initiatives.

With member-state commitment and longevity, regional institutions acquire legitimacy and a tradition. Legitimacy and tradition are powerful shapers of political choice and a basis for cooperation. Legitimacy can sustain patterns of behavior long after the original basis for institution creation has disappeared. Actors value their reputations, and costs are exacted if they choose to defy tradition and regionally legitimized practices (Stein, 1990: 52).

As we have seen, the organizations of this study were quite embryonic in their development when Chilean, Nigerian, and Philippine elites were confronted with their policy decisions. A tradition of cooperation had yet to be developed and the organizations' legitimacy yet to be established. Member-state elites had not had sufficient time to acquire high levels of socialization and commitment. In each case, the country's leadership that participated in the initial founding of the organization had been replaced by leaders less committed to the ventures.

When effective institutions exist, with reasonable certainty of routinized interaction, and when an agenda is formulated toward the achievement of multiple goals, cooperation may be enhanced by linkage within and across issue areas. Issue linkage may be used to alter the payoff structure. The quantity of benefits deriving from cooperation in one issue area may be drawn on to facilitate cooperation in another. Actors likely will have preferences of differing intensity. In what is often referred to as "log-rolling," participants may trade cooperation in a less valued issue area for their partners' cooperation in a more highly valued area. Iterativeness and shadow of the future are enhanced (Axelrod and Keohane, 1985: 239; Oye, 1985: 21).

The existence of effective institutions lengthen the shadow of the future; they make it possible for member-state elites to consider not just the utilities of cooperation within the context of a single immediate transaction, but reshape their calculations in terms of longer-term relations, which may engender collective goods that cannot be achieved individually (Stein, 1992: 207).

It should not be assumed that the establishment of effective institutions will result in the abandonment of national bases for utility calculations. Instead, they change the payoff structure within which national decisions are made. National elites may conclude that joint maximization of interests is a more effective means of achieving personal or national interests than autonomous behavior. They may come to consider partners' interests as well as their own in the taking of decisions. After binding themselves together out of self-interest, for various reasons national decision makers may come to accept the pursuit of regional interests as an imperative (Stein, 1990: 52–53).

Ultimately, the transformation in the way developing country elites assess their utilities may coalesce to yield a sense of "community." This concept refers to an advanced stage of socialization in which incongruity between the goals of the regional economic organization and individual member states no longer impedes institutional effectiveness. Community decision makers hold common or compatible values and beliefs. Communication and relations among them are direct and multifaceted. There is mutual predictability of behavior among them, and they practice generalized as well as balanced reciprocity. A community provides collective and national goods without having to resort to threats of coercion or sanctions (Deutsch, 1957; Taylor, 1987: 23). The creation of a community is in the distant future for most regional economic organizations among developing countries. However, longevity and success in accomplishing both regional and national objectives will move developing country elites toward this level of cohesion. Evidence of this possibility is provided by the European Union and, I believe, the ASEAN of today.

To summarize, effective institutions may intervene between the framework of utilities associated with cooperation within the regional economic organization and the framework out of which developing country elites take their decisions. Effective institutions may change the payoff structure, stabilize expectations, provide good information, alleviate or reduce risk and uncertainty, and codify norms and rules. In time, the effective institution may educate and socialize developing country elites such that, rather than engaging in self-maximization on an absolute or relative basis, they come to evaluate payoffs in terms of joint maximization.

POLITICAL LEADERSHIP AND ENTREPRENEURSHIP—A SOLUTION TO INCONGRUENT PAYOFF STRUCTURES

Effective executive leadership for regional economic organizations cannot derive from the usual political power attributes, because policy-making authority ultimately resides with the member states. Each possesses veto power over proposed regional integration initiatives. Instead, regional executive personnel must exercise leadership by demonstrating intellectual, administrative, and political entrepreneurial acumen. Executive heads of regional economic organizations may be selected on the basis of personal charisma, experience, expertise, negotiating and/or administrative abilities, and the reputation that they bring to regional integration processes. These personal attributes legitimize for member-state elites the executives' authority to propose, analyze, and implement policy.

The regional executive may exercise intellectual leadership by shaping and controlling the organizational agenda that delineates the issues, problems, and goals to be considered by regional decision makers; this agenda structures all subsequent negotiations. The executive may act to promote common understandings of regional problems and goals, and cultivate a consensus as to how these policy areas should be conceptualized, including the cause-and-effect relationships underlying them. The regional executive may exercise intellectual leadership by generating ideas and policy proposals that reshape the member-states' assessment of their national and personal interests. Collective policies that also address national and personal needs should be delineated. Particularly if the executive is able to persuade member states that he or she possesses unique knowledge and understanding of regional problems, then it is likely that his or her view will be embraced by the group. The roles played by Maurice Strong and Mustafa Tolba in environmental policy deliberations under the auspices of the United Nations Environment Programme provide strong illustrations of the power that expertise may assign to international executives (Haas, 1990: 226, Footnote 3).

Political entrepreneurship also plays a role in the agenda-setting and consensus-building processes. The executive engages in activities that mobilize relevant regional constituencies, thus drawing potential collaborators and allies into discussions over proposed cooperative efforts. Once the various policy alternatives have been delineated, the regional executive may identify potential areas of agreement and broker compromises among the member states' divergent views. When the policy-formulation stage is completed, the effective executive secretariat must then arrange the necessary coordination to ensure implementation and compliance (Haas, 1990: 135; Sandholtz, 1993: 249–252; Young, 1991).

These theoretical admonishments seem to contradict the empirical realities of the usual quality of regional executive leadership and the constraints under which they must perform. An unassuming and self-effacing leadership is the predominant pattern. Member states are often unwilling to appoint regional leadership that may acquire an independent status in regional policy deliberations. During the formative years, the organizations may be plagued by crises: political, even-armed conflict between members; members' tardiness or failure to implement regional policies; and reneging on contribution obligations. Under crisis conditions, it is difficult for regional personnel to exert intellectual and entrepreneurial leadership. Regional leaders react rather than generate proactive policies. Energy and time are devoted to crisis management, to "putting out fires." Regional leadership may become risk averse. It is axiomatic but true that periods of change and crisis present opportunities for progress and achievement as well as stalemate and failure. Thus, it is during times of crisis that the quality of intellectual and entrepreneurial leadership will be most influential in determining the degree to which member-state elites come to frame their policy decisions in terms of collective goals.

Haas (1990: 244, Footnote 11) describes as politician and prophet the idealized roles of personnel who provide intellectual as well as entrepreneurial leadership: "They were able to draw on bodies of expert knowledge and so present it as to fit their personal ideologies and also to meet the political demands of their colleagues. Often such people have a distinct notion of secular time, of historic breakpoints of which they see themselves as exponents and agents."

Perhaps it is unrealistic to expect that regional executive leaders be prophets as well as politicians, but it is reasonable to suggest that high-quality personnel be appointed who bring special expertise and a solid reputation to the regional enterprise. At minimum, member states might avoid establishing ambiguous organizational schemes and competing loci of authority (as evident in the conflicting functions associated with the ECOWAS executive secretariat and the head of the Fund), which mire the organization in internecine battles.

This chapter concludes with some relatively specific policy suggestions as to how regional leaders may take initial steps toward meeting the short-term needs of member-state elites. To the extent possible, concrete examples will be drawn from the case studies under consideration as to how these policy suggestions have been undertaken in various organizational contexts. These suggestions may be interpreted as ranging from the self-obvious (have regularly scheduled meetings) to the superficial (provide opportunities for member-state elites to interact in informal, social settings). It must be reiterated, however, that multiple, interacting, and organization-specific remedies are required to bring congruency to the framework of utilities associated with regional economic cooperation and the way developing country elites conceptualize regional policy decisions.

RECOMMENDATIONS FOR ENHANCED INSTITUTIONAL EFFECTIVENESS AND INTELLECTUAL AND POLITICAL LEADERSHIP

If developing country elites frame participation decisions in terms of short-term national and personal loss avoidance, then organizational procedures and policies and regional leaders must act to reduce member-elites' perceived uncertainty and risk, to lengthen the time frame within which they assess utilities, and to educate and socialize them as to how collective means may enhance their ability to meet national and personal needs. To a large extent, the benefits forthcoming from such strategies overlap and interact.

As noted in the preceding theoretical discussion, effort should be expended to ensure that organizational rules and policies are clearly delineated. Concise goal identification and policy provisions clarify for participants what constitutes cooperation and noncooperation. If policy provisions and compliance expectations are clear, monitoring of implementation and compliance is facilitated. Monitoring of policy implementation and compliance must be consistent. A clear delineation of organizational policy goals and a strict monitoring and publication of compliance records will facilitate the creation of expectations for compliance with regional initiatives.

Compliance records must be well publicized to garner incentives associated with reputation. In the realm of international economic diplomacy, even among developing countries, member states desire to foster and preserve a reputation for assuming regional leadership and regional cooperation. This reputation-enhancement function is unlikely to supersede in importance such framing components as short-term survival needs or strongly held ideological views within the cognitive framing of developing country elites, but it may figure among other less significant utility assessments.

One deceptively simple way to reduce perceived uncertainty and risk is to establish and maintain a regular schedule of formal meetings of the organization's functional units and informal meetings among member-state elites. Regular meetings give regional goals and policies priority on national leaders' agendas. Formal discussions of regional policies clarify and emphasize in participants' minds the enlarged pool of benefits to be derived from regional collaboration. Routinized interaction suggests to developing country elites that even if they do not receive immediate tangible economic benefits from regional cooperation, future interactions and policies will yield national benefits. Routinized interaction also facilitates linkage among policy issues as well as performing education and socialization functions. Regional meetings and summits provide developing country elites with the opportunity to be portrayed in their national media as occupying prominent roles in regional and international deliberations. Such public relations benefits may enhance their prospects for political survival.

Informal interactions among member-state elites should not be underestimated. Regularized face-to-face interaction provides opportunity for personally acquainted member-state elites to discuss bilateral disputes. As was pointed out, ASEAN meetings provided a forum for Philippine and Malaysian leaders to address their dispute over Sabah, which was characterized by sword rattling and the suspension of diplomatic relations. Similarly, a 1975 border dispute between Benin and Togo was resolved as a consequence of ECOWAS efforts. It is generally acknowledged that ASEAN intraorganizational problems have been ameliorated by member-state leaders' interactions during golf games that precede foreign ministerial meetings.[4]

Meetings should be well planned and administered. They provide an opportunity for the executive secretariat staff to exert intellectual and political leadership and to demonstrate administrative effectiveness. Short-term organizational difficulties or intermember disputes should not be allowed to interfere with regularly scheduled regional meetings. The potential for lapsed meetings is well illustrated in the Andean Pact and ASEAN cases, when Chilean intransigence interfered with personnel succession and scheduled meetings, and the Philippine-Malaysian dispute over Sabah resulted in the suspension of ASEAN meetings between October 1968 and May 1969. Regular, well-orchestrated, and productive informal and formal meetings generate expectations for continued regional interactions and cooperation. It contributes to elite socialization and community building.

Regional executive leadership must proactively head off bilateral disputes threatening regional cooperation. Developing member states have not had centuries of political independence in which to sort out regional territorial disputes. Consequently, bilateral territorial and other substantive disputes commonly threaten the survival of regional organizations. As was noted, multiple political and territorial disputes characterized relations among ECOWAS members. Armed conflict between El Salvador and Honduras contributed to the collapse of the *Mercado Commun Centroamericana*. And, of course, the Malaysian-Philippine dispute over Sabah was a serious deterrent to ASEAN progress. The opportunities for the exercise of regional executive leadership are clear: preemptive action to defuse intermember disputes contributes to regional cooperation and provides short-term national and personal benefits to developing country elites.

The task of providing good analysis to support the formulation of regional policies is a realm in which the regional secretariat might contribute to the reduction of perceived uncertainty and risk. Good policy analysis enables developing country elites to make informed judgments and to have confidence that they fully comprehend the consequences of their policy choices. The clearest illustration of the dangers of formulating policy without fully comprehending the possible negative consequences provided in this study was ECOWAS' promulgation of the Protocol on Free Movement of Persons. Regardless of whether their influx was actually exacerbated by the ECOWAS policy, Nigeria was unprepared to provide employment and social services to large numbers of alien workers. The ill-designed and possibly premature policy created a focal point for dissatisfaction among Nigeria's citizens for the entire concept of regional cooperation and leadership.

The policy process and attendant educational processes should explicate that an enhanced pool of resources will be available in the short term to help developing country elites address national political and economic needs. As demonstrated in the cases of this study, it is not enough to designate funding for an industrial undertaking to a particular member state. Andean Pact members had agreed on the allocation among themselves of metalworking and petrochemical manufacturing enterprises. The Philippines had been designated the primary regional producer of fertilizers. The immediate promise of benefits from these industrial allocations was not sufficient to affect the way developing country elites framed their participation decisions. To accommodate for the short-term aspect of developing country elites' framing of decisions, the regional organization should address highly salient emergency needs and specific national needs that could not be met by the member states on their own. This is not as difficult as might be presumed. Two excellent examples of these types of undertakings are the ASEAN's creation of oil and rice emergency provision mechanisms and the ECOWAS' funding of a telecommunications network linking the capitals of each member state and the outside world. In the former case, the availability of rice or oil from regional sources during times of crisis cannot fail to convince developing country elites of the short-term, national and personal, political and economic benefits of regional cooperation. In the latter case, ECOWAS members had not unilaterally provided efficient communication capabilities for domestic, regional, and international service for their governments, business communities, and citizenry. Participation within the ECOWAS made these services available, providing highly concrete evidence of the immediate national and personal economic and political benefits. The multiplier effect from this level of infrastructure investment is immense in terms of short-term public relations and long-term economic benefits.

Effective institutions and regional leaders may contrive to lengthen the shadow of the future in member-state elites' utility assessments. Ideally, regional policy should meet the short-term national and personal needs of developing country elites while facilitating the attainment of long-term regional economic goals. As noted, policies that made emergency rice and oil resources available to member states and infrastructure projects such as telecommunications systems met long- and short-term national and collective needs. Well-designed policy initiatives and effective regional meetings build expectations among developing country elites that regional initiatives will bear fruit. To the extent that regional cooperation helps meet immediate national and personal needs, commitment and socialization are enhanced. These factors lengthen the shadow of the future in the way developing country elites frame their participation decisions.

Although some of the framing components discussed in this study are more typical of decision making among developing country elites, (the extreme tendency toward loss avoidance and survival needs), the conclusions of this study have ramifications for integration efforts in advanced industrial contexts such as the European Union and the North American Free Trade Agreement. Those wishing to facilitate cooperation in these contexts will do well to consider how national decision makers frame and assess the utilities associated with policy decisions.

Ultimately, effective institutions and regional executive leadership aspire to change the bases on which developing country elites frame their participation questions and calculate their utilities. In the short term, this means undertaking measures to educate and socialize member-state elites to expect short- and long-term collective national and personal utilities from regional cooperation. In the long term, developing country elites may conclude that collective policies are the best means to achieve national and personal goals. Over time, cooperative norms may be established to the extent that each new regional policy initiative does not elicit a reassessment of the benefits of cooperation. Elites may come to automatically assume that the solutions to their problems may be found on the regional level. Policy decisions may come to be framed habitually on the collective level. At this point, a community in the Deutschian sense will have been achieved.

NOTES

1. Chile's Junta came to power as a result of a 1973 military *coup d'état*. Shagari's government in Nigeria was democratically elected; however, it was preceded by four military regimes: JTU Aguyi-Ironsi, January 15–July 29, 1966; Yakubu Gowon, July 19, 1966–July 29, 1975; Murtala Muhammed, July 29, 1975–February 13, 1976; and Olusegun Obasanjo, February 13, 1976–October 1, 1979 (Maduagwe, 1993: 67–68). Although successful military coups are not part of the political tradition in the Philippines, armed insurgencies are. In addition to the Muslim insurgency in the South, Philippine governments have been challenged by communist guerrilla activities throughout the country's history.

2. Keohane (1989: 4, 6) discusses three measures of institutionalization: (1) *commonality*, the degree to which expectations about appropriate behavior and understandings about how to interpret actions are shared by system participants; (2) *specificity*, the degree to which these expectations are clearly specified in the form of rules; and (3) *autonomy*, the extent to which the institution can promulgate or alter its own rules rather than rely on outside agents to do so. These criteria are suggested by Samuel Huntington (1968: 20), who defines autonomy as "the development of political organizations and procedures that are not simply expressions of the interest of particular social groups." Huntington's three other criteria for institutionalization include adaptability, coherence, and complexity. Although some level of institutionalization is required for effectiveness, institutionalization does not necessarily guarantee effectiveness. Highly institutionalized structures and procedures may become rigid or irrelevant.

3. Social incentives, such as those associated with reputation, derive from the concurrent desires to gain or maintain approval and avoid censure; they work

through mechanisms such as criticism and shaming by fellow members and others. It is generally assumed that these incentives are effective only in relatively small groups; however, these benefits may be fostered by decomposing larger organizations into subgroups (Taylor, 1987: 13).

Discussing various deterrents to collective action, Hardin (1982: 213) points out the difficulty of cultivating a reputation for trustworthiness in a system in which there is a very low incidence of trustworthy behavior: "If almost no one is trusted, then I will not be trusted even if I am—alas, known only to me—utterly trustworthy . . . . This much we have in common with used cars: the incidence of enough lemons among us will wreck the reputations of us all." Unfortunately, a general dearth of trustworthiness may obtain in the early stages of regional interaction among developing countries.

4. The *New York Times* reported in 1975 (May 14) that since 1967 golf clubs and related equipment have been the most commonly given symbols of friendship among Asean foreign ministers.

Appendix

Africa

1959 MALI FEDERATION

Established: January 1959, headquarters Dakar.

Goals: Inter-federation and inter-African economic development and cooperation

Members: Benin (Dahomey), Mali (Soudan), Senegal, and Burkina Faso (Upper Volta).

Difficulties:

- Organization disintegrated shortly after its inception with the January and February 1959 withdrawal of Dahomey and Upper Volta, respectively.

- Senegal and Soudan espoused divergent ideals and goals.

Current Status: Defunct.
(Foltz, 1965: 109, 117-118, 160)

1961 ORGANISATION COMMUNE AFRICAINE ET MALGACHE (OCAM)

Established: Charter ratified at Tananarive 27 June 1966.

Goals: To accelerate members' economic social, technical, and cultural development. Organisation will seek to harmonize members' policy in these fields, to coordinate their development programs and to facilitate policy consultations between them.

Members: Burkina Faso, Cameroon, Central African Republic, Chad, Congo, *Cote d'Ivoire*, Dahomey, Gabon, Malagasy Republic, Mali, Niger, Rwanda, Senega, Togo, and Zaire.

Accomplishments: Sugar agreement and Air Afrique.

Difficulties:

- Conflict among members
- Half of membership had dropped away before the organization's demise.
- French President Charles DeGaulle pursued imperialistic designs via the organization.

Status: Defunct, as of 1985.

1964 UNION DOUANIERE ET ECONOMIQUE DE L'AFRIQUE CENTRALE (UDEAC)
or Customs Union of Central African States

Established: treaty signed 8 December 1964; into force 1 January 1966.

Members: Cameroon, Central African Republic, Chad, Congo, and Gabon.

Goals: Customs union; proposes to stimulate industrialization by replacing import duties on materials needed for manufacture with a lower "single tax" and to build up a fund from which compensation can be paid to members for lost revenues; unification of investment code.

Accomplishments: Solidarity Fund (of insignificant size) established to reduce economic disparities among member states (Robson, 1990).

Difficulties:

● Unevenness of development led withdrawal of Chad and Central African Republic 1 January 1969; later rejoined
● No discernible positive effect on trade
● "[T]he single tax system and investment code have strengthened the market dominance of the foreign owned-companies, have guaranteed their profitability, have eliminated incentives to efficient production, have promoted capital and import-intensive production and have encouraged duplication of plants and products throughout the region." (Mytelka, 1984: 146)

Status: In 1990 still operational; yet policy reforms needed to upgrade participation benefits in relation to costs (Robson, 1990: 8).

1967 EAST AFRICAN COMMUNITY (EAC)

Established: 1967, Secretariat housed in Arusha.

Members: Kenya, Tanzania and Uganda

Accomplishments:

● Some important infrastructural projects such as East African Railways and East African Airways
● Technical cooperation in several areas has continued, e.g., the East African Marine Fisheries Institute
● Established precedence of intraregional cooperation.

Difficulties:

● Ideological differences between Kenya and Tanzania over social and economic paths
● Predominance of outside investment in Kenya relative to other members
● Pre-Community economic dominance of Kenya
● Perceived inequitable distribution of benefits
● Decade of political instability in Uganda
● Inherent difficulty in the "rule of three"

Status: collapsed 1977
(Onwuka and Sesay, 1985)

1970 COMMUNAUTE ECONOMIQUE DE L'AFRIQUE DE L'OUEST (CEAO)
   or West African Economic Community

Established: May 1970; headquarters Ouagadougou, Burkina Faso; became operational
1 January 1974

Members: *Cote d'Ivoire,* Mali, Mauritania, Niger, Senegal, Upper Volta (Burkina Faso);
Guinea and Togo are observers

Goals:

● To create a regional common market
● To encourage intra-community trade in manufactured goods
● To improve regional infrastructure

Accomplishments:

● Fish purchasing and marketing company established
● Successful in operating partial free-trade area for industrial products (Robson, 1990: 8)
● By 1976, intra-regional trade was considerably enhanced
● Establishment of a Community Development Fund 1 January 1976 to finance development
   projects and to compensate members suffering negative consequences from Community's
   economic and social policies (Asante, 1985b)

Difficulties:

● Corruption scandal uncovered by President Sankara of Burkina Faso in 1985
● No industrial specialization within the region

Status: CEAO member states were urged to join the ECOWAS as the larger organization
purportedly offered greater benefits; as of 1985, Senegal and *Cote d'Ivoire* remained in
opposition to this move.

1973 MANO RIVER UNION (MRU)

Established: Mano River Declaration signed 3 October 1973; headquarters Freetown, Sierra Leone.

Members: Liberia, Sierra Leone; Guinea joined October 1980

Goals: Customs union; trade expansion; harmonization of tariff and trade policies; promote joint development projects and secure fair distribution of benefits for members

Accomplishments:

- Relations with several other intergovernmental organizations
- Common external tariff instituted between Liberia and Sierra Leone April 1977, extension to Guinea envisaged
- Trade liberalization program for specific goods of local origin entered into force 1 May 1981

Difficulties:

- Member states' small size and low level of development fosters extreme dependence on developed countries for security, financial and technical assistance
- Internal rivalries, ethnic and social instability and violence
- Balance of payments difficulties in Sierra Leone forced postponement of establishment of customs union
- Incompatible infrastructures
- The Union was the product of an interdisciplinary committee set up by the United Nations Development Program; therefore, policy making in the MRU was influenced from the beginning by outside actors (Onwuka and Sesay, 1985)

Status: In 1992 under duress, but operational
(YEARBOOK OF INTERNATIONAL ORGANIZATIONS, 1993/1994: 1230)

1976 COMMUNAUTE ECONOMIQUE DES PAYS DES GRANDS LACS (CEPGL)
or Economic Community of the Great Lakes Countries

Establishment: Founded 20 September 1976; headquarters Gisenyi, Rwanda

Members: Burundi, Rwanda and Zaire

Goals: A regional common market and to ensure security of its members

Accomplishments:

- Monetary arrangement among central banks signed March 1981
- Social Security Convention signed September 1978
- Agreement on free movement of diplomats and businessmen and on postal organization signed 1980
- Created Development Bank of the Great Lakes States 9 September 1977, Institute of Agricultural and Zootechnical Research 9 December 1979; also instrumental in setting up Multinational Programming and Operational Centre
- Cooperates with the United Nations
- Publishes CEPGL QUARTERLY REVIEW, *JOURNAL OFFICIEL DE LA CEGL* (annually)

Status: Active
(YEARBOOK OF INTERNATIONAL ORGANIZATIONS, 1993/94: 388)

1979 SOUTHERN AFRICAN DEVELOPMENT COORDINATION CONFERENCE (SADCC)

Established: Lusaka Declaration adopted 1979; took effect 1 April 1980; headquarters Gaberone

Members: Angola, Botswana, Lesotho, Malawi, Mozambique, Swaziland, Tanzania, Zambia, and Zimbabwe.

Goals: To enable sympathetic Western states to assist in developing alternative infrastructure to member-states' dependence upon South Africa, particularly in overland transportation and imports. Regional integration of economies.

Accomplishments:

● Program of action focuses on ten sectors, each the responsibility of a single member state
● Primary infrastructure activity is rehabilitation of the 200 mile Beira corridor, consisting of rail, highway, and pipeline links between Mozambican port of Beira and the interior
● By 1987, 400 or 500 proposed projects had been approved by members at the projected cost of US$5.4 billion; more than one-third of this amount had been pledged by Western donors by early 1987
● In 1988-89, member-states averaged real growth in Gross Domestic Product of 4.5%, exceeding a 3.2% rate of population growth
● SADCC has fostered the emergence of a "regional mentality" and established itself as an essential participant in international and regional fora

Difficulties:

● Members are economically dependent in South Africa, particularly for employment
● South African-supported RENAMO guerillas wrought havoc with already-faltering Mozambican economy
● Heteogeneity of membership includes type of regime, level of economic development, ideological inclinations, degree of dependence upon South Africa, and geography
● SADCC has had difficulty moving beyond coordination of national policies to the formulation of regional policies

Status: Independence for Namibia and end of civil wars in Angola and Mozambique will improve the organization's prospects; with the end of South Africa's system of apartheid, donor sympathy for SADCC may fade and aid decline. Reduced European Communities' support for SADCC projects is already evident (Tjonneland, 1992: 109-110)

1981 PREFERENTIAL TRADE AREA FOR EAST AND SOUTHERN AFRICA (PTA)

Established: November 1981; headquarters Lusaka

Members: Original signatories are Comoros, Djibouti, Ethiopia, Kenya, Malawi, Mauritius, Somalia, Uganda, and Zambia; subsequent members include Burundi, Lesotho, Rwanda, Swaziland, Tanzania, and Zimbabwe. In 1991, Angola, Botswana, Madagascar, Mozambique, and the Seychelles had not yet ratified the treaty.

Goals: Coordinate regional development and tariff reduction. Trade and development bank has been proposed.

Accomplishments: In 1989 common travelers' checks were issued by member states, denominated in Special Drawing Rights (AFRICA REPORT 1985, 30: 1)

Difficulties:

- Unrealistic assessment of immediacy of benefits
- Lack of commitment and enthusiasm on the part of the member-states
- Nonpayment of contributions
- Polarization of benefits around economically stronger members Kenya and Zimbabwe

Status: Operational, but organizational reform needed to enhance and equitably distribute benefits (Takirambudde, 1991: 53-57)

1981 COMMUNAUTE ECONOMIQUE DES ETATS DE L'AFRIQUE CENTRALE (CEEAC)
or Economic Community of Central African States (ECCAS)

Established: December 1981, during a conference of the Heads of State of Central African Customs and Economic Union as recommended by the Organization of African Union's Plan of Action and the final Act of Lagos (1980). Treaty was adopted 18 October 1983 in Libreville and entered into force 18 December 1984.

Members: Burundi, Cameroon, Central African Republic, Chad, Congo, Equatorial Guinea, Gabon, Rwanda, Sao Tome-Principe, and Zaire; Angola holds observer status.

Goals:

- The elimination of customs duties and other import/export taxes among members
- The elimination of quantitative restrictions and other deterrents to trade among members
- The establishment of a common commercial policy with respect to third countries
- Progressive elimination among members of obstacles to free movement of persons, goods, services, capital and right of establishment
- Promoting common activities in industry, transport and communications, energy, agriculture, natural resources, trade, currency, etc.
- Creation of a cooperation and development fund

Accomplishments:

- New non-tariff barriers in intra-community trade are prohibited
- A CEEAC clearing house was established in February 1989
- Legislation on road transport is being harmonized, as are flight schedules and air transport tariffs
- Interconnection of telecommunication networks within Pan African Telecommunications Network

Status: active, as of 1993
(YEARBOOK OF INTERNATIONAL ORGANIZATIONS, 1993/94: 388)

Latin America

1960 MERCADO COMUN CENTROAMERICANO (MCCA)

Established: General Treaty on Central American Economic Integration signed in Managua on 13 December 1960; Secretariat in Guatemala City

Members: El Salvador, Guatemala, Honduras, Nicaragua; Costa Rica joined 23 September 1963

Goals: Customs union

Accomplishments:

- Central American Central Banks System (SBCC) created 25 February 1964
- By mid-1969, tariff duties on 95% of the tariff items applicable to intrazonal trade had been abolished; a common external tariff covered 95% of tariff items

Difficulties:

- Conflict between El Salvador and Honduras, caused discontinuation of trade from July 1969 until October 1980
- Honduras withdrew in January 1971
- Some members fear that industrial growth may result in industrial concentration in Guatemala and El Salvador, especially as foreign capital is used in most cases to buy out existing firms
- Coordination of agricultural development programs has proven impossible

Status: Collapsed in the 1980s.

1960 ASOCIACION DE LIBRE COMERCIO (ALALC)
or Latin American Free Trade Association (LAFTA)

Established: Montevideo Treaty signed 18 February 1960; effective 2 June 1961.

Members: Argentina, Brazil, Chile, Mexico, Paraguay, Peru, Uruguay; Colombia and Ecuador joined 1961, Venezuela 1966, and Bolivia 1967.

Goals: Gradual removal of restrictions on trade flows between members over a period not to exceed 12 years

Accomplishments:

- More than 20 industrial complementary agreements concluded; involve specialization in particular products and designed to facilitate reduction of duties and establishment of a common external tariff
- Agreement on multilateral clearing signed in Mexico City, September 1965
- Water Transport Agreement of 30 September 1966, into force May 1974

Difficulties:

- Trade liberalization came to end mid-1960's; in 1967 members failed to agree on list of products in order to liberalize a second 25% of trade
- Absence of progress mainly attributed to wide disparity in members' levels of economic development; alleged that LAFTA is "exercise in Mexican imperialism"

Status: March 1981 replaced by *Asociacion Latinoamericana de Integracion* (ALADI)

1965 CARIBBEAN FREE TRADE ASSOCIATION (CARIFTA)

Established: 15 December 1965 in Dickenson Bay (Antigua-Barbuda) with supplementary agreements signed 18 March 1968 in St. John's (Antigua-Barbuda), 30 April 1968 in St. John's (Antigua-Barbuda), and 13 September 1968 in Georgetown (Guyana).

Status: Inactive, replaced by the Caribbean Community (CARICOM)

1968 EAST CARIBBEAN COMMON MARKET

Established: 11 June 1968 in Grenada

Members: Antigua-Barbuda, Dominica, Grenada, Montserrat, St. Christopher-Nevis, St. Lucia, St. Vincent-Grenadines

Goals: To promote economic integration among members.

Status: Transformed into the Organization of Eastern Caribbean States (OECS) 18 June 1981 (YEARBOOK OF INTERNATIONAL ORGANIZATIONS, 1984/85: 471)

1973 THE CARIBBEAN COMMUNITY (CARICOM)

Established: Treaty of Chaguaramas (Trinidad) signed 4 July 1973, effective 1 August 1973.

Members: Barbados, Guyana, Jamaica, Trinidad and Tobago; Bahamas became a member in July 1983. St. Kitts-Nevis-Anguilla (currently St. Kitts and Nevis) become members in 1974 and Bahamas in July 1983. The treaty became effective for Belize, Dominica, Grenada, Montserrat, St. Vincent and St. Lucia (currently St. Vincent and the Grenadines) 1 May 1974.

Goals:

- Replaced and extended the work of the now inactive CARIFTA
- Intragroup trade liberalization
- Common external tariff and common protective policy for trade with outside countries
- Harmonization of fiscal incentives to industry and taxation arrangements
- Coordinate economic policies and development planning
- Assist less developed countries within the community

Accomplishments:

- Common tariff to be implemented 1 January 1991 for larger members
- Caribbean Development Bank (Caribank) instituted 26 January 1970
- Caribbean Investment Corporation instituted 28 August 1973 to promote industrial development

Status: Active

1975 SISTEMA ECONOMICO LATINOAMERICANO (SELA)

Established: Agreement signed 18 October 1975 as successor to Special Committee for Latin American Coordination (CECLA); entered into force 16 June 1976; headquarters Caracas.

Members: Argentina, Barbados, Belize, Bolivia, Brazil, Chile, Colombia, Costa Rica, Cuba, Dominican Republic, Ecuador, El Salvador, Grenada, Guatemala, Guyana, Haiti, Honduras, Jamaica, Mexico, Nicaragua, Panama, Paraguay, Peru, Suriname, Trinidad-Tobago, Uruguay, Venezuela.

Goals: To create a permanent advisory organ for cooperation and coordination of members' policy stance in international organizations and to promote "the integral, self-sustaining and independent development of the region."

Accomplishments:

- Established PLACIEX, a financing mechanism to support multinational cooperation projects with special emphasis on the pre-investment stage to channel non-reimbursable and reimbursable resources, which became fully operational in 1987 (YEARBOOK OF INTERNATIONAL ORGANIZATIONS, 1993/94: 1205).

Status: Active

Bibliography

Aluko, Olajide. 1985. "The Expulsion of Illegal Aliens from Nigeria: A Study in Nigeria's Decision-Making," *African Affairs* 8A (No. 337, October): 539–550.

Anderson, Charles W. 1967. *Politics and Economic Change in Latin America.* Princeton: Van Nostrand.

Armas, A. 1978. *Philippine Intra-ASEAN Trade Liberalization,* IEDR Discussion Paper No. 78–13, University of the Philippines, School of Economics.

Aronson, Jonathan D. 1985. "Muddling through the Debt Decade," pp. 127–151 in W. Ladd Hollist and F. LaMond, eds. *An International Political Economy.* Boulder, CO: Westview Press.

Asante, S. K. B. 1986. *The Political Economy of Regionalism in Africa: A Decade of the Economic Community of West African States.* New York: Praeger.

———. 1985. "Development and Regional Integration since 1980," pp. 79–99 in Adebayo Adedeji and Timothy M. Shaw, eds. *Economic Crisis in Africa.* Boulder, CO: Lynne Reinner Publishers, Inc.

———. 1985b. "ECOWAS/CEAO: Conflict and Cooperation in West Africa," in Ralph I. Onwuka and Amadu Sesay, eds. *The Future of Regionalism in Africa.* New York: St. Martin's Press.

———. 1982. "Seven Years of ECOWAS: Trade Problems and Prospects," *West Africa* (May 24): 1369–1377.

Asiodu, Phillip C. 1971. "Planning for Further Development in Nigeria," in A. A. Ayida and H. M. A. Onitiri, eds. *Reconstruction in Nigeria.* Ibadan: Oxford University.

Atria, Raul B., et al. 1974. "Chile: actores y agentes politicos internos del proceso de integracion andina," pp. 92–143 in *Variables Politicos de la Integracion Andina.* Santiago: Ediciones Nueva Universidad, Universidad Catolica de Chile.

Axelrod, Robert. 1984. *The Evolution of Cooperation*. New York: Basic Books.

Axelrod, Robert, and Robert O. Keohane. 1985. "Achieving Cooperation under Anarchy: Strategies and Institutions," *World Politics* (October): 226–254.

Balabkins, Nicholas. 1982. *Indigenization and Economic Development; The Nigerian Experience*. Greenwich, CT: JAI Press, Inc.

Balassa, Bela A. 1981. *The Newly Industrializing Countries in the World Economy*. New York: Pergamon Press.

———. 1965. *Economic Development and Integration*. Mexico: Centro de Estudios Monetarios Latinamericanos.

———. 1961. *The Theory of Economic Integration*. Homewood, IL: Richard D. Irwin.

———, and Ardy Stoutjesdijk. 1975. "Economic Integration among Developing Countries," *Journal of Common Market Studies* 14 (September): 37–55.

Bohm-Bawerk, E. V. 1889. *Capital and Interest*. South Holland, IL: Libertarian Press.

———. 1914. *History and Critique of Interest Theories*. South Holland, IL: Libertarian Press.

Bond, Robert D. 1978. "Regionalism in Latin America: Prospects for the Latin American Economic System," *International Organization* 32 (No. 2, Spring): 401–423.

Bonner, Raymond. 1987. *Waltzing with a Dictator: The Marcoses and the Making of American Policy*. New York: Times Books.

Boyd, Gavin. 1984. "Pacific Community Formation: Scope for Innovative Service Enterprises." Paper presented at the Academy of International Business International Meeting, Singapore, June 14–16.

Bull, Hedley. 1971. "The New Balance of Power in Asia and the Pacific," *Foreign Affairs* 49, No. 4 (July): 669–681.

Burns, E. Bradford. 1987. *At War in Nicaragua: The Reagan Doctrine and the Politics of Nostalgia*. New York: Harper and Row.

Buss, Claude A. 1977. *The United States and the Philippines*. Washington, DC: American Enterprise Institute for Public Policy Research.

Calvert, Peter. 1986. *The Foreign Policy of New States*. New York: St. Martin's Press.

———. 1983. *Politics, Power and Revolution: An Introduction to Comparative Politics*. Brighton, Sussex, UK: Harvester.

Caporaso, James A. 1978a. "Introduction," special issue, *International Organization* 32 (Winter): 1–12.

———. 1978b. "Dependence and Dependency in the Global System," special issue, *International Organization* 32 (Winter): 13–43.

Castro, Amado. 1982. "ASEAN Economic Cooperation," pp. 70–91 in Alison Broinowski, ed. *Understanding ASEAN*. New York: St. Martin's Press.

Commission of the European Communities. 1991. *The Countries of the Greater Arab Maghreb and the European Community*. Brussels, Belgium: Europe Information.

Cooper, Richard C. 1972. "Economic Interdependence and Foreign Policies in the 1970's," *World Politics* 24 (January): 158–181.

Davies, Arthur. 1983. "Cost-Benefit Analysis within ECOWAS," *The World Today* 39 (No. 5 May): 170–176.

Deutsch, Karl W. 1969. *Nationalism and Its Alternatives.* New York: Alfred A. Knopf.

——. 1964. "Communication Theory and Political Integration," pp. 46–74 in Philip E. Jacob and James V. Toscano, eds. *The Integration of Political Communities.* Philadelphia, PA: Lippincott.

——, et al. 1957. *Political Community and the North Atlantic Area.* Princeton: Princeton University Press.

——. 1954. *Political Community at the International Level.* Garden City, NY: Doubleday and Company.

——. 1953. *Nationalism and Social Communication: An Inquiry into the Foundations of Nationality.* Cambridge, MA: Technology Press.

Drummond, Stuart. 1982. "Fifteen Years of ASEAN," *Journal of Common Market Studies* XX (No. 4 June): 301–319.

Dudley, Darrel. 1975. *The Andean Movement: An Appraisal.* A Contract Study for the US Department of State. (September)

Eckstein, Harry. 1975. "Case Study and Theory in Political Science," in F. I. Greenstein and N. W. Polsby, eds. *Handbook of Political Science, VII.* Reading, MA: Addison-Wesley.

Economic Community of West African States. 1981. *ECOWAS, Development of the Community, the First Five Years, 1977–81.* Lagos: ECOWAS.

Etzioni, Amitai. 1965. *Political Unification.* New York: Holt, Rinehart and Winston.

Ezenwe, Uka. 1977. "The Distribution of the Gains of Integration: The Case of ECOWAS." Paper presented at the Inaugural Conference of the West African Economic Association, Lagos, December 18–22.

Falola, Toyin, and Julius Ihonvbere. 1985. *The Rise and Fall of Nigeria's Second Republic, 1979–1984.* London: Zed Books.

Fernandez, Alejandro. 1977. *The Philippines and the United States: The Forging of New Relations.* Quezon City: NSDB-UP Research Program.

Ferris, Elizabeth G. 1979. "National Political Support for Regional Integration: The Andean Pact," *International Organization* 33 (No. 1, Winter): 83–104.

——. 1976. *National Support for the Andean Pact: A Comparative Study of Latin American Foreign Policy.* Unpublished dissertation, University of Florida-Gainesville.

Ffrench-Davis, Ricardo. 1982. "Comparative Advantage, Efficiency and Equity in Collective Self-Reliant Industrialization," pp. 101–120 in Gerald K. Helleiner, ed. *For Good or Evil: Economic Theory and North-South Negotiations.* Toronto: University of Toronto Press.

Fifield, Russell H. 1979. *National and Regional Interests in ASEAN: Competition and Cooperation in International Politics.* Singapore: Institute of Southeast Asian Studies.

Fisher, I. 1930. *The Theory of Interest.* New York: Macmillan.

Foltz, William J. 1965. *From French West Africa to the Mali Federation.* Hartford, CT: The Connecticut Printers, Inc.

Fontaine, Roger W. 1977. *The Andean Pact: A Political Analysis.* Beverly Hills, CA: Sage Publications.

Frei, Montalva Eduardo. 1976. "El retiro de Chile, un error irreversible e irreparable," pp. 10–20 in Eduardo Frei Montalva, ed. *Chile y el Pacto Andino.* Santiago.

Friedrich, Carl J. 1968. *Trends of Federalism—Theory and Practice.* London: Allen and Unwin.

Frost, Frank. 1982. "ASEAN and Australia," pp. 144–168 in Alison Broinowski, ed. *Understanding ASEAN.* New York: St. Martin's Press.

———. 1980. "The Origins and Evolution of ASEAN," *World Review,* University of Queensland Press (August).

Fullmer, Robert G. 1973. "The Andean Common Market: Implications for US Business," *Overseas Business Reports* (No. 49, October): 1–17.

Furtado, Celso. 1964. *Development and Underdevelopment.* Translated by Ricardo W. de Aguiar and Eric Charles Drysdale. Berkeley, CA: University of California Press.

Galtung, Johan. 1968. "Structural Theory of Integration," *Journal of Peace Research* V (No. 4).

Gambari, Ibrahim A. 1991. *Political and Comparative Dimensions of Regional Integration: The Case of ECOWAS.* Atlantic Highlands, NJ: Humanities Press International, Inc.

Geertz, Clifford. 1964. "Ideology as a Cultural System," pp. 47–76 in David E. Apter, ed. *Ideology and Discontent.* New York: Free Press.

George, Alexander. 1979. "Case Study and Theory Development: The Method of Structured, Focused Comparison," pp. 43–68 in Paul Gordon, ed. *Diplomacy: New Approaches in History, Theory and Policy.* New York: Free Press.

———. 1974. "Assessing Presidential Character," *World Politics* XXVI (January).

George, Alexander L., and Timothy J. McKeown. 1985. "Case Studies and Theories of Organizational Decision Making," *Advances in Information Processing in Organizations,* II: 21–58.

Goodwin, Barbara. 1987. *Using Political Ideas.* 2nd ed. Chichester: John Wiley & Sons.

Gordon, Bernard K. 1966. *The Dimensions of Conflict in Southeast Asia.* Englewood Cliffs, NJ: Prentice-Hall.

Gravil, Roger. 1985. "The Nigerian Aliens Expulsion Order of 1983," *African Affairs* 84 (No. 337, October): 523–537.

Grieco, Joseph. 1988. "Anarchy and the Limits of Cooperation: A Realist Critique of the Newest Liberal Institutionalism," *International Organization,* 42, No. 3 (Summer): 485–508.

Grisanti, Hugo A. 1976. "Consecuencias de retiro del Pacto Andino," *El Mercurio* (November 18): 2.

Groom, A.J.R., and Paul Taylor, eds. 1975. *Functionalism, Theory and Practice in International Relations.* London: University of London Press Ltd.

Grunwald, Joseph, Miguel Wionczek, and Martin Carnoy. 1972. *Latin American Integration and U.S. Policy.* Washington, DC: The Brookings Institution.

Haas, Ernst B. 1990. *When Knowledge is Power, Three Models of Change in*

International Organizations. Berkeley, CA: University of California Press.

———. 1983. "Words Can Hurt You; Or Who Said What to Whom About Regimes," in Stephen D. Krasner, ed. *International Regimes.* Ithaca, NY: Cornell University Press.

———. 1976. "Turbulent Fields and the Theory of Regional Integration," *International Organization* 30 (No. 2): 173–212.

———. 1971. "The Study of Regional Integration: Reflections on the Joy and Anguish of Pretheorizing," pp. 3–42 in Leon N. Lindberg and Stuart A. Scheingold, eds. *Regional Integration: Theory and Research.* Cambridge, MA: Harvard University Press.

———. 1970. *The Web of Interdependence; the US and International Organizations.* Englewood Cliffs, NJ: Prentice Hall.

———. 1968. "Technology, Pluralism, and the New Europe," pp. 149–176 in Joseph S. Nye, Jr., ed. *International Regionalism.* Boston: Little, Brown.

———. 1967. "The Uniting of Europe and the Uniting of Latin America," *Journal of Common Market Studies* 5 (June): 315–343.

———. 1964. *Beyond the Nation-State: Functionalism and International Organization.* Stanford, CA: Stanford University Press.

———. 1958. *The Uniting of Europe: Political, Economic, and Social Forces, 1950–57.* Stanford, CA: Stanford University Press.

Hanna, Willard A. "Sabotaging Sabah," *Southeast Asia Series* XVI (15): 1–29.

Hardin, Russell. 1982. *Collective Action.* Baltimore, MD: Johns Hopkins University Press for Resources for the Future.

Harf, James E., D. G. Hoovler, and T. E. James, Jr. 1974. "Systemic and External Attributes in Foreign Policy Analysis," in James N. Rosenau, ed. *Comparing Foreign Policies: Theories, Findings, and Methods.* Beverly Hills, CA: Sage.

Hazlewood, Arthur. 1980. "Economic Instrumentalities of Statecraft and the End of the EAC," pp. 141–143 in Christian Potholm and Richard A. Fredland, eds. *Integration and Disintegration in East Africa.* Lanham, MD: University Press of America.

Healey, Derek. 1977. *Integration Schemes among Developing Countries: A Survey.* Adelaide: Centre for Asian Studies.

Ho, Kwon Ping. 1982. "ASEAN: The Five Countries," pp. 196–237 in Alison Broinowski, ed. *Understanding ASEAN.* New York: St. Martin's Press.

Hoffman, Stanley. 1965. *The State of War: Essays on the Theory and Practice of International Politics.* New York: Praeger.

Hojmann, David. 1981. "The Andean Pact: Failure of a Model of Economic Integration?" *Journal of Common Market Studies* XX (No. 2, December): 139–160.

"How Will Multinational Firms React to the Andean Pact's D24?" *Inter-American Economic Affairs* XXV 1971 (Autumn, 2): 55–65.

Huntington, Samuel P. 1968. *Political Order in Changing Societies.* New Haven, CT: Yale University Press.

Indorff, H. H. 1975. *ASEAN: Problems and Prospects.* Occasional Paper No. 38. Singapore: Institute of Southeast Asian Studies (December).

Irvine, David. 1982. "Making Haste Less Slowly: ASEAN from 1975," pp. 37–

69 in Alison Broinowski, ed. *Understanding ASEAN*. New York: St. Martin's Press.

Irvine, Roger. 1982. "The Formative Years of ASEAN: 1967–75," pp. 8–36 in Alison Broinowski, ed. *Understanding ASEAN*. New York: St. Martin's Press.

Jevons, W. S. 1871. *Theory of Political Economy*. London: Macmillan.

Jorgensen-Dahl, Arnfinn. 1982. *Regional Organization and Order in South-East Asia*. New York: St. Martin's Press.

Jurado, Gonzalo M. 1976. "Foreign Trade and External Debt," pp. 262–299 in Jose Encarnacion, Jr., ed. *Philippine Economic Problems in Perspective*. Manila: Institute of Economic Development and Research, School of Economics, University of Philippines.

Kador, Bela. 1984. *Structural Changes in the World Economy*. New York: St. Martin's Press.

Kahneman, Daniel, and Amos Tversky. 1979. "Prospect Theory: An Analysis of Decision under Risk," *Econometrica* 47, No. 2 (March): 263–291.

Kaul, Man Mohino. 1978. *The Philippines and Southeast Asia*. New Delhi: Radiant Publishers.

Kelley, Harold H., and John W. Thibaut. 1978. *Interpersonal Relations: A Theory of Interdependence*. New York: John Wiley & Sons.

Keohane, Robert O. 1990. "Multilateralism: an Agenda for Research," *International Journal* 45 (Autumn): 731–764.

———. 1989. *International Institutions and State Power, Essays in International Relations Theory*. Boulder, CO: Westview Press.

———. 1984. *After Hegemony: Cooperation and Discord in the World Political Economy*. Princeton, NJ: Princeton University Press.

———, and Joseph Nye. 1977. *Power and Interdependence: World Politics in Transition*. Boston: Little, Brown.

Komisar, Lucy. 1987. *Corazon Aquino: The Story of a Revolution*. New York: George Braziller.

Krasner, Stephen D., ed. 1983. *International Regimes*. Ithaca, NY: Cornell University Press.

Krause, Laurence B. 1982. *U. S. Economic Policy Toward the Association of Southeast Asian Nations*. Washington, DC: Brookings Institution.

———, and Joseph S. Nye. 1975. "Reflections on the Economics and Politics of International Economic Organizations," *International Organization* 27 (No. 1, Winter): 323–342.

Kreps, David M., Paul Milgrom, John Roberts, and Robert Wilson. 1982. "Rational Cooperation in the Finitely Repeated Prisoners' Dilemma," *Journal of Economic Theory* 27: 245–252.

Lancaster, Carol. 1985. "ECOWAS at Ten," *Africa Report* (July–August): 69–72.

Lanfranco, Sam. 1980. "Industrial Selections for Regional Integration," *Journal of Common Market Studies* 18 (No. 3, March): 272–283.

Langhammer, Rolf J., and Ulrich Hiemanz. 1990. *Regional Integration Among Developing Countries: Opportunities, Obstacles, and Options*. Ann Arbor: University of Michigan.

Lijphart, Arend. 1971. "Comparative Politics and the Comparative Method," *American Political Science Review* 65 (September): 682–693.

———. 1975. "The Comparative Case Strategy in Comparative Research," *Comparative Political Studies* 8 (July): 158–177.

Lim, Robyn. 1980. "Current ASEAN-Australian Relations," *Southeast Asian Affairs* (Singapore): 37–53.

Lin, Lim Yoon. 1975. "The Philippines—Marcos' 'New Society,'" *Southeast Asian Affairs:* 115–126.

———. 1974. "An Overview of the Philippines," *Southeast Asian Affairs:* 175–202.

Lindberg, Leon N. 1971. "Political Integration as a Multidimensional Phenomenon Requiring Multivariate Measurement," pp. 45–127 in Leon N. Lindberg and Stuart A. Scheingold, eds. *Regional Integration: Theory and Research.* Cambridge, MA: Harvard University Press.

———. 1965. "Decisionmaking and Integration in the European Community," *International Organization* XIX (Winter).

Loewenstein, George, and John Elster, eds. 1992. *Choice over Time.* New York: Russell Sage Foundation.

Loewenstein, George, and Drazen Prelec. 1992. "Anomalies in Intertemporal Choice: Evidence and an Interpretation," pp. 119–145 in George Loewenstein and John Elster, eds. *Choice over Time.* New York: Russell Sage Foundation.

Lopez, Salvador P. 1978. "Trends in Philippine Foreign Policy," pp. 53–71 in M. Rajaretnam, ed. *Trends in the Philippines II.* Singapore: Singapore University Press.

Maduagwe, M. O. 1993. "The Military and the Survival of Democracy in Nigeria," *Stanford Journal of International Affairs* II, Issue 1 (Fall/Winter): 63–83.

Marcos, Ferdinand. 1977. "An Earnest Faith in the ASEAN," statement at the Second ASEAN conference, Kuala Lumpur, Malaysia, August 4. *Presidential Speeches,* 11: 308–310.

Mazrui, Ali. 1972. *Cultural Engineering and Nation-Building in East Africa.* Evanston, IL: Northwestern University Press.

McKeown, Timothy J. 1993. "Decision Processes and Co-operation in Foreign Policy," pp. 202–219 in Janice Gross Stein and Louis W. Pauly, eds. *Choosing to Co-Operate: How States Avoid Loss.* Baltimore, MD: The Johns Hopkins University Press.

McLaughlin, Martin M. 1979. *The United States and World Development: Agenda 1979.* New York: Praeger.

Meadows, Martin. 1962. "The Philippine Claim to North Borneo," *Political Science Quarterly* LXXVII (September, No. 3): 321–335.

Meeker, Guy B. 1971. "Fade-out Joint Venture: Can It Work for Latin America?" *Inter-American Economic Affairs* 24 (Spring): 25–42.

Meerhaeghe, Marcel Alfons Gilbert van. 1992. *International Economic Institutions,* 6th ed. Dordrecht, The Netherlands: Kluwer Academic Publishers.

Mendez, Juan Carlos. 1979. *Chilean Economic Policy.* Chile: Calderon y Cia Ltda.

Middlebrook, Kevin. 1978. "Regional Organizations and Andean Economic Integration, 1969–1975," *Journal of Common Market Studies* 17, No. 1 (September): 62–82.

Mikesell, R. F. 1982. "The Theory of Common Markets as Applied to Regional Arrangements among Developing Countries," pp. 204–227 in John M. Letiche, ed. *International Economic Policies and Theoretical Foundations*. New York: Academic Press.

Milenky, Edward S. 1973. "Developmental Nationalism in Practice: The Problems and Progress of the Andean Group," *Inter-American Economic Affairs* 27 (Spring): 49–68.

———. 1971. "From Integration to Developmental Nationalism: The Andean Group 1965–71," *Inter-American Economic Affairs* 25 (Winter): 77–91.

Mitrany, David. 1966. *A Working Peace System*. Chicago: Quadrangle Press.

Morgenthau, Hans J. 1966 (originally published in 1948). *Politics Among Nations*, 4th ed. New York: Knopf.

Morrell, Jim. 1979. "Aid to the Philippines: Who Benefits?" *International Policy Report*, 2 (October): 1–8.

Morse, Edward S. 1970. "The Transformation of Foreign Policies: Modernization, Interdependence, and Externalization," *World Politics* 22 (April): 371–392.

Mytelka, Lynn Krieger. 1984. "Competition, Conflict and Decline in the Union Douaniere et Economique de l'Afrique Centrale (UDEAC)," in Domenico Mazzeo's *African Regional Organizations*. Cambridge: Cambridge University Press.

———. 1979. *Regional Development in a Global Economy*. New Haven, CT: Yale University Press.

Niksch, L. 1978. *ASEAN: An Emerging Challenge in U. S. Policy Towards Asia*. US Congressional Research Service Report. (November).

Nwanna, Gladson I. 1986. "ECOWAS and Labor Migration in West Africa," *Journal of Social, Political and Economic Studies* 11: 163–174.

Nye, Joseph S., Jr. 1971a. "Comparing Common Markets: A Revised Neo-Functionalist Model," pp. 192–231 in Leon N. Lindberg and Stuart A. Scheingold, eds. *Regional Integration: Theory and Research*. Cambridge, MA: Harvard University Press.

———. 1971b. *Peace in Parts: Integration and Conflict in Regional Organizations*. Boston: Little, Brown.

———. 1970. "East African Integration: A Note on Measurement." Paper presented at the Carnegie Endowment Conference on the Scientific Approach to the Study of International Relations, Geneva.

———. 1968. "Comparative Regional Integration: Concept and Measurement," *International Organization* 22 (No. 4, Autumn): 855–880.

Nyong, Francis Etim. 1983. *Nigeria and ECOWAS: The Prospects for Nigeria's Role in ECOWAS; Objectives, Opportunities, Problems, Leadership and Policy*. Unpublished dissertation, Claremont Graduate School.

Ogunsuyi, Austin. 1982. "200 Women Storm Bendel Assembly," *The Nigerian Observer* (February 17): 1.

Ojo, Olantunde J. B. 1980. "Nigeria and the Formation of ECOWAS," *International Organization* (Autumn): 571–604.

Okolo, Julius Emeka, and Stephen Wright. 1989. *West Africa: Regional Cooperation and Development*. Boulder, CO: Westview Press.

Okolo, Julius Emeka. 1984. "West African Regional Integration: ECOWAS."

Paper presented at the 25th Annual Meeting of the International Studies Association, Atlanta, March 27–April 1.

Olaloku, F. A., et al. 1979. *Structure of the Nigeria Economy*. New York: St. Martin's Press.

Olayiwola, Peter O. 1987. *Petroleum and Structural Change in a Country: The Case of Nigeria*. New York: Praeger.

Olson, Mancur, Jr. 1965. *The Logic of Collective Action*. Cambridge, MA: Harvard University Press.

Onwuka, Ralph I., and Amadu Sesay. 1985. *The Future of Regionalism in Africa*. New York: St. Martin's Press.

Onwuka, Ralph I. 1982. "The ECOWAS Protocol on the Free Movement of Persons: A Threat to Nigerian Security?" *African Affairs* 80 (No. 323, April): 193–203.

———. 1980. "The ECOWAS Treaty: Inching towards Implementation," *The World Today* 36 (February): 52–59.

Onyemelukwe, J. O. C. 1984. *Industrialization in West Africa*. New York: St. Martin's Press.

Ortiz, Pacifico A. 1963. "Legal Aspects of the North Borneo Question," *Philippine Studies* 11 (1, January).

Oye, Kenneth A. 1985. "Explaining Cooperation under Anarchy: Hypotheses and Strategies," *World Politics* 38 (October): 1–24.

Pentland, Charles. 1973. *International Theory and European Integration*. New York: Free Press.

Phanit, Thakur. 1980. *Regional Integration Attempts in Southeast Asia: A Study of ASEAN's Problems and Progress*. Ann Arbor, MI: University Microfilms International.

Prebisch, Raul. 1963. *Towards a Dynamic Development Policy for Latin America*. New York: United Nations.

Przeworksi, A., and H. Teune. 1970. *The Logic of Comparative Social Inquiry*. New York: Wiley-Interscience.

Puchala, Donald S. 1970. "Integration and Disintegration in Franco-German Relations, 1954–1965," *International Organization* 24 (Spring): 183–208.

Puyana de Palacios, Alicia. 1982. *Economic Integration Among Uneven Partners: The Case of the Andean Group*. New York: Pergamon Press.

Quintos, Rolando N. 1968. "Nationalism and the Claim to Sabah," *Solidarity* 3 (August): 1–9.

Rajaretnam, M., ed. 1978. *Trends in the Philippines II*. Singapore: Singapore University Press.

———. 1976. "The Philippines: A Question of Earnest Intentions," *Southeast Asian Affairs:* 253–268.

Riker, William H. 1964. *Federalism: Origin, Operation, Significance*. Boston: Little, Brown.

———. 1962. *The Theory of Political Coalitions*. New Haven, CT: Yale University Press.

Rix, Alan. 1982. "ASEAN and Japan: More than Economics," pp. 144–168 in Alison Broinowski, ed. *Understanding ASEAN*. New York: St. Martin's Press.

Robson, Peter. 1990. "Economic Integration in Africa: A New Phase?" in James

Pickett and Hans Singer, eds. *Towards Economic Recovery in Sub-Saharan Africa*. London: Routledge.

———. 1980. *The Economics of International Integration*. London: Allen & Unwin.

———. 1978. "Regional Economic Cooperation among Developing Countries," *World Development* 6: 771–777.

———. 1971. *International Economic Integration*. London: Penguin Books.

———. 1968. *Economic Integration in Africa*. London: Allen & Unwin.

Rosecrance, Richard. 1973. *International Relations: Peace or War?* New York: McGraw-Hill.

Rosenau, James N. 1980. *The Scientific Study of Foreign Policy*. New York: Nichols.

———, and G. Hoggard. 1974. "Foreign Policy Behavior in Dyadic Relationships: Testing a Pre-theoretical Extension," in James N. Rosenau, ed. *Comparing Foreign Policies: Theories, Findings, and Methods*. Beverly Hills, CA: Sage.

———. 1966. "Pre-theories and Theories of Foreign Policy," pp. 27–92 in R. Barry Farrell, ed. *Approaches to Comparative and International Studies*. Evanston, IL: Northwestern University Press.

Ruggie, John Gerard. 1982. "International Regimes, Transactions, and Change: Embedded Liberalism in the Postwar Economic Order," *International Organization* 36, No. 2 (Spring): 379–345.

Russett, Bruce M. 1967. *International Regimes and the International System: A Study in Political Ecology*. Chicago: Rand McNally.

Samuelson, Paul A. 1937. "A Note on Measurement of Utility," *Review of Economic Studies* 4: 155–161.

Sandholtz, Wayne. 1993. "Institutions and Collective Action, The New Telecommunications in Western Europe," *World Politics* 45, No. 2: 243–270.

Scheingold, Stuart A. 1970. "Domestic and International Consequences of Regional Integration," *International Organization* 24 (Fall): 978–1002.

Schmitter, Philippe C. 1970. "A Revised Theory of Regional Integration," *International Organization* 24 (No. 4): 836–868.

———. 1969. "Further Notes on Operationalizing some Variables Related to Regional Integration," *International Organization* 23 (Spring): 327–336.

Seah, Chee-meow. 1980. "Major Powers in the Search for a New Equilibrium in Southeast Asia," *Asian Pacific Community* (No. 7, Winter).

Segal, Aaron. 1967. "The Integration of Developing Countries: Some Thoughts on East Africa and Central America." *Journal of Common Market Studies* 5 (March).

Senior, N. W. 1836. *An Outline of the Science of Political Economy*. London: Clowes and Sons.

Shaw, Timothy M., and Olajide Aluko, eds. 1984. *The Political Economy of African Foreign Policy*. New York: St. Martin's Press.

Sigmund, Paul E. 1977. *The Overthrow of Allende and the Politics of Chile, 1964–1976*. Pittsburgh: University of Pittsburgh Press.

Simon, Herbert A. 1958. *Administration Behavior*. New York: Macmillan.

———. 1957. "A Behavioral Model of Rational Choice," pp. 241–260 in Simon, ed. *Models of Man: Social and Rational*. New York: Wiley.

————. 1955. "A Behavioral Model of Rational Choice," *Quarterly Journal of Economics*, LXIX (February): 99–118.

Sinaga, Edward Janner. 1974. *ASEAN: Economic, Political and Defense Problems, Progress, and Prospects in Regional Cooperation with Reference to the Role of Major Powers in Southeast Asia*. Ann Arbor, MI: University Microfilms International.

Singer, J. David. 1961. "The Level-of-Analysis Problem in International Relations," pp. 77–92 in Klaus Knorr and Sidney Verba, eds. *The International System*. Princeton, NJ: Princeton University Press.

Snidal, Duncan. 1991. "International Cooperation among Relative Gains Maximizers," *International Studies Quarterly* 35 (December): 387–402.

Spaak, Paul Henry. 1968. *The Crises of the Atlantic Alliance*. Mershon Center Pamphlet Series, No. 5. Columbus, OH: Ohio University Press.

"Special Issue: Chile Blood on the Peaceful Road." 1974. *Latin American Perspectives* I (2), (Summer).

Stein, Arthur A. 1990. *Why Nations Cooperate: Circumstance and Choice in International Relations*. Ithaca: Cornell University Press.

Stein, Janice Gross. 1992. "International Cooperation and Loss Avoidance: Framing the Problem," *International Journal* XLVII (Spring): 202–234.

Sweeney, Jane P. 1984. *The First European Elections*. Boulder, CO: Westview Press.

Takirambudde, Peter N. 1991. "Regional Co-operation and Trade Liberalization," pp. 37–58 in Oliver S. Saasa, ed. *Joining the Future*. Nairobi: ACTS.

Tanco, Arturo R., Jr. 1978. "The Philippines in the 1980s: An Overview," pp. 137–183 in M. Rajaretnam, ed. *Trends in the Philippines II*. Singapore: Singapore University Press.

Taylor, Bryan Wilson, III. 1981. *The Political Economy of Chile under Allende and Pinochet*. Unpublished master's thesis, University of South Carolina.

Taylor, Michael. 1987. *The Possibility of Cooperation*. Cambridge, MA: Cambridge University Press.

Taylor, Paul. 1968. "The Concept of Community and the European Integration Process," *Journal of Common Market Studies* 7 (December): 83–101.

Taylor, Phillip. 1984. *Nonstate Actors in International Politics*. Boulder, CO: Westview Press.

Tijjani, Aminu, and David Williams, eds. 1981. *Shehu Shagari: My Vision of Nigeria*. London: Frank Cass.

Tjonneland, Elling N. 1992. *Southern Africa After Apartheid*. Bergen, Norway: Bergen Print Service.

Tversky, Amos, and Daniel Kahneman. 1986. "Rational Choice and the Framing of Decisions," *Journal of Business* 59 (October): S251–278.

Union of International Associations. *Yearbook of International Organizations*. Munchen: K. G. Sour, various issues.

Vargas-Hildalgo, Rafael. 1979. "The Crisis of the Andean Pact: Lessons for Integration among Developing Countries," *Journal of Common Market Studies* XVII (No. 3, March): 213–226.

Viner, Jacob. 1950. *The Customs Union Issue*. New York: Carnegie Endowment for International Peace.

Vreeland, Nena, Geoffrey B. Hurwitz, Peter Just, Philip W. Moeller, and R. S.

Shinn. 1976. *Area Handbook for the Philippines,* 2nd ed. Washington, DC: US Government Printing Office.

Wardlaw, Andrew B. 1973. *The Andean Movement: A Report Prepared under Contract for the US Department of State.* Washington, DC: Government Printing Office.

Watts, Michael, and Paul Lubeck. 1983. "The Popular Classes and the Oil Boom: A Political Economy of Rural and Urban Poverty," pp. 105–144 in I. William Zartman, ed. *The Political Economy of Nigeria.* New York: Praeger.

Weatherbee, Donald E. 1987. "The Philippines and ASEAN: Options for Aquino," *Asian Survey* XXVII (No. 12, December): 1223–1239.

Williams, David. 1982. *The President and Power in Nigeria: The Life of Shehu Shagari.* London: Totowa.

Wionczek, Miguel. 1968. "Latin American Integration and U. S. Economic Policies," in Robert Gregg, ed. *International Organization in the Western Hemisphere.* Syracuse, NY: Syracuse University Press.

Wright, Martin, ed. 1988. *Revolution in the Philippines? A Keesings' Special Report.* Harlow, Essex, UK: Longman Group UK Limited.

Wright, Stephen. 1982. "Nigeria: A Mid-Term Assessment," *The World Today* (March): 105–113.

Wong, John. 1979. *ASEAN Economies in Perspective.* Philadelphia: Institute for the Study of Human Issues.

Yansane, A. Y. 1977a. "Economic Community of West African States (ECO-WAS)," *Review of Black Political Economy* 7 (Spring): 215–237.

———. 1977b. "West African Economic Integration: Is ECOWAS the Answer?" *Africa Today* 24 (July): 43–59.

Yeats, Alexander J. 1981. *Trade and Development Policies.* London: Macmillan and Company.

Young, Oran. 1991. "Political Leadership and Regime Formation: On the Development of Institutions in International Society," *International Organization* 45 (Summer).

———. 1989. *International Cooperation: Building Regimes for Natural Resources and the Environment.* Ithaca, NY: Cornell University Press.

Zartman, I. William, ed. 1983. *The Political Economy of Nigeria.* New York: Praeger Publishers.

JOURNALS, NEWSPAPERS, AND OTHER PERIODICALS

Africa Diary, Delhi
Africa Now, Cedar Grove, NJ
Africa Report, New York
Africa Research Bulletin, Exeter
Andean Report
Asian Almanac, Singapore
Bank of London and South America Review, London
Business Latin America, New York
Daily Express, Manila

Daily Sketch, Ibadan
Daily Times, Lagos
Eastern Star, Malaysia/Singapore
The Economist, London
El Mercurio, Santiago
Far Eastern Economic Review, Hong Kong
Fookien Times Yearbook
International Herald Tribune, New York
Latin America, London
Latin American Perspective, Riverside, CA
The London Times, London
Manila Times, Manila
National Concord, Lagos
New Nigeria, Kaduna
New Nigerian, Lagos
The New York Times, New York
Nigerian Observer, Benin City
Nigerian Tribune, Ibadan
Nigeria Yearbook
Philippine Daily Express, Manila
Philippine News
Punch, Lagos
South, London
Straits Times, Singapore
Sunday Concord, Lagos
UN Yearbook of International Trade Statistics. New York, 1965–1980.
The Wall Street Journal, New York
Washington Post, Washington
West Africa, London

Index

Agenda, 3, 58, 104, 112, 133, 135, 137, 139
Alessandi, Jorge, 45
Allende, Salvador, 27, 45–47, 49, 50, 53, 54, 67, 69 nn.9, 7, 70 nn.10, 12, 14, 71 nn.14, 16, 132
Aluko, Olajide, 88, 91
Andean Pact, 3, 4, 7, 10, 28, 43, 44, 47–58, 60–61, 63–66, 68, 69 n.9, 71 n.15, 126–129, 131, 132, 140, 141; Agreement of Cartegena, 48, 56, 62; Commission, 49–51, 58, 62
Anderson, Charles W., 18
Argentina, 47, 48, 51, 60, 61
Armas, A., 118
Association of Southeast Asia (ASA), 101, 106, 107, 108, 109, 110, 123 n.3
Association of Southeast Asian Nations (ASEAN), 3–4, 7–10, 78, 94, 99, 102–105, 107–110, 113–122, 123 n.9, 124 nn.10, 11, 126–128, 132, 136, 138–141; Bangkok Declaration, 102, 108
Asante, S. K. B., 77, 79, 83, 94, 95
Atria, Raul B., 69 n.9
Australia, 104, 105, 118, 119, 122
Axelrod, Robert, 19, 21, 40 n.1, 30, 135

Baba, Alhaji Ali, 8, 74, 88, 95 n.2, 91
Balabkins, Nicholas, 84
Balassa, Bela A., 32, 33, 34
Benin (Dahomey), 11, 75, 76, 77, 79, 80, 81, 82, 95, 96 n.9, 139
Bohm-Bawerk, E. V., 42 n.13
Bolivia, 11, 48, 50, 52, 57, 58, 59, 61, 65
Bond, Robert D., 18, 47, 69 n.6
Boyd, Gavin, 17
Brann, C. M. B., 77
Brazil, 47, 48, 57, 61
Brunei, 11, 101, 122; Sultan of, 100
Bull, Hedley, 116
Burns, E. Bradford, 11 n.1
Buss, Claude A., 106, 115

Cambodia, 107, 115
Cameroon, 74, 77, 87, 90, 91
Cape Verde, 11, 81, 96 n.8
Castro, Amado, 123 n.8, 124 n.10
Castro, Sergio de, 50, 54, 61, 62
Center for Studies on Company Development, Chile, 50, 61
Chad, 74, 75, 76, 77, 88
Chile, 3, 4, 7, 10, 11, 23, 24, 27, 28, 38, 43–45, 48–51, 53–63, 65–67, 69 n.7, 70 nn.10, 11, 13, 14, 71 n.14,

Chile (*continued*)
72 n.17, 127, 128, 129, 130, 131, 132, 135, 140; Aylwin, Patricio, 70 n.14; Christian Democrats, 45, 52, 54, 56, 60, 66, 68, 70 n.14, 71 n.14, 131, 132; copper, 44–46, 48, 53, 64, 68 nn.1, 3, 70 n.11; debt, 43, 45–47, 69 n.4; Decree Law 600 (D600), 55, 57–59, 63; human rights in , 47, 55, 60, 68; Junta, 7, 43, 46, 47, 50, 54–57, 60, 61, 63, 66, 68, 70–71 nn.14, 16, 126, 131, 132, 142 n.1; Socialist leadership of, 49, 53, 54, 66–68, 69 n.9; (un)employment in, 43, 45, 47, 53, 61, 63, 69 n.4

Club of Paris, 46, 47

Coalition, 16, 18, 19, 68 n.2, 71 n.16, 89, 122

Cognitive framing model, 3, 5, 10, 13, 14, 18, 19, 21–24, 27–28, 31, 36, 126, 127

Collective good(s), 20, 21, 135, 136

Colombia, 11, 44, 47, 48, 49, 58, 59, 61, 62

Communaute Economique de l'Afrique de l'Ouest (CEAO), 5, 80, 81

Community, 69 n.9, 80, 136, 140, 142

Confrontation, The 107, 109

Cooper, Richard C., 40 n.4

Corregidor Affair, 102, 109

Customs union(s), 32–35, 80; theory, 28, 31, 36, 38, 120, 125, 130, 131

Côte d'Ivoire, 11, 77, 78, 79, 96 n.9

Davies, Arthur, 96 n.9

Decision 24 (Statute on the Common Treatment of Foreign Capital, Trademarks, Patents, Licensing Agreements, and Royalties, D24), 7, 23, 28, 43, 48, 50–54, 56–66, 68, 69 n.9, 70 nn.10, 12, 71 n.16, 126, 127, 128, 129, 130, 131, 132

de Overbeck, Baron, 100–101, 122 n.2

Dependency, 132; theory, 131

de Tocqueville, Alexis, 42 n.14

Deutsch, Karl W., 17, 18, 136

Diaby-Ouattara, Aboubakar, 78, 96 n.11

Economic Community of West African States (ECOWAS), 3, 4, 7, 8, 10, 73–74, 76—83, 86, 88–89, 91–95, 96 nn.4, 5, 6, 9, 10, 97 nn.13, 14, 126, 127, 128, 132, 138, 139, 140, 141; Authority of Heads of State and Government, 76, 81–82, 88, 96; Fund for Cooperation, Compensation, and Development, 82, 95, 96 n.11, 138; Pan African Telecommunications Project, 95, 141; Treaty of the, 76, 81, 93, 95, 96 nn.4, 5

Ecuador, 11, 48, 52, 57, 58, 59, 61, 64, 65

El Mercurio, 54, 60, 63, 69–70 n.10

Elster, John, 29, 41 n.8, 42 nn.13, 14

Entrepreneurship (political), 125, 133, 136–137

Etzioni, Amitai, 17

European Communities/Union, 1, 2, 17, 47, 51, 76, 94, 117, 118, 136, 142

Falola, Toyin, 73, 85, 90, 91

Fernandez, Alejandro, 116

Ferris, Elizabeth G., 55, 56

Fifield, Russell H., 106, 109, 110, 119

Fisher, I., 42 n.13

Fontaine, Roger W., 47, 49, 52, 58, 64

France, 79, 80, 83, 96 n.7

Free trade, 2, 7, 20, 32–35, 118, 125; theory, 29, 31, 36, 38, 120, 125, 130, 131

Frei Montalva, Eduardo, 45, 47, 48, 53, 54, 56, 60–61, 63, 70–71 n.14, 131, 132

Functionalism, 1, 3, 5, 16, 17, 18, 40 n.4

Gambari, Ibrahim A., 81, 96 n.9

Geertz, Clifford, 28

George, Alexander L., 6, 11 n.4

Ghana, 8, 11, 73, 74, 75, 76, 77, 82, 88, 89, 91, 96 n.9, 97 n.13

Goodwin, Barbara, 27

Gowon, Yakubu, 78, 79, 80, 142 n.1

Gravil, Roger, 75, 91, 92, 96 n.7

Greater Malay Confederation ("Maphilindo"), 101, 106, 107, 108, 109

Grieco, Joseph, 19, 21
Guinea, 11, 77, 95, 96 nn.8, 9, 97 n.13
Guinea-Bissau, 11, 81, 96 n.9

Haas, Ernst B., 17, 18, 40 n.4, 80, 134, 137, 138
Hanna, Willard A., 101, 103
Hardin, Russell, 143 n.3
Hazlewood, Arthur, 17, 18
Healey, Derek, 18
Hegemon(y), 19, 20, 21, 121
Hoffman, Stanley, 16
Hojmann, David, 57
Huntington, Samuel P., 18, 37, 142 n.2

Ideology, 3, 6, 7, 10, 14, 18, 22, 26–28, 36, 38, 56, 57, 60, 66, 94, 105, 120, 126, 131–132, 138, 139; Friedmanite, 28, 43, 46, 53, 54, 67, 126, 127, 132
Ihonvbere, Julius, 73, 85, 90, 91
Indonesia, 11, 101, 105–107, 109, 111, 116–118
Institution(s), effective, 10, 19, 20, 29, 30, 133, 135, 136, 138, 141–142
Institutionalization, 18, 21, 39, 106, 134, 135, 142 n.2
Integration 1, 5, 7, 9, 17, 33–35, 38, 39, 47–51, 57, 59, 63, 66, 68, 69 n.9, 79, 81; regional, 125, 128, 129, 131–133, 136, 143 n.3; theory, 28, 31, 34, 36, 38, 120
Interdependence, 1, 17, 19, 21; theory/literature, 16, 19, 40 n.4
Irvine, David, 118, 119, 124 n.10
Irvine, Roger, 106, 107, 108, 109, 118
Islam(ism), 100–102, 112–113, 121, 123 n.5; insurgency, 8, 24, 27, 99, 104, 111–112, 114, 120, 127, 128, 129, 130, 131, 142 n.1
Iteration, 21, 30, 135

Japan, 51, 115, 117, 118, 119, 122
Jevons, W. S., 42 n.13
Jorgensen-Dhal, Arnfinn, 100, 105, 109

Kahneman, Daniel, 24, 25, 41 n.11
Kaul, Man Mohino, 106
Kelley, Harold H., 21, 22
Keohane, Robert O., 15, 16, 18, 19, 30, 39 n.1, 40 nn.4, 5, 133, 135, 142 n.2
Khaddafy, Muammar, 112, 113
Komisar, Lucy, 123 n.6
Krasner, Stephen D., 19
Krause, Laurence B., 17

Lancaster, Carol, 82, 95, 96 n.11
Lanfranco, Sam, 18
Latin American Free Trade Association (LAFTA), 47–49, 51, 69 nn.5, 6, 131
Leadership, 15, 17, 28, 39, 60, 65, 66, 68, 70, 139; entrepreneurial, 137–138; intellectual, 136–138, 140; political, 1, 4, 10, 35, 37, 125–126, 133, 136, 138, 140; regional, 3, 32, 67, 73, 99, 105, 116, 127, 134, 139, 142
Legitimacy, 39, 135
Liberalism, 2, 5, 10, 13, 14, 15, 16, 19, 21, 32, 47, 65, 66, 126, 127; economic, 76, 126; economic theory, 28, 32, 46, 65, 76, 127; economic neoliberalism, 7, 47, 66, 68
Libya, 112, 113, 121
Lin, Lim Yoon, 112
Lindberg, Leon N., 17, 18, 40 n.4
Linkage (issue) 18, 135, 139
Loewenstein, George, 29, 41 n.8, 42 nn.13, 14
Loss, 3, 6, 8, 13, 14, 24, 25, 35–38, 93, 94, 120, 127–130, 132; avoidance/aversion, 4, 9, 10, 22, 24, 26, 37, 60, 64, 66–68, 92, 120, 121, 125, 126, 128–130, 133, 138, 141
Lubeck, Paul, 85

Macapagal, Diosdado, 101, 103, 106, 109, 111,
Maduagwe, M. O., 142 n.1
Malaysia, 8, 9, 11, 99–107, 109–114, 117, 119, 120, 121, 126, 139, 140; Rahman, Tunku Abdul (Prime Minister), 101, 106, 109; Razak, Tun Abdul (Foreign Minister/Deputy

Malaysia (*continued*)
  Prime Minister/Premier), 102, 103,
  107, 109, 113
Mali, 5, 11, 81, 96 n.9
Malik, Adam (Foreign Minister), 107,
  110, 116
Mano River Union, 51, 81
Maphilindo. *See* Greater Malay Con-
  federation
Marcos, Ferdinand, 9, 24, 27, 37, 99–
  100, 102–105, 107, 109–122, 126,
  127, 128, 129, 130, 131
Marcos, Imelda, 112, 113, 126, 130
Mazrui, Ali, 17
McKeown, Timothy J., 6, 14, 25, 41
  n.10
McLaughlin, Martin M., 11 n.1
Meadows, Martin, 100
Meeker, Guy B., 57
Mendez, Juan Carlos, 44, 68 n.4, 69
  n.5
Mexico, 47, 48, 51, 57, 69 n.9, 84
Middlebrook, Kevin, 51
Mikesell, R. F., 35
Mindanao, 101, 104, 111, 113, 131
Misuari, Nur(ralaji), 111, 113, 123 n.6
Mitrany, David, 18, 40 n.4
Morganthau, Hans J., 15
Moro National Liberation Front
  (MNLF), 8, 111–114, 121
Morse, Edward S., 40 n.4
Muhammed, (General) Murtala, 81,
  142 n.1
Muslims. *See* Islam
Mytelka, Lynn Krieger, 49, 50, 57,
  65, 69 n.9, 70 n.10

Nationalism, 18, 38, 69 n.9, 100, 120
Neofunctionalism, 1, 3, 5, 16–19, 36,
  40 n.4
New York Times, 108, 143 n.4
New Zealand, 104, 118, 119, 122
Niger, 11, 77, 82
Nigeria, 3, 4, 7, 8, 10, 11, 24, 26, 27,
  37, 73–95, 95 n.1, 96 nn.7, 9, 97
  n.13, 126, 127, 128, 129, 130, 131,
  132, 135, 140, 142 n.1; crime, 87–
  88, 91, 93, 95; (un)employment, 74–

75, 85–88, 91–94, 140; Great Nige-
  rian People's Party, 89–90; (im)mo-
  rality, 87–88, 91; National Party of
  Nigeria (NPN), 89–90; Nigerian
  People's Party, 78, 89–90
Nixon, Richard M., 114–115, 121
Norms, 19, 21, 30, 39, 40 n.5, 54, 134,
  136, 142
North Atlantic Treaty Organization
  (NATO), 121, 123 n.7
Nye, Joseph S., Jr., 17, 18, 19, 40 n.4
Nyong, Francis Etim, 17

Obasanjo, (General) Olusegun, 81,
  142 n.1
Ojo, Olantunde, J. B., 79, 80
Okolo, Julius Emeka, 78, 81
Olayiwola, Peter O., 84
Olson, Mancur, 18
Onwuka, Ralph I., 78, 82
Onyemelukwe, J. O. C., 95
Organization of Oil Exporting Coun-
  tries (OPEC), 83, 84
Osundare, Nije, 88
Oye, Kenneth A., 30, 134, 135

Padjak, 101, 122–123 n.2
Payoff(s), 10, 15, 21–22, 26, 28–31,
  37, 40–41 nn.6, 11, 132, 134; structure, 13, 21–22, 30, 36–37, 133,
  135, 136
People's Republic of China (PRC),
  107, 108, 115, 116, 121
Peru, 11, 47, 48, 55, 58, 59, 61, 62, 70
  n.13
Philippines, 3, 8–9, 27, 37, 99–107,
  109, 110–122, 122 nn.1, 2, 123 n.7,
  124 n.11, 125, 126, 127, 130, 131,
  132, 135, 139, 140, 141, 142 n.1;
  Congress, 101, 102, 103; Garcia,
  Carlos P. (President), 106, 109; Mutual Defense Treaty (1951), 121, 123
  n.7; Tanco, Arturo R., Jr. (Secretary of Agriculture), 114, 124 n.11
Pinochet Ugarte (General), 27, 46, 53,
  54, 62, 71, 71 n.16, 132
Policy: compliance, 19, 20, 77, 86, 93,
  97 n.13, 126, 129, 131, 134, 135,

137, 139; implementation, 18, 49, 73, 76, 77, 83, 91, 93, 100, 104, 113, 118, 126, 132, 134, 136, 137, 139
Probability, 3, 6, 11, 13, 14, 22, 25–26, 36, 38, 67, 94, 120, 129, 130
Prospect theory, 21, 25
Protocol on Free Movement of Persons, Right of Residence, and Establishment (ECOWAS) (1979), 7, 8, 73, 76–79, 89, 91–95, 126, 127, 128, 140
Przeworski, A., 7
Puchala, Donald S., 18
Puyana de Palacios, Alicia, 69 n.7

Rajaretnam, M., 113, 114
Ramos, Narciso, 103, 109, 110
Rationality, 15, 16, 20, 21, 22, 26, 30, 39 n.2; instrumental, 19, 39 n.2
Realism, 5, 15, 16, 19, 20
Reciprocity, 20, 136
Regime(s), 20, 21, 24, 27, 37, 133, 134; theory 16, 19, 21
Reputation, 68, 134, 135, 136, 138, 139, 142–143 n.3
Riker, William H., 18
Risk, 3, 6, 10, 13, 14, 22, 24–26, 36–38, 41, 41 n.11, 67, 93, 94, 120, 125, 129, 130, 133, 134, 136, 138, 139, 140; aversion/avoidance, 36, 38, 41, 125, 133, 137
Robson, Peter, 18, 32, 35
Romulo, Carlos, 104, 105, 110, 116, 117
Rosecrance, Richard, 26
Rosenau, James N., 11 n.3, 36
Ruggie, John Gerard, 2
Russett, Bruce M., 17

Sabah (North Borneo), 3, 5, 8, 9, 37, 99–107, 109, 110, 111, 113, 114, 117, 119, 120–122, 125, 126, 127, 128, 129, 130, 139, 140; Mustapha, Tun (Chief Minister), 104, 111; Salleh, Datuk Harris (Chief Minister), 104, 114
Saez, Raul, 48, 54, 55, 58, 70 n.11
Samuelson, P., 42 n.13

Sandholtz, Wayne, 18, 137
Sanfuentes, Emilio V., 63, 72 n.17
Sarawak, 101, 106
Scheingold, Stuart A., 17, 40 n.4
Schmitter, Philippe C., 17, 18
Segal, Aaron, 18
Senegal, 11, 81, 95, 96 n.9
Senior, N. W., 42 n.13
Shadow of the future, 30, 133, 135, 141
Shagari, Shehu, 26, 37, 84, 88–93, 97 n.12, 127, 128, 129, 130, 142 n.1
Sierra Leone, 11, 77, 81, 97 n.13
Sigmund, Paul E., 70 n.14
Singapore, 11, 101, 104, 108, 109, 114, 117, 118, 119, 122
Snidal, Duncan, 39 n.3
Socialization, 18, 67, 128, 133, 134, 135, 136, 138, 139, 140, 141
Sociedad de Fomento Fabril (SOFOFA), 48, 54, 69 n.9
Southeast Asia Treaty Organization (SEATO), 104, 115, 121
Soviet Union, 2, 115, 116, 121
Spaak, Paul Henry, 17
Spain, 44, 51, 103
"Spillover," 17, 18, 78
(In)Stability: political 17, 38, 44, 49, 50, 57, 67, 73, 93, 99, 120, 121, 123 n.6, 125, 126, 127, 128, 129, 133; social, 8, 27, 38, 42, 73, 87, 88, 93, 125, 128, 129, 131, 133
Stein, Arthur A., 16, 22, 26, 27, 29, 30, 135
Stein, Janice Gross, 19, 22, 24, 29, 30, 39 n.3, 134, 135
Stoutjesdijk, Ardy, 34
Sulu, 102, 104, 111, 112, 113, 114; Sultan of, 100, 101, 102
Sweeney, Jane P., 17, 18
Survival, 3, 6, 8, 10, 14, 15, 16, 22, 24, 26–27, 30, 36, 37, 38, 67, 92, 93, 94, 116, 120, 125, 126, 129, 130, 131, 132, 133, 139, 141, 142

Taylor, Bryan Wilson, III, 46, 47
Taylor, Michael, 21, 29, 41 n.6, 136, 143 n.3

Taylor, Paul, 18
Taylor, Phillip, 47, 69 n.6, 108, 122
Technology transfer, 52, 59, 62, 63, 71 n.15
Teune, H., 7
Thailand, 11, 105, 106, 107, 108, 115, 117, 119
Thaler, Richard, 29
Thibaut, John W., 21, 22
Tijjani, Aminu, 89
Time, 3, 6, 13, 14, 15, 19, 42 n.13, 118, 134, 135, 136, 137, 138, 142; horizon(s), 22, 25, 28–30, 35, 36, 38, 67, 120, 132
Togo, 11, 75, 76, 77, 80, 81, 82, 95, 96 nn.9, 11, 139
Transnational corporations, 19, 33, 52, 54, 65, 70 n.10, 96 n.9, 127
Tversky, Amos, 24, 26, 41 n.11

United Kingdom (UK, Great Britain), 9, 76, 96 n.7, 99, 100, 101, 104, 107, 115, 121, 122 n.2
United Nations (UN), 51, 76, 80, 90, 92, 103, 106, 137

United States (US), 2, 9, 20, 23, 46, 48, 49, 55, 61, 76, 99, 103, 107, 110, 114, 115, 116, 121, 122, 123 nn.2, 7
University of Chicago, 54, 66, 72 n.17, 132
Upper Volta, 11, 96 n.9

Venezuela, 11, 48, 49, 54, 58, 59, 62, 64, 69 n.9, 70 n.13
Vietnam, 107, 114, 115, 117
Viner, Jacob, 32, 33
Vreeland, Nena, 104, 107, 112, 115, 123 n.7

Watts, Michael, 85
Weatherbee, Donald E., 100
Williams, David, 87, 90, 91
World Bank, 47, 82
Wright, Stephen, 87

Yeats, Alexander, J., 18, 33
Young, Oran, 134, 137

Zartman, I. William, 84

About the Author

M. LEANN BROWN teaches in the Department of Political Science at the University of Florida. She studies regional integration efforts among advanced industrial and developing countries and European Community policymaking. Professor Brown formerly served as Program Coordinator for the International Studies Association.

ISBN 0-275-94960-5

90000>

EAN

9 780275 949600

HARDCOVER BAR CODE